Undergraduate Topics in Computer Science

Undergraduate Topics in Computer Science' (UTiCS) delivers high-quality instructional content for undergraduates studying in all areas of computing and information science. From core foundational and theoretical material to final-year topics and applications, UTiCS books take a fresh, concise, and modern approach and are ideal for self-study or for a one- or two-semester course. The texts are all authored by established experts in their fields, reviewed by an international advisory board, and contain numerous examples and problems. Many include fully worked solutions.

Also in this series

Iain D. Craig
Object-Oriented Programming Languages: Interpretation
978-1-84628-773-2

Max Bramer
Principles of Data Mining
978-1-84628-765-7

Hanne Riis Nielson and Flemming Nielson
Semantics with Applications: An Appetizer
978-1-84628-691-9

Michael Kifer and Scott A. Smolka
Introduction to Operating System Design and Implementation: The OSP 2 Approcah
978-1-84628-842-5

Phillip J. Brooke and Richard F. Paige
Practical Distributed Processing
978-1-84628-840-1

Frank Klawonn

Introduction to Computer Graphics

Using Java 2D and 3D

 Springer

Frank Klawonn, MSc, PhD
Department of Computer Science
University of Applied Sciences Braunschweig/Wolfenbuettel
Germany

Series editor
Ian Mackie, École Polytechnique, France and King's College London, UK

Advisory board
Samson Abramsky, University of Oxford, UK
Chris Hankin, Imperial College London, UK
Dexter Kozen, Cornell University, USA
Andrew Pitts, University of Cambridge, UK
Hanne Riis Nielson, Technical University of Denmark, Denmark
Steven Skiena, Stony Brook University, USA
Iain Stewart, University of Durham, UK
David Zhang, The Hong Kong Polytechnic University, Hong Kong

British Library Cataloguing in Publication Data
A catalogue record for this book is available from the British Library

Library of Congress Control Number: 2007939533

Undergraduate Topics in Computer Science ISSN 1863-7310
ISBN: 978-1-84628-847-0   e-ISBN: 978-1-84628-848-7

Printed on acid-free paper

9 8 7 6 5 4 3 2 1

springer.com

Preface

Early computer graphics started as a research and application field that was the domain of only a few experts, for instance in the area of computer aided design (CAD). Nowadays, any person using a personal computer benefits from the developments in computer graphics. Operating systems and application programs with graphical user interfaces (GUIs) belong to the simplest applications of computer graphics. Visualisation techniques, ranging from simple histograms to dynamic 3D animations showing changes of winds or currents over time, use computer graphics in the same manner as popular computer games. Even those who do not use a personal computer might see the results of computer graphics on TV or in cinemas where parts of scenes or even a whole movie might be produced by computer graphics techniques.

Without powerful hardware in the form of fast processors, sufficiently large memory and special graphics cards, most of these applications would not have been possible. In addition to these hardware requirements efficient algorithms as well as programming tools that are easy to use and flexible at the time are required. Nowadays, a standard personal computer is sufficient to generate impressive graphics and animations using freely available programming platforms like OpenGL or Java 3D. In addition to at least an elementary understanding of programming, the use of such platforms also requires basic knowledge about the underlying background, concepts and methods of computer graphics.

Aims of the book

The aim of this book is to explain the necessary background and principles of computer graphics combined with direct applications in concrete and simple examples. Coupling the theory with the practical examples enables the reader to apply the technical concepts directly and to visually understand what they mean.

Java 2D and Java 3D build the basis for the practical examples. Wherever possible, the introduced concepts and theory of computer graphics are immediately followed by their counterparts in Java 2D and Java 3D. However, the intention of this book is not to provide a complete introduction to Java 2D or Java 3D, which would both need a multivolume edition themselves without even touching the underlying theoretical concepts of computer graphics.

In order to directly apply computer graphics concepts introduced in this book, the book focusses on the parts of Java 2D and Java 3D that are absolutely relevant for these concepts. Sometimes a simple solution is preferred over the most general one so that not all possible options and additional parameters for an implementation will be discussed. The example programs are kept as simple as possible in order to concentrate on the important concepts and not to disguise them in complex, but more impressive scenes.

There are some selected additional topics—for instance the computation of shadows within computer graphics—that are introduced in the book, although Java 3D does not provide such techniques yet.

Why Java?

There are various reasons for using Java 2D and Java 3D as application platforms. The programming language Java becomes more and more popular in applications and teaching so that extensions like Java 2D/3D seem to be the most obvious choice. Many universities use Java as the introductory programming language, not only in computer science, but also in other areas so that students with a basic knowledge in Java can immediately start to work with Java 2D/3D. Specifically, for multimedia applications Java is very often the language of first choice.

Overview

The first chapters of the book focus on aspects of two-dimensional computer graphics like how to create and draw lines, curves and geometric shapes, handling of colours and techniques for animated graphics.

Chapter 5 and all following chapters cover topics of three-dimensional computer graphics. This includes modelling of 3D objects and scenes, producing images from virtual 3D scenes, animation, interaction, illumination and shading. The last chapter introduces selected special topics, for example special effects like fog, sound effects and stereoscopic viewing.

Guidelines for the reader

In order to be able to apply the computer graphics concepts introduced in this book, the reader will need only very elementary knowledge of the programming language Java. The example programs in this book use Java 3D but also Java 2D in the first chapters, since two-dimensional representations are essential for computer graphics and the geometrical concepts are easier to understand in two dimensions than in three. The necessary background of Java 2D and Java 3D is included as application sections in this book.

Although the coupling of theory and practice was a main guideline for writing this book, the book can also be used as an introduction to the general concepts of computer graphics without focussing on specific platforms or learning how to use Java 2D or Java 3D. Skipping all sections and subsections containing the word "Java" in their headlines, the book will remain completely self-contained in the sense of a more theoretical basic introduction to computer graphics. For some of the computer graphics concepts introduced in this book it is assumed that the reader has basic knowledge about vectors, matrices and elementary calculus.

Supplemental resources

Including the complete source code of all mentioned example programs would have led to a thicker, but less readable book. In addition, no one would like to take the burden of typing the source code again in order to run the examples. Therefore, the book itself only contains those relevant excerpts of the source code that are referred to in the text. The complete source code of all example programs and additional programs can be downloaded from the book web site at

http://public.rz.fh-wolfenbuettel.de/~klawonn/computergraphics

This online service also provides additional exercises concerning the theoretical background as well programming tasks including sketches of solutions, teaching material in the form of slides and some files that are needed for the example programs. The links mentioned in the appendix and further links to some interesting web sites can also be found at the online service of this book.

Acknowledgements

Over the years, the questions, remarks and proposals of my students had a great influence on how this book was written. I cannot list all of them by name, but I would like to mention at least Daniel Beier, Thomas Weber, Jana Volkmer and especially Dave Bahr for reading the manuscript and their extremely helpful comments. I also would like to thank Katharina Tschumitschew and Gerry Gehrmann for designing the online service of the book and for some 3D models that I could use in my programs. The book was first published in German and without the encouragement and support of Catherine Brett from Springer Verlag in London this English version would have been impossible. Thanks also to Frank Ganz from Springer, who seems to know everything about LaTeX. My very personal thanks go to my parents and my wife Keiko for their love and for always accepting my sometimes extremely heavy overload of work.

Wolfenbüttel   Frank Klawonn
September 2007

Contents

List of Figures

1
Introduction

Computer graphics provides methods to generate images using a computer. The word "image" should be understood in a more abstract sense here. An image can represent a realistic scene from the real world, but graphics like histograms or pie charts as well as the graphical user interface of a software tool are also considered as images. The following section provides a brief overview on typical application fields and facets of computer graphics.

1.1 Application fields

Graphical user interfaces can be considered as an application of computer graphics, although they do not play an important role in computer graphics anymore. On the one hand, there are standard programming tools and APIs (Application Programming Interfaces) for the implementation of graphical user interfaces and on the other hand the main emphasis of user interfaces is the construction of user-friendly human computer interfaces and not the generation of complex graphics.

In advertising and certain fields of art pictures are sometimes designed using the computer only or photos serve as a basis and are modified or changed with computer graphics techniques.

Large amounts of data are collected in business, industry, economy and science. In addition to suitable data analysis techniques, methods for visualising high-dimensional data are needed. Such visualisation techniques reach much further than simple representations like graphs of functions, pie or bar charts—graphics that can already be generated by today's standard spreadsheet tools. Two- or three-dimensional visualisations of high-dimensional data, problem-specific representations of the data [28, 39, 43] or animations that show dynamic aspects like the flow of currents or the change of weather phenomena belong to this class of applications of computer graphics.

Apart from constructing and representing such more abstract graphics, the generation of realistic images and sequences of images—not necessarily of the real world—are the main application field of computer graphics. Other areas, that were the driving force in the early days of computer graphics, are CAD/CAM (Computer-Aided Design/Manufacturing) for the design and construction of objects like cars or chassis. The objects are designed using a suitable computer graphics software and their geometry is stored in computers. Nowadays, not only industrial products are designed in the computer, but also buildings, gardens or artificial environments for computer games. Very often, real existing objects have to be modelled and combined with hypothetical objects, for instance when an architect wants to visualise how a possible extension of an old house might look. The same applies to flight or driving simulators, where existing landscapes and cities need to be modelled in the computer.

The possibilities of designing, modelling and visualising objects play an important role in computer graphics, but also the generation of realistic models and representations of objects based on measurement data. There are various techniques to obtain such data. 3D laser scanners can be used to scan the surface of objects or a set of calibrated cameras allows to reconstruct 3D information of objects from their images. Medical informatics [11] is another very important application field of computer graphics where measurements are available in the form of X-ray images or data from computerised tomography and ultrasonic testing. Such data allows a 3D visualisation of bones or viscera.

The combination of real data and images with techniques from computer graphics will probably gain more importance than it has today. Computer games allow to navigate through scenes and to view the scenes from different angles. For movies, as they are shown on TV or in cinemas, the choice of the viewpoint is not possible anymore once the movie has been produced. Even if various cameras where used to capture the same scene from different angles, one can only choose between the perspectives of the different cameras. But it is not possible to view the scene from a position between the cameras. The elementary techniques allowing a free choice of the viewpoint are available in principle today [4]. However, this will not only need "intelligent" TV sets, but also the processing of the movie from several perspectives. In order to view a scene from a viewpoint different from the cameras, the 3D scene is reconstructed using image processing methods exploiting the information coming from the different perspectives of the cameras. Once the scene is reconstructed, computer graphics techniques can show it from any viewpoint, not only from the camera perspectives. For this application, a combination of image analysis and image recognition techniques with image synthesis methods—i.e., computer graphics algorithms—is required [46].

Other important fields of application of computer graphics are virtual reality [27], where the user should be able to move and act more or less freely in a virtual 3D world, and augmented reality [23], where the real world is enriched by additional information in the form of text or virtual objects.

1.2 From a real scene to an image

The various application examples of computer graphics discussed in the previous section demonstrate already that a large variety of different problems and tasks must be solved within computer graphics. Figure 1.1 illustrates crucial steps that are needed in order to generate an image from a real or virtual scene.

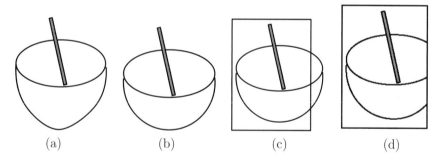

(a)   (b)   (c)   (d)

Figure 1.1   From a scene to an image

As a first step, the objects in the scene in figure 1.1(a) have to be modelled with the techniques and methods provided by a computer graphics tool. In general, these models will not be exact copies of the real or virtual objects of the scene, but only approximations of them. Depending on how detailed the objects should be modelled, how much effort one wants to invest and on the techniques provided by the computer graphics tool, the approximation of the objects can be almost exact or very rough only. Figure 1.1(b) illustrates this problem of approximation by assuming that the computer graphics tool is very restricted and the bowl in the real scene can only be approximated by a semisphere.

The modelled objects usually cover a much larger region than the part that is visible for the virtual viewer from his viewpoint. The model might for instance include a group of buildings surrounded by gardens and the viewer can move in the buildings and through the gardens. When the viewer is in a room of one of the buildings looking into the room, but not outside the window, he can only see a very small fraction of the objects of this virtual world. Most of the objects can therefore be neglected, when the image is generated. Taking the viewer's position and the direction of his view into account, a three-dimensional region must be defined that determines which objects might be visible for the viewer (see figure 1.1(c)). The computation of which objects belong completely or at least partly to this region is called *clipping* or, more specifically, *3D-clipping*. Not all objects located in the clipping region might be visible for the viewer, since some of them might be hidden from the viewer's view by other objects that are closer to the viewer.

The visible objects in the clipping region need to be projected onto a two-dimensional plane in order to obtain a flat pixel image as shown in figure 1.1(d) that can be printed out or shown on a computer screen. This projection requires the application of hidden line and hidden surface algorithms in order to find out whether objects or parts of the objects are visible or hidden by other objects. The effects of light like shading, shadows and reflection are extremely important issues for the generation of realistic images. *2D-clipping* is also necessary to decide which parts of the projection of an object in the 3D-clipping region lie within the projection plane.

The whole process of generating a pixel image from a three-dimensional virtual scene is called *rendering*. The successive composition of the single techniques that are roughly outlined in figure 1.1 is also referred to as the *rendering pipeline*. The details of the rendering pipeline depend on the chosen techniques and algorithms, for instance whether shadows can be neglected or not. In [18] five different rendering pipelines are explained only within the context of lighting and shading.

1.3 Organisation of the book

The organisation of the book reflects the structure of the rendering pipeline. Chapters 2, 3 and 4 cover fundamental aspects of the last part of the rendering pipeline focussing exclusively on two-dimensional images. On the one hand, the techniques for two-dimensional images comprise one part of the rendering of three-dimensional virtual scenes. On the other hand, they can be viewed on their own for instance as a drawing tool.

Chapter 2 outlines the basic principles of vector and raster graphics and simple modelling techniques for planar objects and their animation including a short introduction to Java 2D for the illustrative examples.

Chapter 3 provides an overview on algorithmic aspects for raster graphics that are of high importance for drawing lines and curves. Chapter 4 covers the representation and drawing of areas, a rough outline on the problems of drawing letters and numbers using different fonts as well an overview on colour representation.

The next chapters are devoted to modelling, representation and rendering of three-dimensional virtual scenes and provide in parallel an introduction to Java 3D. Chapters 5 and 6 discuss the basic principles for modelling and handling three-dimensional objects and scenes in computer graphics.

Various techniques for the hidden line and hidden surface problem—i.e., to identify which objects are hidden from the view by other objects—are described in Chapter 7.

In order to generate photo-realistic images, it is necessary to incorporate lighting effects like shading, shadows and reflections. Chapter 8 deals with this important topic.

Finally, Chapter 9 covers a selection of further interesting techniques and topics like special effects, interaction and stereoscopic viewing which is required for the understanding of virtual reality applications.

The appendix contains links to web pages that might be of interest to the reader of this book. All example programs mentioned in this book are also listed in the appendix including references to the pages where they are discussed in more detail.

2

Basic principles of two-dimensional graphics

This chapter introduces basic concepts that are required for the understanding of two-dimensional graphics. Almost all output devices for graphics like computer monitors or printers are pixel-oriented. Therefore, it is crucial to distinguish between the representation of images on these devices and the model of the image itself which is usually not pixel-oriented, but defined as scalable vector graphics, i.e., floating point values are used for coordinates.

2.1 Raster versus vector graphics

Before an object can be shown on a computer monitor or a printer, a model describing the object's geometry is required, unless the object is an image itself. Modelling of geometrical objects is usually done in the framework of *vector-oriented* or *vector graphics*. A more complex object is modelled as a combination of elementary objects like lines, rectangles, circles, ellipses or arcs. Each of these elementary objects can be defined by a few coordinates, describing the location of the object, and some parameters like the radius for a circle. A very simple description of the house in figure 2.1(a) in terms of vector graphics is shown in figure 2.1(b). The house can be defined as a sequence of points or vectors. It must also be specified within the sequence of points whether two neighbouring points should be connected by a line or not. Dotted lines in figure

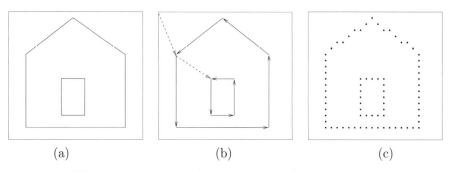

(a)   (b)   (c)

Figure 2.1 Original image, vector and pixel graphics

2.1(b) refer to points in the sequence that should not be connected by a line.

The vector graphics-oriented description of objects is not directly suitable for the representation on a purely pixel-oriented device like an LCD monitor or printer. From a theoretical point of view, it would be possible to display vector graphics directly on a CRT[1] monitor by running the cathode ray—or, in case of colour display, the three cathode rays—along the lines defined by the sequence of points and switch the ray on or off, depending on whether the corresponding connecting line should be drawn. In this case, the monitor might not be flicker free anymore since the cathode ray might take too long to refresh the screen for a more complex image in vector graphics, so that fluorescent spots on the screen might fade out, before the cathode ray returns. Flicker-free monitors should have a refresh rate of 60 Hz. If a cathode ray were to run along the contour lines of objects represented in vector graphics, the refresh rate would depend on how many lines the objects contain, so that a sufficiently fast refresh rate could not be guaranteed in this operational mode. Therefore, the cathode ray scans the screen line by line leading to a guaranteed and constant refresh rate, independent of the image to be drawn.

Computer monitors, printers and also various formats for storing images like bitmaps or JPEG are based on *raster* or *raster-oriented graphics*, also called *pixel* or *pixel-oriented graphics*. Raster graphics uses a pixel matrix of fixed size. A colour can be assigned to each pixel of the raster. In the simplest case of a black-and-white image a pixel takes one of the two values black or white.

In order to display vector-oriented graphics in the form of raster graphics, all geometrical shapes must be converted into pixels. This procedure is called *scan conversion*. On the one hand, this can lead to high computational efforts. A standard monitor has more than one million pixels. For each of them, it must be decided which colour to assign to it for each image. On the other hand, undesired *aliasing effects* occur in the form of jagged edges, known as

---
[1] Cathode ray tube.

jaggies or *staircasing*. The term *aliasing effect* originates from the field of signal processing and refers to artifacts, i.e., superficial undesired effects that can occur, when a discrete sampling rate is used to measure a continuous signal. A grey-scale image can be viewed as a two-dimensional signal. In this sense, a coloured image based on the three colours red, green and blue, is nothing else than three two-dimensional signals, one for each colour.

Even if an image will be displayed in terms of raster-oriented graphics, it still has advantages to model and store it in a vector-oriented format. Raster graphics is bound to a specific resolution. Once the resolution is fixed, the full information contained in the vector-oriented image cannot be recovered anymore, leading to serious disadvantages, when the image is displayed on a device with a different resolution or when the image needs to be enlarged or scaled down. Figure 2.2 shows the tip of an arrow and its representation in the form of raster graphics for two different resolutions. If only the more coarse pixel image in the middle is stored, it is impossible to reconstruct the refined pixel image on the right-hand side without additional information. One could only produce an image appearing in the same form as the one in the middle by simply identifying four pixels of the refined image with one pixel in the coarser image. If the quotient of the pixel resolution is not an integer number, the transformation from a raster graphics with one resolution to a raster graphics with another resolution becomes even more complicated and will lead to new aliasing effects, even if the new resolution is higher than the original one.

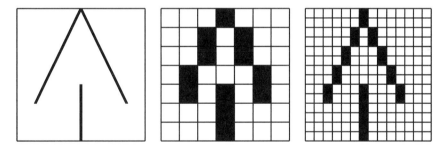

Figure 2.2 The tip of an arrow drawn as raster graphics in two different resolutions

In most cases, when a pixel matrix is considered in this book, each pixel is represented by a square between the lines of a grid as shown in figure 2.2. However, sometimes another representation is more convenient where pixels are illustrated as circles on the points where the lines of the grid cross. Figure 2.3 shows the pixel with the grid coordinates (5,3).

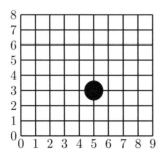

Figure 2.3 An alternative representation for pixels

2.2 The first Java 2D program

Before modelling of two-dimensional objects is discussed in more detail, a short introduction into how Java 2D can be used to generate images in general is provided. The first chapters of this book dealing exclusively with problems and questions of two-dimensional graphics refer to Java 2D. Chapter 5 and the latter chapters will use Java 3D for three-dimensional modelling, animation and representations.

It is not the aim of this book to provide a complete introduction to Java 2D and Java 3D. Instead, the main intention of this book is to enable even those readers with only very basic knowledge in Java to use and apply the more theoretical concepts of computer graphics immediately within the framework of Java 2D and Java 3D. For this reason, the example programs are kept as simple as possible and not all available options and settings will be explained in detail, in order to better focus on the main aspects and concepts. For readers who are already more familiar with Java programming the book provides an introduction to Java 2D and 3D that enables the reader to study the more advanced options and possibilities of these two Application Programming Interfaces (APIs) with the help of specific literature and the API documentations.

Detailed information concerning Java 2D can be found in books like [24, 29], in the API documentation and the Java tutorial, that are available on the Internet (see the appendix).

Java 2D is an API belonging to the kernel classes of the Java 2 (formerly JDK 1.2) and later platforms so that it is not necessary to carry out additional installations to use Java 2D classes, as long as a Java platform is installed on the computer.

Java 2D extends some of the AWT[2] packages of Java by additional classes and also introduces new packages within AWT. Java 2D can be viewed as a

---

[2] Abstract Windowing Toolkit.

component under Java's graphics components AWT and Swing (see figure 2.4).

Although AWT is seldom used anymore, the introductory examples for Java 2D in this book are based on AWT. The reason is that within AWT it is easily possible to program simple animations without the technique of double buffering that will be used later on in this book.

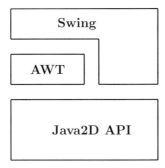

Figure 2.4 The Java 2D API extends AWT

AWT components that are displayed on the computer screen contain a `paint` method with a `Graphics` object as its argument. In order to use the facilities of Java 2D for the corresponding AWT component, it is necessary to cast this `Graphics` object into a `Graphics2D` object. The class `Graphics2D` within Java 2D extends the class `Graphics`. The following simple Java class `SimpleJava2DExample.java` demonstrates this simple casting procedure. In order to keep the printed code examples short, comments are only included in the programs that can be downloaded from the web site of this book, but not in the printed versions. The result of this program is shown in figure 2.5.

Figure 2.5 The result of the first Java 2D program

```java
import java.awt.*;

public class SimpleJava2DExample extends Frame
{
  SimpleJava2DExample()
  {
    addWindowListener(new MyFinishWindow());
  }

  public void paint(Graphics g)
  {
    Graphics2D g2d = (Graphics2D) g;
    g2d.drawString("Hello world!",30,50);
  }

  public static void main(String[] argv)
  {
    SimpleJava2DExample f = new SimpleJava2DExample();
    f.setTitle("The first Java 2D program");
    f.setSize(350,80);
    f.setVisible(true);
  }
}
```

The method `addWindowListener`, called in the constructor, enables the closing of the window by clicking on the cross in the upper right corner. The method uses a simple additional class `MyFinishWindow.java`, that can also be downloaded from the web site of this book. The `main` method generates the corresponding window, defines the title of the window, determines its size by 350 pixels in width and 80 pixels in height and finally displays it. This structure of the `main` method will be used for all Java 2D examples in this book. For other programs, it will only be necessary to replace `SimpleJava2DExample` by the corresponding class name and—if desired—to change the title of the window and its size.

The image or graphics to be displayed is defined within the `paint` method. The first line of this method will always be the same in all examples here: It carries out the casting of the `Graphics` object to a `Graphics2D` object. The remaining code lines in the `paint` method depend on what is to be displayed and will be different for each program. In the example here, only the text "Hello worl" is printed at the window coordinates (30,50).

When specifying window coordinates, the following two aspects should be taken into account.

– The point (0,0) is located in the upper left corner of the window. The window
  extends to the right (in the example program 350 pixels) and downwards (in
  the example program 80 pixels). This means that the y-axis of the coordinate
  system does not point upwards, but downwards since the pixel lines in the
  window are counted from the top to the bottom. How to avoid this problem
  of an inverted y-axis will be explained later on.

– The window includes margins on all its four sides. Especially the upper margin, containing the title of the window, is quite broad. It is not possible to
  draw anything on or outside these margins within the `paint` method. Trying
  to draw an object on the margin or outside the window will not lead to an
  error or exception. The clipping procedure will simply make sure that the
  object or its corresponding part is not drawn. Therefore, when a window
  of a size of 350×80 pixels is defined as in the example program, a slightly
  smaller area is available for drawing. The width of the margins depends on
  the operating system platform. The example programs avoid this problem
  by defining a window that is large enough and by not drawing objects too
  close to any of the margins. The exact width of the margins can also be
  determined within the class, for instance within the `paint` method using

```
Insets ins = this.getInsets();
```

The width of the left, right, upper and lower margin in pixels is given by
`ins.left`, `ins.right`, `ins.top` and `ins.bottom`, respectively.

The first example of a Java 2D program did not require any additional
computations before the objects—in this case only text—could be drawn. For
real graphics it is usually necessary to carry out more or less complicated
computations in order to define and position the objects to be displayed. Java
2D distinguishes between the definition of objects and drawing objects. An
object that has been defined will not be drawn or shown in the corresponding
window, until a `draw`- or `fill` method is called with the corresponding object
as argument. Therefore, Java 2D also differentiates between modelling objects
based on vector graphics using floating point arithmetics and displaying or
drawing objects on the screen based on raster graphics with scan conversion
and integer arithmetics.

In order to keep the example programs in this book as simple and under-
standable as possible, the computations required for defining and positioning
the geometric objects are carried out directly in the `paint` method. For more
complex animated graphics, i.e., for graphics with moving or changing objects,
this can lead to flickering effects and also to the effect that the window might
react very slowly, for instance when it should be closed while the animation is
still running. Java assigns a high priority to the `paint` method so that other

events like closing of the window cannot be carried out immediately. In order to avoid this undesired effect, one can carry out all computations to construct or position objects outside the `paint` method and instead call the `repaint` method only, when objects have to be drawn. The double buffering technique, introduced later on in section 4.2, provides an even better solution.

2.3 Basic geometric objects

The basic geometric objects in computer graphics are usually called *primitives* or *graphics output primitives*. They include geometric entities like points, straight and curved lines and areas as well as character strings. The basic primitives are the following ones.

Points that are uniquely defined by their x- and y-coordinate. Points are usually not drawn themselves. Their main function is the description of other objects like lines that can be defined by their two endpoints.

Lines, *polylines* or *curves* can be defined by two or more points. Whereas for a line two points are needed, curves require additional control points. Polylines are connected sequences of lines.

Areas are usually bounded by *closed polylines* or *polygons*. Areas can be filled with a colour or a texture.

Figure 2.6 A self-overlapping, a nonconvex and a convex polygon

The simplest curve is a line segment or simply a line. A sequence of line where the following line starts where the previous one ends is called a *polyline*. If the last line segment of a polyline ends where the first line segment started, the polyline is called a *polygon*. For various applications—for instance for modelling surfaces—additional properties of polygons are required. One of such properties is that the polygon should not overlap with itself. *Convexity* is another important property that is often needed. A polygon or, more generally, an area or a region is *convex* if whenever two points are within the region the connecting line between these two points lies completely inside the region as well. Figure 2.6 shows a self-overlapping polygon, a nonconvex polygon and a convex polygon. For the nonconvex polygon two points inside the polygon are chosen and connected by a dotted line that lies not completely inside the polygon.

In addition to lines and piecewise linear polylines, curves are also common in computer graphics. In most cases, curves are defined as parametric polynomials that can also be attached to each other like lines in a polyline. The precise definition and computation of these curves will be postponed until chapter 6. Here it is sufficient to understand the principle of how the parameters of a curve influence its shape. In addition to the endpoints of the curve, one or more *control points* have to be specified. Usually, two control points are used leading to a cubic curve or only one control point is used in order to define a quadratic curve. The curve begins and ends in the two specified endpoints. In general, it will not pass through control points. The control points define the direction of the curve in the two endpoints.

In the case of a quadratic curve with one control point one can imagine the lines connecting the control point with the two endpoints. The connecting lines are the tangents of the quadratic curve in the two endpoints. Figure 2.7 illustrates the definition of a quadratic curve on the left-hand side. The quadratic curve is given by two endpoints and one control point through which the curve does not pass. The tangents in the endpoints are also shown here as dotted lines. For a cubic curve as shown on the right-hand side of the figure, the tangents in the two endpoints can be defined independently by the two control points.

Figure 2.7 Definition of quadratic and cubic curves

When fitting quadratic or cubic curves together in order to form a longer, more complicated curve, it is not sufficient to simply use the endpoint of the previous curve as a starting point for the next curve. The resulting joint curve would be continuous, but not smooth, i.e., sharp bends might occur. In order to avoid sharp bends, the tangent of the endpoint of the previous curve and the following curve must point into the same direction. This means the endpoint, which is equal to the starting point of the next curve, and the two control points defining the two tangents must be collinear. This means they must lie on the same line. Therefore, the first control point of a succeeding curve must be on the line defined by the last control and endpoint of the previous curve.

In the same way a curve can be fitted to a line without causing a sharp bend by locating the first control point on the prolongation of the line. Figure 2.8 illustrates this principle.

Figure 2.8 Fitting a cubic curve to a line without sharp bends

Other important curves in computer graphics are circles, ellipses and circular and elliptic arcs.

In the same sense as polygons, circles and ellipses define areas. Areas are bounded by a closed curve. When only the shell or margin of the area should be drawn, there is no difference to drawing arbitrary curves. In contrast to lines and simple curves, areas can be filled by colours and textures. From the algorithmic point of view, filling of an area is very different from drawing curves.

Axes-parallel rectangles, whose sides are parallel to the coordinate axes, play an important role in computer graphics. Although they can be understood as special cases of polygons, they are simpler to handle since it is already sufficient to specify two opposing vertices.

Instead of specifying a polygon or the boundary directly in order to define an area, it is sometimes more convenient to construct a more complicated area by combining previously defined areas using set-theoretic operations. The most important operations are union, intersection, difference and symmetric difference. The *union* joins two areas to a larger area whereas their *intersection* consists of the part belonging to both areas. The *difference* of an area with another removes all parts from the first area that also belong to the second area. The *symmetric difference* corresponds to a pointwise exclusive OR-operation applied to the two areas. The symmetric difference is the union of the two areas without their intersection. Figure 2.9 shows the results of applying these operations to two areas in the form of a circle and a rectangle.

Figure 2.9 Union, intersection, difference and symmetric difference of a circle and a rectangle

Geometric transformations like scalings will be discussed in section 2.5. They provide another way of constructing new areas from already existing ones.

2.4 Basic geometric objects in Java 2D

All methods for generating geometric objects as they were described in the previous section are also available within the Java 2D framework. The abstract class `Shape` with its various subclasses allows the construction of various two-dimensional geometric objects. Vector graphics is used to define `Shape` objects, whose real-valued coordinates can either be given as `float`- or `double`-values. Shapes will not be drawn until the `draw` or the `fill` method is called with the corresponding `Shape` as argument in the form `graphics2d.draw(shape)` or `graphics2d.fill(shape)`, respectively. The `draw` method draws only the margin or circumference of the `Shape` object, whereas the whole area defined by the corresponding `Shape` object is filled, when the `fill` method is called.

The abstract class `Point2D` for points is not a subclass of `Shape`. Points cannot be drawn directly. If one wants to draw a point, i.e., a single pixel, then a line from this point to the same point can be drawn instead. Objects of the class `Point2D` are mainly used to specify coordinates for other geometric objects. In most cases, it is also possible to define these coordinates also directly by two single values determining the x- and the y-coordinate. Therefore, the class `Point2D` will not occur very often in the example programs. The abstract class `Point2D` is extended by the two classes `Point2D.Float` and `Point2D.Double`. When using the abstract class `Point2D` it is not necessary to specify whether coordinates are given as `float`- or `double`-values. The same concept is also used for most of the other geometric objects.

The elementary geometric objects in Java 2D introduced in the following extend the class Shape, so that they can be drawn by applying one of the methods draw or fill.

The abstract class Line2D defines lines. One way to define a line from point (x_1, y_1) to point (x_2, y_2) is the following:

```
Line2D.Double line = new Line2D.Double(x1,y1,x2,y2);
```

The parameters x1, y1, x2 and y2 are of type double. Similarly, Line2D.Float requires the same parameters, but of type float. It should be emphasised again that the defined line will not yet be drawn. Only when the method g2d.draw(line) is called, will the line appear on the screen.

Analogously to lines, quadratic curves are modelled by the abstract class QuadCurve2D. The definition of a quadratic curve requires two endpoints and one control point. The quadratic curve is constructed in such a way that it connects the two endpoints (x_1, y_1) and (x_2, y_2) and the tangents in the endpoints meet in the control point (crtlx,crtly), as illustrated by the left curve in figure 2.7. One way to define quadratic curves in Java 2D is the following:

```
QuadCurve2D.Double qc = new QuadCurve2D.Double(x1,y1,
                                 ctrlx,ctrly,
                                 x2,y2);
```

Cubic curves need two control points instead of one in order to define the tangents in the two endpoints independently as shown by the right curve in figure 2.7. Java 2D provides the abstract class CubicCurve2D for modelling cubic curves. Analogously to the cases of lines and quadratic curves, CubicCurve2D.Double is a subclass of CubicCurve2D allowing to define a cubic curve in the following way:

```
CubicCurve2D.Double cc =
            new CubicCurve2D.Double(x1,y1,
                                 ctrlx1,ctrly1,
                                 ctrlx2,ctrly2,
                                 x2,y2);
```

The program CurveDemo.java demonstrates the usage of the classes Line2D.Double, QuadCurve2D.Double and CubicCurve2D.Double.

The class GeneralPath allows the construction not only of polylines, i.e., sequences of lines, but also mixed sequences of lines, quadratic and cubic curves in Java 2D. A GeneralPath starts in the origin of the coordinate system, i.e., in the point (0,0). The class GeneralPath provides four basic methods for defining a sequence of lines, quadratic and cubic curves. Each method will append a corresponding line or curve to the endpoint of the last element in the sequence of the GeneralPath. The methods lineTo, quadTo and curveTo append a line, a quadratic and a cubic curve, respectively, as the next element in the sequence of the GeneralPath. These methods are used within GeneralPath in the same way as in Line2D, QuadCurve2D and CubicCurve2D except that the definition of the first endpoint of the line or curve is omitted since this point is already determined by the endpoint of the previous line or curve in the GeneralPath. The coordinates of the points must be specified as float-values. In addition to these three methods for curves and lines, the class GeneralPath also contains the method moveTo that allows to jump from the endpoint of the previous curve to another point without connecting the points by a line or curve. A GeneralPath must always start with the method moveTo, defining the starting point of the general path.

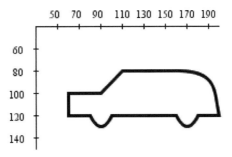

Figure 2.10   An example for a GeneralPath

Figure 2.10 shows the outline of a car that was generated by the following GeneralPath:

```
GeneralPath gp = new GeneralPath();

//Start at the lower left corner of the car
gp.moveTo(60,120);
gp.lineTo(80,120); //front underbody
gp.quadTo(90,140,100,120); //front wheel
gp.lineTo(160,120); //middle underbody
gp.quadTo(170,140,180,120); //rear wheel
gp.lineTo(200,120); //rear underbody
gp.curveTo(195,100,200,80,160,80); //rear
gp.lineTo(110,80); //roof
gp.lineTo(90,100); //windscreen
gp.lineTo(60,100); //bonnet
gp.lineTo(60,120); //front
```

```
g2d.draw(gp); //Draw the car
```

The coordinate system shown in figure 2.10 refers to the window coordinates, so that the y-axis points downwards. The complete class for drawing the car can be found in the example program `GeneralPathCar.java`.

An area can be defined by its boundary that might be specified as a `GeneralPath` object. In addition to the class `GeneralPath` Java 2D also provides classes for axes-parallel rectangles and ellipses as basic geometric objects.

By the class `Rectangle2D.Double`, extending the abstract class `Rectangle2D`, an axes-parallel rectangle can be defined in the following way:

```
Rectangle2D.Double r2d =
          new Rectangle2D.Double(x,y,width,height);
```

The rectangle is determined by its opposite corners (x, y) and $(x + width, y + height)$ on the diagonal. Taking into account that the y-axis in the window where the rectangle will be drawn points downwards, a rectangle is defined whose upper left corner is located at the position (x, y) and whose lower right corner is at $(x + width, y + height)$. Figure 2.11 shows a rectangle on the left-hand side that was defined by

```
Rectangle2D.Double r2d =
          new Rectangle2D.Double(50,60,150,100);
```

It should be emphasised again that this constructor will only define the rectangle in the same way as for all other `Shape` objects that were introduced so far. It is still necessary to call the method `g2d.draw(r2d)` in order to show the rectangle in the corresponding window.

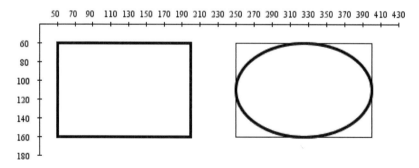

Figure 2.11 An example for a rectangle and an ellipse

In the same way as rectangles, axes-parallel ellipses can be defined in Java 2D. An ellipse is determined by its bounding rectangle which can be specified with the same parameters as `Rectangle2D` objects. The ellipse shown in figure 2.11 on the right-hand side was generated by

```
Ellipse2D.Double elli =
           new Ellipse2D.Double(250,60,150,100);
```

For illustration purposes the bounding rectangle that was used to generate the ellipse is also shown in figure 2.11. The figure was generated by the class `RectangleEllipseExample.java`.

A circle is a special case of an ellipse, where the bounding rectangle is a square. A circle with centre point (x, y) and radius r can be generated by

```
Ellipse2D.Double circle =
           new Ellipse2D.Double(x-r,y-r,2*r,2*r);
```

With the class `Arc2D` elliptic arcs and, of course, circular arcs can be defined.

```
Arc2D.Double arc = new
           Arc2D.Double(rect2D,start,extend,type);
```

– `rect2D` specifies the bounding rectangle of the corresponding ellipse in the form of a `Rectangle2D`.

– `start` is the angle where the arc is supposed to start relative to the bounding rectangle viewed as a square. The angle is given as a `float`-value in terms of degrees.[3] The angle corresponds to the angle with the x-axis only in the special case when a circular arc is defined, i.e., when the bounding rectangle is a square. Otherwise, the angle is determined relative to the rectangle. For example, a starting angle of $45°$ means that the starting point of the arc lies on the connecting line from the centre of the rectangle to its upper right corner.

– `extend` is the opening angle of the arc, i.e., the arc extends from the start angle `start` to the angle `start` + `extend`. Analogously to the `start` angle, `extend` corresponds to the true angle of the arc only in the case of a circular arc. The angle `start` + `extend` is again interpreted relative to the bounding rectangle in the same way as `start`. `extend` must also be specified as a `float`-value in degrees.

– `type` can take one of the three values `Arc2D.OPEN`, `Arc2D.PIE` and `Arc2D.CHORD`, specifying whether only the arc itself, the corresponding segment or the arc with the chord of the ellipse, respectively, should be constructed.

---

[3] `Arc2D` is the only exception where angles are specified in the unit radians. Otherwise angles in Java 2D and Java 3D must be specified in radiant.

Figure 2.12 shows from left to right an arc of an ellipse, a segment and an arc together with the corresponding chord. In all cases a starting angle of 45° and an opening angle of 90° were chosen. For illustration purposes the bounding rectangle is also shown in the figure. One can see clearly that the arc starts on the intersection of the ellipse with the line from the centre of the bounding rectangle to its upper right corner, according to the choice of the starting angle of 45°. Obviously, the line defined by the centre point of the rectangle and the starting point of the ellipse meets the x-axis in a smaller angle than 45° since a flat, but long bounding rectangle was chosen. The same applies to the opening angle. The actual opening angle is not 90°, but it corresponds to the angle between the lines from the centre of the bounding rectangle to its upper right and to its upper left corner. An example for using the class Arc2D can be found in the file ArcExample.java, which was also used to generate figure 2.12.

Figure 2.12 An arc of an ellipse, a segment and an arc with its corresponding chord

An area can be defined as a rectangle, an ellipse or in the form of a GeneralPath. At the end of section 2.3 a technique for defining areas based on the set-theoretic operations union, intersection, set difference and symmetric difference was explained. Applying these operations to already defined areas, new shapes of areas can be defined. Java 2D offers the class Area for this purpose. From a Shape object s, for instance a Rectangle2D, an Ellipse2D, a closed GeneralPath or an Arc2D, representing the segment of an ellipse or an ellipse arc with its chord, an Area object with the same outline can be defined by

```
Area a = new Area(Shape s);
```

The above-mentioned set-theoretic operations can be applied to such Area objects to generate new areas. Given two Area objects areaA and areaB, the following methods are available, implementing the corresponding set-theoretic operations.

− areaA.add(areaB) computes the union of areaA and areaB.

− areaA.intersect(areaB) computes the intersection of areaA and areaB.

– `areaA.subtract(areaB)` yields `areaA` without the parts lying in `areaB`, i.e.,
their difference.

– `areaA.exclusiveOr(areaB)` constructs the union of `areaA` and `areaB` without their intersection, i.e., their symmetric difference.

The `Area` object `areaA` contains the result of the application of the corresponding set-theoretic operation. An `Area` object can be used as an argument of the
methods `draw`, which will only draw the outline of the area, and `fill`, which
will fill the whole area, in the same way as these methods are used for `Shape`
objects. The file `AreaExample.java`, which was also used to generate figure 2.9
on page 17, demonstrates the use of `Area` objects.

2.5 Geometric transformations

In addition to geometric objects, geometric transformations play a crucial role
in computer graphics. Geometric transformations can be used to position objects, i.e., to shift them to another position or to rotate them, to change the
shape of objects, for instance to stretch or shrink them in one direction, or to
move objects or change the shape of objects step by step in animated scenes.

Before discussing geometric transformations in more detail, it is necessary
to explain some general conventions. In computer graphics, *points* as well as
vectors are used. From a purely mathematical point of view, both can be represented as elements of the space $\mathbb{R}^n$, i.e., as a tuple of real numbers. Especially in
physics, it is very important to distinguish clearly between these two concepts
of points and vectors. In the framework of this book and from the viewpoint
of computer graphics, it is very common to switch between the interpretations
of a tuple of real numbers as a point and as a vector, giving more flexibility in
handling certain matters. A tuple $(x_1, \ldots, x_n) \in \mathbb{R}^n$ might occur in one equation as a point and in the next equation it might be interpreted as a vector.
Hopefully, physicists will tolerate the abuse of notation in the context of this
book. For equations within this book, column vectors will be used consistently.
Within the text, points are sometimes written as row vectors in order to avoid
stretching of text lines. In those cases where a point is explicitly understood
as a column vector, the symbol for transposing vectors will be used, i.e., the
point will be written as $(x, y)^\top \in \mathbb{R}^2$ and $(x, y, z)^\top \in \mathbb{R}^3$, respectively.

The *dot product* of two vectors $\mathbf{u}$ and $\mathbf{v}$ will be denoted in the following way, which is also very common in statistics:

$$\mathbf{u}^\top \cdot \mathbf{v} = (u_1, \ldots, u_n) \cdot \begin{pmatrix} v_1 \\ \vdots \\ v_n \end{pmatrix} = \sum_{i=1}^{n} u_i \cdot v_i.$$

The most important geometric transformations are scaling, rotation, shearing and translation.

A *scaling* leads to *stretching* or *shrinking* of objects in the direction of the x- and the y-axis. A scaling $S(s_x, s_y)$ maps the point (x, y) to the point (x', y') given by

$$\begin{pmatrix} x' \\ y' \end{pmatrix} = \begin{pmatrix} s_x \cdot x \\ s_y \cdot y \end{pmatrix} = \begin{pmatrix} s_x & 0 \\ 0 & s_y \end{pmatrix} \cdot \begin{pmatrix} x' \\ y' \end{pmatrix}.$$

s_x is the scaling factor in the direction of the x-axis. If $|s_x| > 1$ holds, then a stretching in the direction of the x-axis is carried out. For $|s_x| < 1$ shrinking takes place. If s_x is negative, in addition to stretching or shrinking in the x-direction, a reflection with respect to the y-axis is applied. In the same way, s_y leads to stretching or shrinking in the direction of the y-axis and a negative value of s_y incorporates an additional reflection with respect to the x-axis.

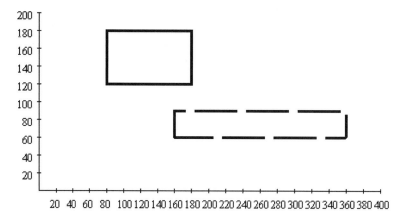

Figure 2.13 Scaling applied to a rectangle

Applying a scaling to an object means that the scaling is carried out pointwise. The same holds for all other geometric transformations. They carry out pointwise transformations of objects. As an example, the translation with the scaling factors $s_x = 2$ and $s_y = 0.5$ is considered, stretching along the x-axis by the factor 2 and shrinking in the direction of the y-axis by the factor 0.5. The application of this scaling to the rectangle whose lower left corner is located at the point (80,120) and whose upper right corner is at (180,180) yields a rectangle whose width has doubled with half the original height. But in addition, the centre of the rectangle is also transformed so that the transformed rectangle is shifted to the lower right compared to the original rectangle. Figure 2.13[4] shows the original rectangle and the rectangle after scaling by dashed lines. A scaling is always carried out with respect to the origin of the coordinate system. Applying a scaling to an object that is not centred around the origin of the coordinate system will lead to a translation of the (centre of the) object in addition to the scaling.

Another important group of geometric transformations are *rotations* that are determined by a single parameter, the rotation angle. The rotation is carried out anticlockwise around the origin of the coordinate system in case of a positive angle. A negative angle means that the rotation is carried out in a clockwise manner. The rotation $R(\theta)$ by the angle θ maps the point (x, y) to the point (x', y') given by

$$\left(\begin{array}{c} x' \\ y' \end{array} \right) = \left(\begin{array}{c} x \cdot \cos(\theta) - y \cdot \sin(\theta) \\ x \cdot \sin(\theta) + y \cdot \cos(\theta) \end{array} \right) = \left(\begin{array}{cc} \cos(\theta) & -\sin(\theta) \\ \sin(\theta) & \cos(\theta) \end{array} \right) \cdot \left(\begin{array}{c} x \\ y \end{array} \right).$$

A rotation is always carried out around the origin of the coordinate system. Therefore, a similar shifting effect as in the case of scalings happens, when an object is not centred around the origin. In figure 2.14 a rotation by an angle of 45° was carried out, mapping the original rectangle to the rectangle drawn with dashed lines.

The *shear transformation* is another elementary geometric transformation that causes a certain deformation of objects. Similar to scalings, the shear transformation requires two parameters, however, not on the main diagonal of the transformation matrix, but on the other two positions. Applying a shear transformation $Sh(s_x, s_y)$ to a point (x, y) yields the point (x', y') with the new coordinates

$$\left(\begin{array}{c} x' \\ y' \end{array} \right) = \left(\begin{array}{c} x + s_x \cdot y \\ y + s_y \cdot x \end{array} \right) = \left(\begin{array}{cc} 1 & s_x \\ s_y & 1 \end{array} \right) \cdot \left(\begin{array}{c} x \\ y \end{array} \right).$$

As in the case of scalings and rotations, shear transformations are carried out with respect to the origin of the coordinate system, so that an object that is not centred around the origin will not only be deformed by a shear transformation, but also shifted. The dashed rectangle is obtained from the original rectangle in figure 2.15 by applying a shear transformation with the parameters $s_x = 1$ and $s_y = 0$.

---

[4] The figure is drawn in the usual representation and not in the standard Java 2D window coordinate representation where the y-axis would point downwards.

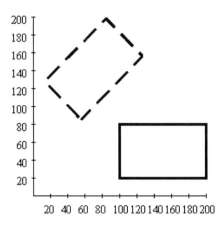

Figure 2.14 A rotation applied to a rectangle

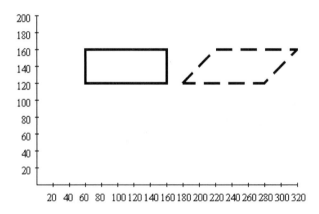

Figure 2.15 A shear transformation applied to a rectangle

Since $s_y = 0$ was chosen for this shear transformation, the shearing takes place in the direction of the y-axis. When the shearing should be carried out in the direction of the x-axis, $s_x = 0$ must hold.

The last elementary or primitive geometric transformation to be considered here is very simple, but differs from the other three types of elementary transformations that were introduced so far in an important aspect. A *translation* $T(d_x, d_y)$ causes a shift by the vector $\mathbf{d} = (d_x, d_y)^\top$. This means the translation maps the point (x, y) to the point

$$\begin{pmatrix} x' \\ y' \end{pmatrix} = \begin{pmatrix} x + d_x \\ y + d_y \end{pmatrix} = \begin{pmatrix} x \\ y \end{pmatrix} + \begin{pmatrix} d_x \\ d_y \end{pmatrix}.$$

In figure 2.16 a translation defined by the vector $\mathbf{d} = (140, 80)^\top$ is applied to a rectangle, mapping it to the dashed rectangle.

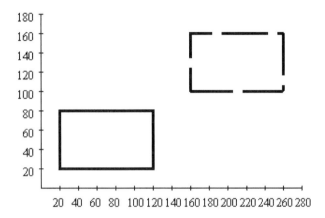

Figure 2.16 Translation of a rectangle

In contrast to the other transformations introduced so far, translations are not linear, so that they cannot be represented in terms of matrix multiplication. A matrix multiplication will always leave the zero vector unchanged, whereas a translation will shift all points including the origin of the coordinate system corresponding to the zero vector. Translations are affine, but not linear mappings.

Within computer graphics, more complex transformations are usually described or generated as compositions of elementary geometric transformations. A transformation composed of scalings, rotations and shear transformations can be specified by a single matrix, obtained as the product of the matrices encoding the corresponding elementary transformations. When also translations are involved, the composition of transformation can no longer be computed by simple matrix multiplication and represented by a single matrix. If all this was possible within matrix calculus, this would be a great advantage in terms of memory— just a single matrix is required to represent a complex transformations—and in terms of computational efficiency since all that would be needed for fast computations are efficient implementations of matrix operations.

In order to represent also translations in matrix form, another representation of the coordinates of points is introduced. The next section will discuss this alternative representation called homogeneous coordinates in more detail.

2.6 Homogeneous coordinates

This section introduces the representation of points in the two-dimensional plane in homogeneous coordinates. The same concept will also be applied later on to points in the three-dimensional space for the same reason, to allow the representation of 3D translations in matrix form. *Homogeneous coordinates* use an additional dimension for the representation of points. The point (x, y, z) in homogeneous coordinates is identified with the point $\left(\frac{x}{z}, \frac{y}{z}\right)$ in Cartesian coordinates. The z-component of a point in homogeneous coordinates must not be zero. When the point (x_0, y_0) in Cartesian coordinates has to be transformed into homogeneous coordinates, the representation $(x_0, y_0, 1)$ can be used. This is, however, not the only way to represent the point (x_0, y_0) in homogeneous coordinates. Any representation of the form $(z \cdot x_0, z \cdot y_0, z)$ where $z \neq 0$ encodes also the same point. The points $\{(x, y, z) \in \mathbb{R}^3 \mid (x, y, z) = (z \cdot x_0, z \cdot y_0, z)\}$ lie on a line in the space $\mathbb{R}^3$ passing through the origin of the coordinate system. The line is given by the system of equations

$$
\begin{aligned}
x - x_0 \cdot z &= 0, \\
y - y_0 \cdot z &= 0.
\end{aligned}
$$

Any point on this line, except the origin of the coordinate system, is a representative in homogenous coordinates of the point (x_0, y_0) in Cartesian coordinates. Fixing a value for z for the representation in homogeneous coordinates, for instance $z = 1$, the Cartesian x/y-plane is represented by a parallel plane with the corresponding constant z-value.

Figure 2.17 illustrates these relations. All points on the line shown in figure 2.17 represent the same point in the two-dimensional Cartesian plane $\mathbb{R}^2$. Choosing a constant value for z, for instance one of the planes shown in figure 2.17, the corresponding plane is a homogeneous representative of the Cartesian plane $\mathbb{R}^2$.

The origin of the Cartesian coordinate system corresponds to any point of the form $(0, 0, z)$ $(z \neq 0)$ in homogeneous coordinates. This point is no longer a necessary fixed point of a linear mapping in terms of homogeneous coordinates, i.e., a linear mapping from $\mathbb{R}^3$ to $\mathbb{R}^3$. The linear mapping can map this point to another point in homogeneous coordinates.

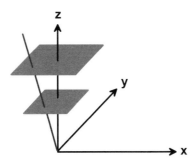

Figure 2.17 Homogeneous coordinates

In homogeneous coordinates a translation can now be written as matrix multiplication:

$$\begin{pmatrix} x' \\ y' \\ 1 \end{pmatrix} = \begin{pmatrix} x + d_x \\ y + d_y \\ 1 \end{pmatrix} = \begin{pmatrix} 1 & 0 & d_x \\ 0 & 1 & d_y \\ 0 & 0 & 1 \end{pmatrix} \cdot \begin{pmatrix} x \\ y \\ 1 \end{pmatrix}.$$

The other elementary transformation can be extended to homogeneous coordinates in a straightforward manner, leading to the following set of transformation matrices:

transformation	notation	matrix
translation	$T(d_x, d_y)$	$\begin{pmatrix} 1 & 0 & d_x \\ 0 & 1 & d_y \\ 0 & 0 & 1 \end{pmatrix}$
scaling	$S(s_x, s_y)$	$\begin{pmatrix} s_x & 0 & 0 \\ 0 & s_y & 0 \\ 0 & 0 & 1 \end{pmatrix}$
rotation	$R(\theta)$	$\begin{pmatrix} \cos(\theta) & -\sin(\theta) & 0 \\ \sin(\theta) & \cos(\theta) & 0 \\ 0 & 0 & 1 \end{pmatrix}$
shear transformation	$S(s_x, s_y)$	$\begin{pmatrix} 1 & s_x & 0 \\ s_y & 1 & 0 \\ 0 & 0 & 1 \end{pmatrix}$

Rotations and translations preserve lengths and angles. Scalings and shear transformations do not preserve lengths and angles in general, but at least parallel lines will be mapped to parallel lines again.

With this matrix representation in homogeneous coordinates, the composition of geometric transformations can be computed by matrix multiplication.

All matrices, introduced for the elementary geometric transformations are of the form

$$\begin{pmatrix} a & c & e \\ b & d & f \\ 0 & 0 & 1 \end{pmatrix}. \tag{2.1}$$

It is easy to verify that the product of two such matrices results again in a matrix of the same form. Therefore, geometric transformations are usually represented and stored in this way in computer graphics. This does not only apply to transformations that operate on the two-dimensional plane, but also to transformations in the three-dimensional space that will be discussed in chapter 5. It is now obvious that a graphics card of a computer must—among other things—be able to carry out matrix operations as fast as possible.

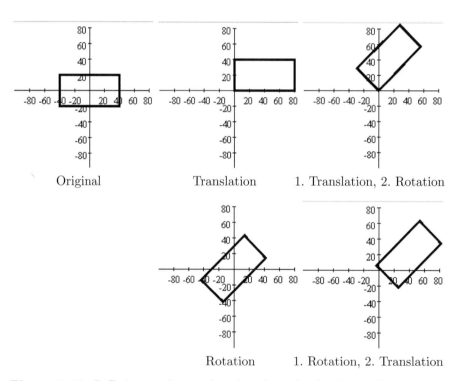

Figure 2.18 Differing results on changing the order for the application of a translation and a rotation

For the composition of transformations it should be taken into account that the order in which the transformations are applied is of importance. Matrix multiplication is a noncommutative operation. The right part of figure 2.18 shows the different results that are obtained, when the order in which translation and rotation are applied is changed. When first a translation with the translation vector $(40, 20)^\top$ and afterwards a rotation by $45°$ is applied, then the rectangle on the left-hand side of figure 2.18 is mapped to the upper rectangle on the right. When the rotation is carried out first and afterwards the translation, the result is the lower right rectangle. This effect occurs in general in all cases, when geometric transformations of different types are combined. Only when transformations of the same type, i.e., only rotations, only translations, only scalings or only shear transformations, are composed, the order in which the transformations are applied is of no importance.

It should also be taken into account that transformations in matrix notation or as compositions of mappings are carried out from right to left. The transformation

$$(T(d_x, d_y) \circ R(\theta))(\mathbf{v})$$

or in matrix notation

$$\begin{pmatrix} 1 & 0 & d_x \\ 0 & 1 & d_y \\ 0 & 0 & 1 \end{pmatrix} \cdot \begin{pmatrix} \cos(\theta) & -\sin(\theta) & 0 \\ \sin(\theta) & \cos(\theta) & 0 \\ 0 & 0 & 1 \end{pmatrix} \cdot \mathbf{v}$$

means that first the rotation $R(\theta)$ and then the translation $T(d_x, d_y)$ is applied to the point $\mathbf{v}$.

2.7 Applications of transformations

This section introduces typical applications and problems that can be solved using geometric transformations.

In computer graphics it is common to define objects in an arbitrary coordinate system in floating point arithmetics, the so-called *world coordinates*. In order to generate an image of specific objects on the computer screen or another output device, a rectangular clipping region, called *viewport*, must be specified. The viewport determines which region of the "object world" is visible. Therefore, it is necessary to find a transformation that maps the objects in the viewport, given in world coordinates, to the window coordinates of the computer screen.

Figure 2.19 illustrates the problem and its solution. The rectangle with the lower left corner at $(x_{\min}, y_{\min})$ and the upper right corner at $(x_{\max}, y_{\max})$ in the upper left part of the figure defines the viewport or the clipping region, a window specified in the world coordinate system. This part of the object world

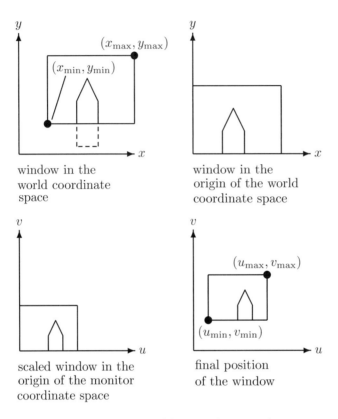

Figure 2.19 From world to window coordinates

should be shown on the computer screen in a window defined by the rectangle with $(u_{\min}, v_{\min})$ as its lower left and $(u_{\max}, v_{\max})$ as its upper right corner, given in the coordinates of the computer monitor. These two windows can have different sizes. Even the shape of the two rectangles does not have to coincide.

The mapping from the viewport to the computer monitor can be realized as a composition of the following transformations. In the first step, the viewport window is shifted to the origin of the coordinate system by a suitable translation. In the next step, the viewport window is scaled in such a way that it matches the size of the window on the computer screen. Finally, another translation will position the scaled window at the correct location on the computer screen. Altogether, the following sequence of elementary geometric transformations has to be carried out:

$$T(u_{\min}, v_{\min}) \circ S\left(\frac{u_{\max} - u_{\min}}{x_{\max} - x_{\min}}, \frac{v_{\max} - v_{\min}}{y_{\max} - y_{\min}}\right) \circ T(-x_{\min}, -y_{\min}). \quad (2.2)$$

In equation (2.2) ∘ denotes the composition or concatenation of mappings. It should be noted again that the transformations are carried out from right to left in this formula.

As mentioned before, rotations $R(\theta)$ defined by a rotation matrix as described on page 29 will always carry out the rotation around the origin of the coordinate system. When the centre of the rotation is supposed to be another point (x_0, y_0), one can achieve this by applying first a translation shifting the point (x_0, y_0) to the origin of the coordinate system, then carry out the rotation around the origin and afterwards reverse the initial translation. This means that a rotation through the angle θ around the point (x_0, y_0) can be implemented by the following composition of transformations:

$$R(\theta, x_0, y_0) \;=\; T(x_0, y_0) \circ R(\theta) \circ T(-x_0, -y_0). \qquad (2.3)$$

In the same way, a scaling can be carried out with respect to the point (x_0, y_0) instead of the origin of the coordinate system, by simply replacing the rotation in (2.3) by the corresponding scaling.

Pixel coordinates within a window on the computer screen are usually specified in such a way that the first component refers to the pixel column, whereas the second component refers to the pixel row, where pixel rows are counted from top to bottom. As a consequence, the x-axis points as usual from left to right, but the y-axis is oriented in a reverse manner, i.e., it points downwards instead of upwards. When the specification in standard Cartesian coordinates is preferred, one can simply apply suitable geometric transformations, before drawing objects in the window coordinate system. In order to reverse the direction of the y-axis, a reflection with respect to the x-axis has to be carried out. After this reflection, the y-axis points upwards, but the origin of the coordinate system of the window still remains in the upper left corner, so that only objects with negative y-components would be visible. Therefore, after the reflection a translation is also carried out. The translation is a shift in y-direction by the height h of the window, measured in pixels. In this way, the origin of the coordinate system is mapped to the lower left corner of the window. The reflection is a scaling with the parameters $s_x = 1$ and $s_y = -1$. Altogether the transformation is given by

$$T(0, h) \circ S(1, -1). \qquad (2.4)$$

2.8 Geometric transformations in Java 2D

The class `AffineTransform` is the basis for geometric transformations in Java 2D where geometric transformations are also implemented by matrices in homogeneous coordinates. The most important constructors are:

- `AffineTransform id = new AffineTransform()`
  generates the identical transformation, that is encoded by the unity matrix.
  This default constructor generates a transformation that maps every point
  to itself.

- The constructor

      `AffineTransform at = new AffineTransform(a,d,b,e,c,f)`

  allows the specification of an arbitrary transformation matrix. The arguments
  $a, \ldots, f$ define the six `Double`-parameters of the transformation matrix. The
  matrix (2.1) on page 30 shows the assignment of the arguments to the corresponding matrix parameters.

  The elementary geometric transformations can be generated in the following
way:

Rotation:

- For rotations the class `AffineTransform` provides the two methods
  `affTrans.setToRotation(angle)` that defines the transformation
  `affTrans` as a rotation through the angle `angle` around the origin of
  the coordinate system and `affTrans.setToRotation(angle,x,y)` setting the transformation `affTrans` to a rotation through the angle `angle`
  around the point (x, y), respectively.

- The method `affTrans.rotation(angle)` and the corresponding method
  `affTrans.rotation(angle,x,y)` extend the transformation
  `affTrans` by a rotation around the origin of the coordinate system or
  around the point (x, y). This means that the matrix that encodes the
  original transformation `affTrans` is multiplied from the right by a matrix for the corresponding rotation. As a consequence, when `affTrans` is
  applied to an object, the rotation is carried out first and afterwards the
  original transformation in `affTrans` is applied.

Scaling:

- The method `affTrans.setToScale(sx,sy)` defines the transformation
  `affTrans` as a scaling with the scaling factors `sx` for the x- and `sy` for
  the y-axis with respect to the origin of the coordinate system.

- The method `affTrans.scale(sx,sy)` extends the transformation
  `affTrans` by a corresponding scaling. The extension is to be understood
  in the same way as in the case of rotations, i.e., as a matrix multiplication
  from the right.

Shear transformation:

- The method `affTrans.setToShear(sx,sy)` defines the transformation `affTrans` as a shear transformation with the shear values `sx` for the x- and `sy` for the y-axis with respect to the origin of the coordinate system.

- The method `affTrans.shear(sx,sy)` extends the transformation `affTrans` by a corresponding shear transformation, again in terms of matrix multiplication from the right.

Translation:

- The method `affTrans.setToTranslation(dx,dy)` defines the transformation `affTrans` as translation by the vector $(dx, dy)^\top$.

- The method `affTrans.translate(dx,dy)` extends the transformation `affTrans` by a corresponding translation in the same manner as for rotations, scalings and shear transformations, i.e., as matrix multiplication from the right.

The following methods for the composition of such affine transformations are available in the class `AffineTransform`:

- By `at1.concatenate(at2)` the affine transformation `at2` is appended to the affine transformation `at1` in terms of matrix multiplication from the right, so that first `at2` and then the original transformation `at1` is carried out.

- By `at1.preConcatenate(at2)` the affine transformation `at2` is combined with the affine transformation `at1` in the sense of matrix multiplication from the left. This means that first the original transformation `at1` and then `at2` is carried out.

In both cases, the composition of the two transformations is stored in `at1`.

An affine transformation that is defined as an instance `affTrans` of the class `AffineTransform` can be applied to a `Shape` object `s` in the following way:

```
Shape transformedShape = affTrans.createTransformedShape(s);
```

The method `createTransformedShape` returns the transformed object again as an instance of the class `Shape`.

In the same way, affine transformations can be applied to an **Area** object `a`, for instance in the form

```
Area transformedArea = affTrans.createTransformedArea(a);
```

An affine transformation can also be applied to the `Graphics2D` object `g2d` by

```
g2d.transform(affTrans);
```

In this case, the corresponding affine transformation will be applied to all objects before they are drawn.

Figures 2.13–2.16 and the images in figure 2.18 were generated using these methods in the following programs:

- ScalingExample.java,

- RotationExample.java,

- ShearingExample.java,

- TranslationExample.java,

- TransformationOrderExample.java,

- TransformationOrderExampleT.java,

- TransformationOrderExampleRT.java,

- TransformationOrderExampleR.java and

- TransformationOrderExampleTR.java.

In all of these figures a standard Cartesian coordinate system instead of the window coordinate system was used for the representation of the objects, so that the y-axis points upwards in the window. In order to achieve this effect, an affine transformation according to (2.4) was applied to the Graphics2D object yielding the desired orientation of the y-axis and the desired location of the origin of the coordinate system.

```
AffineTransform yUp = new AffineTransform();
yUp.setToScale(1,-1);
AffineTransform translate = new AffineTransform();
translate.setToTranslation(xOffset,windowHeight-yOffset);
yUp.preConcatenate(translate);
g2d.transform(yUp);
```

In (2.4) the values xOffset and yOffset do not occur. This means they are assumed to be zero there. Setting both values to zero means that the origin of the coordinate system is in the lower left corner of the window, a point that is on the margin of the window and therefore, it is not possible to draw this point. Thus, the origin of the coordinate system was slightly shifted to the interior of the window by choosing xOffset=140 and yOffset=150, so that the origin of the coordinate system is visible inside the window.

2.9 Animation and movements based on transformations

So far, geometric transformations were only applied in a static manner in order to map one coordinate system to another or to describe positioning and deformation of objects. Geometric transformations are also suitable to model moving objects, for instance moving the hands of a clock carrying out a rotation of 6° per second or per minute or 30° per hour. Continuous movements must be decomposed into small stepwise movements which can be described by geometric transformations. The stepwise changes between two images must be small enough and the time between two images in a sequence must be short enough in order to let the movement appear as a continuous or floating movement and not as jumps from one state to another.

Once the movement of an object is modelled by suitable geometric transformations, the object must be drawn, the transformed object has to be computed, the old object must be deleted and the new transformed object has to be drawn again. Deleting the old object causes problems for raster graphics. Deleting means in this case to overwrite the object. In order to overwrite the pixels of the old object a background image must be specified. For more complex objects, overwriting the pixels belonging to the old object would require to render the object again in order to determine which pixels were covered by the old object. Therefore, instead of overwriting single moving objects it is common to write the complete image buffer again, instead of modifying the old one. However, the new image is usually not written directly into the window buffer, but into a virtual buffer which will be copied to the window buffer after the image has been completed. This technique is also called *double buffering* and will be explained in more detail in section 4.2.

As a simple example for a moving object, a moving clock with a single hand for the seconds is considered sliding from the lower left to the upper right of a display window. The clock itself consists of a quadratic frame and the single rectangular hand for the seconds. The hands for minutes and hours could be modelled in the same way, but are not included here for reasons of simplicity. A translation is needed in order to move the quadratic frame of the clock from the lower left to the upper right corner of the window. This translation must also be applied to the hand for the seconds. In addition to the translation, the hand must also rotate. Figure 2.20 shows some snapshots of the moving clock.

Assuming that the clock should move in each step two units to the right and one unit up, this could be modelled by a translation

$$T_{\text{clock,step}} = T(2,1).$$

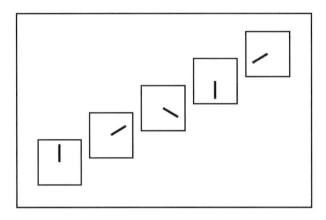

Figure 2.20 A moving clock with a rotating hand

For the hand a rotation of the form

$$T_{\text{hand,step}} \;=\; R(-\pi/180)$$

is needed in order to turn the hand by $-\pi/180$, i.e., by $6°$ clockwise in each step. One end of the hand is fixed in the centre of the clock which is therefore also the centre of the rotation. Even if the clock were initially centred in the origin of the coordinate system, it would move out of the origin after one step already and the centre of rotation for the hand would no longer be the origin.

There are two possible strategies to describe and handle such composed movements as in the case of the hand, where a translation as well as a rotation has to be carried out. One way would be to track the position of the corresponding object—in this case the hand of the clock—and to shift the centre of the rotation accordingly. In the general case, it is not sufficient to track only the translation of an object. If, for instance, the object is also supposed to be scaled along one of its axes, it is also necessary to know the orientation of the object in order to apply the scaling properly. As an example, the hand of the clock could get longer or shorter while it is rotating without changing its width. In the beginning, the corresponding scaling had to be a scaling along the y-axis. But once the hand starts to rotate, the axis of scaling must also be rotated. Otherwise the hand would not only become longer or shorter, but also thicker or thinner.

Although this strategy for modelling continuous movements of objects is applicable, the following second strategy seems to be more convenient and simpler to implement. The principle of this second strategy is to leave the objects in their initial positions and to compute accumulated geometric transformations which are applied to the objects before they are drawn. For the example of the clock one could use three more transformations in addition to the above-mentioned two transformations:

$$T^{(\text{new})}_{\text{clock,accTrans}} \;=\; T_{\text{clock,step}} \circ T^{(\text{old})}_{\text{clock,accTrans}}$$

$$T^{(\text{new})}_{\text{hand,accRotation}} \;=\; T_{\text{hand,step}} \circ T^{(\text{old})}_{\text{hand,accRotation}}$$

$$T_{\text{hand,acc}} \;=\; T_{\text{clock,accTrans}} \circ T_{\text{hand,accRotation}}.$$

$T_{\text{clock,accTrans}}$ and $T_{\text{hand,accRotation}}$ are initialized by the identical transformations and are then updated in each step according to the specified equations. $T_{\text{clock,accTrans}}$ specifies the translation which has to be carried out in order to shift the clock from the initial position to the actual position. $T_{\text{clock,accTrans}}$ is applied to the initial frame of the clock that is centred in the origin of the coordinate system. $T_{\text{hand,accRotation}}$ describes the rotation around the origin of the coordinate system that must be applied to the hand of the clock in order to reach its actual position within the clock centred around the origin. In addition to this rotation, the hand must also move along with the clock. Therefore, after rotating the hand around the origin, the corresponding translation $T_{\text{clock,accTrans}}$ is also applied to the hand. It is important that the rotation is carried out first and only then the translation is applied.

Scenegraphs as they are introduced in chapter 5 provide a more convenient alternative to this way of modelling movements and animations.

2.10 Movements via transformations in Java 2D

This section explains how to implement the simple example of the moving clock of the previous section in Java 2D. Within the book, only the most essential parts of the source code are shown. The full source code for this example can be found in the class NonSynchronizedClock.java.

In order to specify the location of the objects and the transformations in standard coordinates with the y-axis pointing upwards, the transformation yUp introduced on page 36 is applied to the Graphics2D object.

Initially, the frame of the clock will be centred in the origin of the coordinate system. It is represented by the object clockFrame of the class Rectangle2D. The single hand of the clock named clockHand is also generated as an object from the class Rectangle2D. Its initial position is chosen in such a way that it starts in the origin of the coordinate system and points upwards with the y-axis as its centre axis.

The transformations $T_{\text{clock,step}}$, $T_{\text{hand,step}}$, $T_{\text{clock,accTrans}}$, $T_{\text{hand,accRotation}}$ and $T_{\text{hand,acc}}$ as described above are represented by the objects singleTranslation, singleRotation, accumulatedTranslation, accumulatedRotation and handTransform, respectively, all belonging to the class AffineTransform.

The transformation singleTranslation is defined as a translation by the vector $(2, 1)^\top$, whereas singleRotation is a clockwise rotation by an angle of 6°. Both transformations remain unchanged, while the program is running.

The transformation accumulatedRotation is initialised as the identity. The transformation accumulatedTranslation could also be initialised as the identity. But this would lead to the effect that the clock starts its movement centred in the lower left corner of the window, so that in the beginning only the upper left quarter of the clock would be visible. Therefore, a suitable translation is chosen for the initialisation of accumulatedTranslation ensuring that the clock is fully visible, when the animation is started.

A loop is used to compute the stepwise changing positions of the clock and the hand. In this loop, the transformations accumulatedTranslation, accumulatedRotation and handTransform are updated according to the equations specified on page 39. This is realised by the following lines of code:

```
accumulatedTranslation.preConcatenate(singleTranslation);
accumulatedRotation.preConcatenate(singleRotation);
handTransform.setTransform(accumulatedRotation);
handTransform.preConcatenate(accumulatedTranslation);
```

The first line corresponds to the first equation, the second line to the second equation and the last two lines implement the last equation.

After the transformations have been updated in this way, the old image must be deleted and afterwards the frame of the clock and its hand have to be drawn again. Before these objects are drawn, the corresponding transformations are applied to them making sure that they are positioned at their updated locations.

```
g2d.draw(accumulatedTranslation.createTransformedShape(
                                          clockFrame));
```

```
g2d.fill(handTransform.createTransformedShape(clockHand));
```

The initial objects clockFrame and clockHand for the frame of the clock and for its hand, respectively, are not changed in the loop. Only the transformations applied to them change and the updated transformations are used to generate new objects of the class Shape that are drawn in each step.

The implementation proposed here has various disadvantages. Since all computations for the animation are carried within the paint method, this might lead to flickering and it might also be difficult to stop the animation since the paint method has a high priority in order to avoid showing half-ready images.

For MAC computers the animation might not work at all since all computations in the `paint` method will be carried out completely, before anything is drawn on the screen. The program `NonSynchronizedClock.java` also uses a very primitive `sustain` method for the intermediate time between two frames. This method implements active waiting which should be avoided in programming. The double buffering technique introduced in section 4.2 offers a much better solution than the one provided here which was only presented for reasons of simplicity.

2.11 Interpolators for continuous changes

The previous two sections have demonstrated how moving objects can be modelled on the basis of suitable transformations. Single stepwise transformations describe the changes of the objects from one image frame to the next one. The composition of these stepwise transformations determines the complete movement of an object.

But there are also other ways to model movements or changes of objects in animated graphics. An alternative approach is based on the two descriptions of the initial state of the considered object and of its desired final state. The aim is then to find an animation that shows a continuous transition of the object from the initial to its final state. The movement of an object along a line can either be modelled by small stepwise translations to be carried out between two image frames as in the previous two sections or by simply specifying the initial and the end position of the object and then carrying out interpolations between these two positions. In the example of the clock from the previous two sections, one would not define the transformation $T_{\text{clock,step}} = T(2,1)$ to be applied repeatedly to the clock in a sequence of, for instance, 100 images. Instead, it would be sufficient to specify the initial and the end position of the object, say $\mathbf{p}_0 = (0,0)^\top$ and $\mathbf{p}_1 = (200, 100)^\top$.

The points $\mathbf{p}_\alpha$ on the connecting line between the points $\mathbf{p}_0$ and $\mathbf{p}_1$ are simply the *convex combinations* of these two points given by

$$\mathbf{p}_\alpha = (1 - \alpha) \cdot \mathbf{p}_0 + \alpha \cdot \mathbf{p}_1, \qquad \alpha \in [0,1].$$

$\alpha = 0$ yields the initial point $\mathbf{p}_0$, $\alpha = 1$ leads to the end point $\mathbf{p}_1$ and $\alpha = 0.5$ defines the point in the middle between $\mathbf{p}_0$ and $\mathbf{p}_1$.

This principle of convex combinations can be applied not only to points or vectors, but also to matrices. Later on, in section 4.7 the principle of convex combinations will also be applied to colours to generate continuous changes from one colour to another.

In order to understand how convex combinations applied to matrices can be used to generate animations, two affine transformations are considered, given by the matrices M_0 and M_1 in homogeneous coordinates. The convex combination M_α of the two matrices is defined as

$$M_\alpha = (1 - \alpha) \cdot M_0 + \alpha \cdot M_1, \qquad \alpha \in [0, 1].$$

Note that M_α is again a matrix describing an affine transformation in homogeneous coordinates. In the simplest case, the two matrices encode translations mapping an object to its initial and its desired final position. The matrices M_α correspond to intermediate translations. M_α places the object on the points on the line connecting the initial and the end position. For $\alpha = 0$, M_α maps the object to its initial position and for $\alpha = 1$ to its final position.

However, convex combinations are not restricted to translations. In principle, the matrices M_0 and M_1 can represent any two affine transformations that do not even have to belong to the same type of transformation. One could be a rotation, the other a scaling combined with a shearing.

In this way, a continuous transformation can be implemented between two objects obtained from the same object by applying two different transformations. Figure 2.21 illustrates this process for two ellipses that were both generated from the same basic object—also an ellipse—by applying different scalings and transformations. The ellipse in the upper left corner is obtained from the basic ellipse by applying the first transformation, whereas the second transformation yields the ellipse in the lower right corner. Applying convex combinations of these two transformations to the basic ellipse leads to the ellipses in between.

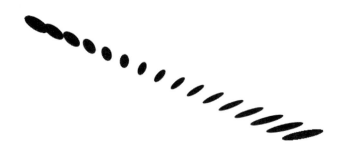

Figure 2.21 Changing one ellipse to another by convex combinations of transformations

Another technique for continuous interpolation between two objects S and S' assumes that both objects are determined by n points $P_1 = (x_1, y_1), \ldots, P_n = (x_n, y_n)$ and $P'_1 = (x'_1, y'_1), \ldots, P'_n = (x'_n, y'_n)$, respectively, and by lines or

quadratic and cubic curves defined using these points. It is important that the
lines or curves in both objects are determined by the corresponding points.
This means, if a quadratic curve defined by the points P_1, P_3 and P_8 is part of
object S, then the corresponding quadratic curve defined by the points P_1', P_3'
and P_8' must be part of object S'.

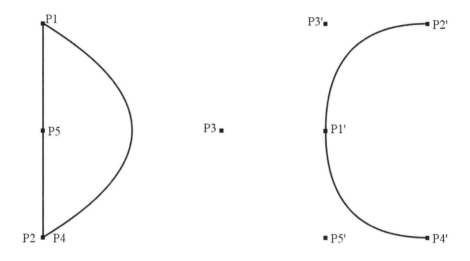

Figure 2.22 Two letters each defined by five points and two quadratic curves

Figure 2.22 shows two simple objects in the form of the two letters D and C.
For each of them five control points $P1,\ldots,P5$ and $P1',\ldots,P5'$, respectively,
are specified. Both letters are described by two quadratic curves:

– One curve uses the corresponding first and second point as endpoints and
the third point as control point. In the case of the letter D the three points
are $P1$, $P2$ and $P3$, respectively, for the letter C the corresponding points
are $P1'$, $P2'$ and $P3'$, respectively.

– The other quadratic curve of each letter has the corresponding first and
fourth point as endpoints and the corresponding fifth point as control point.

In order to continuously transform the two objects—in this case the letters
D and C—into each other, convex combinations are applied again. Instead of
having convex combinations of transformations as in the previous example of
the ellipses, here convex combinations between pairs of corresponding points
P_i and P_i' are considered.

$$P_i^{(\alpha)} \;=\; (1-\alpha)\cdot P_i + \alpha\cdot P_i'.$$

For an intermediate image $\alpha \in [0, 1]$ the corresponding lines or curves are now drawn on the basis of the points $P_i^{(\alpha)}$. In the example of transforming the letter D into the letter C one would draw two quadratic curves, one defined by the points $P_1^{(\alpha)}$, $P_2^{(\alpha)}$ and $P_3^{(\alpha)}$, the other defined by the points $P_4^{(\alpha)}$, $P_5^{(\alpha)}$ and $P_3^{(\alpha)}$.

Figure 2.23 shows intermediate images obtained for the convex combinations with $\alpha = 0, 0.2, 0.4, 0.6, 0.8, 1$ based on the points and the corresponding quadratic curves as illustrated in figure 2.22.

Figure 2.23   Stepwise transformation of two letters into each other

Further applications of interpolators in connection with colours and raster graphics will be introduced in section 4.7.

2.12 Implementation of interpolators in Java 2D

This sections explains in more detail how the two techniques for interpolators introduced in the previous section can be implemented in Java 2D.

The first example of a continuous transition from one ellipse to another as illustrated in figure 2.21 is realised in the class `ConvexCombTransforms.java`. In the first part of the program the basic ellipse `elli` and two affine transformations `initialTransform` and `finalTransform` are defined. The two transformations transform the basic ellipse into the initial ellipse in the beginning of the animation and the final ellipse at the end of the animation. In order to compute the convex combinations of the two transformations the corresponding matrices are required. They are obtained by applying the method `getMatrix` to `initialTransform` and `finalTransform`.

```
double[] initialMatrix = new double[6];
initialTransform.getMatrix(initialMatrix);
```

```
double[] finalMatrix = new double[6];
finalTransform.getMatrix(finalMatrix);
```

The coefficients of the two matrices are stored in the one-dimensional arrays `initialMatrix` and `finalMatrix` according to the representation of transformation matrices (2.1) on page 30. The intermediate images are generated in a loop where in each step a new convex combination of the two arrays is computed. The arrays are treated in the same way as vectors[5] so that their convex combination yields an array of the same length. The elements of this new array can again be interpreted as the coefficients of a transformation matrix in homogeneous coordinates. This transformation is then applied to the basic ellipse and in each step of the loop the resulting transformed ellipse is drawn.

The transformation of the letter D into the letter C is implemented in the class `DToCMorphing.java`. Figure 2.22 showing the initial state—the letter D—and the final state—the letter C—was generated by the classes `SimpleLetterD.java` and `SimpleLetterC.java`. For the transformation of the two letters into each other, two arrays are defined for each letter, one array for the x-coordinates of the control points and one array for the y-coordinates. Another two arrays are needed for the computation of the convex combinations of the control points. In each step of the loop the new convex combination is computed and the computed control points are used to draw the corresponding quadratic curves to generate the corresponding intermediate image.

2.13 Single or double precision

For longer animated graphics with moving objects a large number of transformations have to be applied successively. This means that a large number of matrix multiplications must be carried out. Although the roundoff error for a single matrix multiplication might be negligible, roundoff errors can accumulate over time and might lead to undesired effects. In most cases such roundoff errors will be noticeable in the graphics to be drawn since the numerical computations to be carried out in computer graphics are usually not critical from the numerical point of view. Inverting a matrix to reverse a transformation is an example for an exception where roundoff errors might have serious effects on the graphics, when the matrix is badly conditioned. But most of the calculations in computer graphics do not encounter such problems.

For illustration purposes the example of the second hand of a clock is considered. The hand is 100 units or pixels long. The tip of the hand is at the point

---

[5] Vectors in the mathematical sense, not as the class `Vector` in Java.

time	x	y
	double	
1 minute	99.99999999999973	-4.8572257327350600E-14
2 minutes	99.99999999999939	-9.2981178312356860E-14
3 minutes	99.99999999999906	-1.3739009929736312E-13
4 minutes	99.99999999999876	-1.4571677198205180E-13
5 minutes	99.99999999999857	-2.2204460492503130E-13
6 minutes	99.99999999999829	-2.9143354396410360E-13
7 minutes	99.99999999999803	-3.1641356201816960E-13
8 minutes	99.99999999999771	-3.7331249203020890E-13
9 minutes	99.99999999999747	-4.2604808569990380E-13
10 minutes	99.99999999999715	-4.5657921887709560E-13
8 hours	99.99999999986587	-2.9524993561125257E-11
	float	
1 minute	100.00008	-1.1175871E-5
2 minutes	100.00020	-1.4901161E-5
3 minutes	100.00032	-1.8626451E-5
4 minutes	100.00044	-1.1920929E-5
5 minutes	100.00056	-8.9406970E-6
6 minutes	100.00068	-3.1292439E-5
7 minutes	100.00085	-5.3644180E-5
8 minutes	100.00100	-7.2270630E-5
9 minutes	100.00108	-8.0466270E-5
10 minutes	100.00113	-8.4191560E-5
8 hours	100.00328	-1.9669533E-4

Table 2.1   Effects of roundoff errors

$(100, 0)$ in the beginning. The hand is rotated clockwise around the origin by $6°$ per second. This means that the transformation $R(-6°)$ in terms of a rotation matrix is applied each time. After every full minute—after 60 multiplications of the rotations matrix by itself—the hand should return to its original position.

Table 2.1 shows the computed positions of the tip of the hand after various time intervals using double (`double`) and single (`float`) precision. In both cases the roundoff errors are negligible, especially when taking into account that drawing in raster graphics will require rounding to integer values in the end anyway. Even after eight hours demanding 28800 matrix multiplications, single precision will still be sufficient to obtain the exact values in terms of raster graphics. This is only valid if the accumulated rotation is applied to the hand in its initial position or if the new position of the hand is stored in vector graphics, i.e., using floating point arithmetic, and every second a single rotation by 6° is applied to the updated position of the hand. If the coordinates of the hand are stored in raster graphics using only integer values and a single rotation by 6° is applied to the updated hand in pixel coordinates every second, already after one minute a wrong position of $(95, -2)$ instead of $(100, 0)$ is calculated.

Although computations with double precision values are less error-prone, the accuracy of single precision is sufficient for most applications in computer graphics taking into account that raster graphics will require rounding numbers to integer values in the end, so that numerical errors less than 0.5 are invisible anyway.

Especially for three-dimensional scenes with complex objects a very large number of points is needed to define the objects. In this case the memory requirements very often have a higher priority and single precision is preferred over double precision in order to reduce the amount of memory needed for storing the objects.

2.14 Exercises

Exercise 2.1

Use a `GeneralPath` to draw a rectangle with rounded corners.

Exercise 2.2

A simple two-dimensional solar system model with one sun and one planet should be animated. The centre of the sun is located in the origin of the coordinate system. The spherical planet with a radius of 10 units rotates anticlockwise around the sun on a circular orbit with constant speed. The radius of the planet's orbit (the distance between the centres of the sun and the planet) is 200 units. In the beginning of the animation the centre of the planet is located at the point $(200, 0)$. During one rotation around the sun, the planet rotates 365 times anticlockwise around its own axes. Consider the point on the planet that is closest to the sun in the beginning of the animation. Use geometric transformations to describe where the point will be located after the planet has finished one third of its orbit.

Exercise 2.3

Choose the constant c in the matrix

$$\begin{pmatrix} c & 0 & 6 \\ 0 & c & 4 \\ 0 & 0 & c \end{pmatrix}$$

in such a way that the matrix represents a translation by the vector $(3, 2)^\top$ in homogeneous coordinates.

Exercise 2.4

Use Java 2D for an animation illustrating the movement of the point in exercise 2.2.

Exercise 2.5

Use Java 2D to animate a beating heart that moves along a line in a window on the computer screen.

Exercise 2.6

Apply the technique for transforming one letter into another as illustrated in figure 2.22 for the letters D and C to other letters, for instance your initials.

3

Drawing lines and curves

The previous chapter has introduced basic objects and geometric transformations for two-dimensional computer graphics using the principles of vector graphics. As already mentioned in the introduction, drawing geometric objects in a raster graphics framework requires efficient algorithms. This chapter illustrates the basic problems and solutions in the context of drawing lines and curves within raster graphics.

3.1 Lines and pixel graphics

Drawing a line connecting the points (x_0, y_0) and (x_1, y_1) within a raster graphics framework seems to be a very simple task. However, it will turn out that a naïve approach can lead to inefficient algorithms or even unacceptable results. For reasons of simplicity, it is assumed that the two points to be connected by the line lie on the pixel raster. This means their coordinates are given by integer values. Without loss of generality it is assumed that the first point is not located right of the second point. This means that $x_0 \leq x_1$ holds. If this is not satisfied, the two points can simply be exchanged for drawing the line.

The naïve approach to drawing the corresponding line on the pixel raster would step incrementally through the x-coordinates starting from x_0 and ending at x_1 and compute the corresponding y-value for each x-value. Since the y-value will usually not be an integer value, it must be rounded to the closest integer value in order to draw the closest pixel on the raster with the corresponding x- and the rounded y-value. Figure 3.1 describes this strategy in pseudocode.

```
void drawLine(int x0, int y0, int x1, int y1)
{
  int x;
  double dy = y1 - y0;
  double dx = x1 - x0;
  double m  = dy/dx;
  double y  = y0;

  for (x=x0; x<=x1; x++)
  {
    drawPixel(x, round(y));
    y = y + m;    //or: y = y0 + m*(x - x0);
  }
}
```

Figure 3.1 Pseudocode for a naïve line drawing algorithm

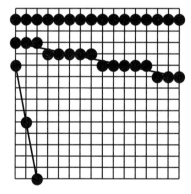

Figure 3.2 Lines resulting from the naïve line drawing algorithm

First of all, it should be noted that this algorithm will fail in the case of a vertical line where $x_0 = x_1$ holds, leading to a division by zero error when the slope m of the line is computed. Of course, this special case could easily be treated separately. Although the algorithm will no longer have problems with division by zero it will still fail to draw acceptable lines as can be seen in figure 3.2. The upper, horizontal line is as perfect as can be expected in raster graphics. The line below with a slightly negative slope is also drawn correctly in terms of raster graphics, taking into account that—at least at the moment—pixels can either be drawn in full black colour or they can be left white. The ideal line that is approximated by the drawn pixels is also included in the figure for illustration purposes.

However, the line in the lower left with the highly negative slope is not drawn correctly, even in terms of the necessary discretisation for raster graphics. A number of pixels are missing that should be drawn for the raster graphics representation of the line. The problem is caused by the fact that the increment for the x-values is one, but due to the large absolute slope of the line the y-value of the line will change by more than one. This leads to the gaps in the representation of the line in raster graphics, since the increments, or the jumps, in the y-values are larger than one. The same effect will occur for all lines with an absolute slope larger than one. The higher the slope of the line, the larger the gaps in the pixel representation will be.

Exchanging the roles of the x- and the y-axis for drawing lines with an absolute slope greater than one solves the problem. This means that instead of incrementing the x-values by one and computing the corresponding y-value, the y-values are incremented and the corresponding rounded x-values are computed for the line. This also solves the previously mentioned problem of division by zero for vertical lines. A vertical line with infinite slope becomes a horizontal line with slope zero, when the coordinate axes are exchanged.

Drawing a line on a pixel raster is a task within computer graphics which has to be carried out many times even for a single image. Therefore, efficient line drawing algorithms are needed to speed up drawing images. One could use the naïve line drawing algorithm described in figure 3.1 and extend it by the necessary exchange of the coordinate axes for lines with absolute slope larger than one. But there are still two choices in the last line of the pseudocode. The first formula requires only a single addition to compute the y-value of the line for the next step. The second one needs two additions[1] and one multiplication. A multiplication demands more computation time than an addition. Therefore, the first version for the computation of the y-value should be preferred. The only disadvantage of this formula is the danger of accumulated roundoff errors. However, this can be neglected, since the number of iterations in the loop is limited by the number of pixels on the x- and the y-axis. So even in the case of a larger high-resolution monitor, the loop cannot contain more than a few thousand iterations. Because rounding to an integer number must be carried out in the end anyway, even the accumulated roundoff error can be neglected.

---

[1] To be precise: One addition and one subtraction.

3.2 The midpoint algorithm for lines

Drawing lines can be carried out in a way much faster than the naïve line drawing algorithm from the previous section. The naïve line drawing algorithm is based on floating point arithmetic for determining rounded integer pixel coordinates. Since integer arithmetic is much faster than floating point arithmetic, a considerable speed-up of the line drawing algorithm could be achieved, if floating point arithmetic could be avoided completely. A line drawing algorithm relying only on integer arithmetic was introduced by J.E. Bresenham [5]. This algorithm will be explained in the following.

When examining the naïve line drawing algorithm in detail, it was already noted that it should be ensured that the line to be drawn has an absolute slope of at most one. For a line with absolute slope greater than one, the roles of the coordinate axes are exchanged for drawing, leading to a line with absolute slope less than one in the modified coordinate system. So in any case, before starting to compute the actual pixels representing a line, the first step is to decide which coordinate axis should be considered as the x-axis in order to ensure that the line has an absolute slope of at most one. Therefore, it is assumed for the following considerations that a line with absolute slope less than one should be drawn. The considerations are even restricted to the case that the slope is between 0 and 1. For lines with a slope between 0 and -1 a corresponding algorithm can be developed analogously.

If a line with slope between 0 and 1 is drawn pixel by pixel and the last pixel which was drawn is located at (x_p, y_p), then there are only two choices for the next pixel. It is obvious that the x-coordinate of the next pixel is $x_{p+1} = x_p + 1$. Since the line has a nonnegative slope, the next y-value cannot be smaller than the previous one. On the other hand, the slope of the line is bounded by one so that it cannot jump over two pixels in the y-direction, when the x-coordinate is incremented by one. Altogether, this means that the pixel to be drawn after the pixel (x_p, y_p) can only be one of the two pixels $(x_{p+1}, y_{p+1}) = (x_p + 1, y_p)$ or $(x_{p+1}, y_{p+1}) = (x_p + 1, y_p + 1)$. Therefore, in each step of the line drawing algorithm there are only two choices for the pixel to be drawn.

Figure 3.3 illustrates the situation. The right ("eastern") neighbouring pixel of (x_p, y_p) is marked by E, the neighbouring pixel to the upper right ("northeastern") by NE.

The pixel to be drawn is the one closer to the point Q on the ideal line with x-coordinate $x_p + 1$. In order to decide whether the pixel E or NE is the correct choice, the midpoint M between these two pixels is considered. If M lies below the ideal line, the upper pixel must be drawn, i.e., NE is the correct choice. If M is above the line, E should be chosen. In case M lies exactly on the line, one can choose either of the two pixels. The decision for pixel NE corresponds

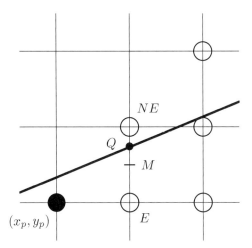

Figure 3.3 The two candidates for the next pixel for the line drawing algorithm

to rounding 0.5 to one, the decision for E corresponds to rounding 0.5 to zero. It is not important which of the two alternatives is chosen. But once a choice is made, one should always stick to the same alternative, when the midpoint lies exactly on the line.

The above considerations reduce the choice for the pixel to be drawn in each step of a line drawing algorithm to two alternatives. In the following, this reduction to two alternatives will be further exploited to avoid floating point arithmetic and use only integer computations in order to decide whether the midpoint M is above or below the ideal line, inducing which pixel should be drawn.

A line considered as a function in the mathematical sense is usually specified in the form

$$y = f(x) = m \cdot x + b. \tag{3.1}$$

This notation reflects the intuition of a computational procedure. For any given x-value the corresponding unique y-value can be calculated using this simple equation. In the context of computer graphics, this representation is not always the most suitable one. On the one hand, vertical lines cannot be represented in the notation of equation (3.1). On the other hand, this notation is not very useful to follow the considerations above that involve the location of the midpoint between two pixels with respect to the line. Of course, it would be possible to calculate the corresponding y-value on the line by equation (3.1) and then compare it with the y-value of the midpoint. However, the comparison then becomes superfluous, since there is no need to consider the midpoint anymore, because the pixel to be drawn can be obtained directly by rounding the computed y-value. Therefore, another representation of lines than (3.1) is preferred.

Any function $y = f(x)$, especially a simple function like a line, can be rewritten in implicit form as

$$F(x,y) = 0. \tag{3.2}$$

The implicit form does no longer consider the function in terms of an explicit computational procedure, but as a definition for the graph of the function. The graph of a function consists of all points belonging to the set

$$\{(x,y) \in \mathbb{R}^2 \mid F(x,y) = 0\}.$$

This is the set of pairs (x,y) that fulfil the implicit equation (3.2) defining the function. A line can be written in implicit representation in the form

$$F(x,y) = A \cdot x + B \cdot y + C = 0. \tag{3.3}$$

For example, the line $y = m \cdot x + b$ can be rewritten as

$$F(x,y) = m \cdot x - y + b = 0. \tag{3.4}$$

This representation is much better suited for the purpose of determining whether a point, especially the midpoint M that will be considered here, is above, below or on a given line. Inserting the point (x_M, y_M) into equation (3.4) leads to three possible outcomes, assuming $m \geq 0$.

– $F(x_M, y_M) = 0$: The point (x_M, y_M) is on the considered line.

– $F(x_m, y_m) > 0$: If the point would be on the line, the corresponding value y_M had to be greater. In other words, y_M is too small, so that the point (x_M, y_M) lies below the line.

– $F(x_m, y_m) < 0$: In this case, if the point would be on the line, the corresponding value y_M had to be smaller. Therefore, the point (x_M, y_M) lies above the line.

This means that it is sufficient to know the sign of $F(x_M, y_M)$ in order to decide where the point (x_M, y_M) lies with respect to the line defined by the implicit equation (3.4). Making use of this implicit equation it is now possible to avoid floating point arithmetic for the determination of the location of the midpoint. Taking into account that the connecting line between the given pixels (x_0, y_0) and (x_1, y_1) should be drawn, equation (3.4) can be reformulated, so that only integer operations are needed for the computation. The line through the points (x_0, y_0) and (x_1, y_1) can be written in the form

$$\frac{y - y_0}{x - x_0} = \frac{y_1 - y_0}{x_1 - x_0}.$$

Solving for y and defining the integer values[2] $dx = x_1 - x_0$ and $dy = y_1 - y_0$, leads to

$$y = \frac{dy}{dx}x + y_0 - \frac{dy}{dx}x_0.$$

This gives the implicit form

$$0 = \frac{dy}{dx}x - y + y_0 - \frac{dy}{dx}x_0.$$

Multiplication of this equation by the factor dx yields the final implicit form

$$F(x, y) = dy \cdot x - dx \cdot y + C = 0 \qquad (3.5)$$

where

$$C = dx \cdot y_0 - dy \cdot x_0.$$

The aim of these considerations and calculations was to restrict the computations for drawing a line to integer arithmetic. Based on the underlying assumption that the line has a slope between zero and one, it could be concluded that for the pixel to be drawn in each step there are only two choices. In order to decide which of the two pixels is the correct one, the location of the line with respect to the midpoint M between the two pixels is considered as illustrated in figure 3.3 on page 53. For this purpose, the representation of the line in implicit form is very useful. Inserting the midpoint into the implicit equation, the resulting sign indicates the location of the midpoint with respect to the line. The midpoint $M = (x_M, y_M)$ lies on the raster in the x-direction and in the middle between two raster points in the y-direction. Therefore, its x-coordinate x_M is an integer value, whereas the y-coordinate y_M has the form

$$y_M = y_M^{(0)} + \frac{1}{2}$$

where the value $y_M^{(0)}$ is also an integer value. Using the implicit form (3.5) for the line and inserting the value y_M, floating point operations are still required. However, multiplying equation (3.5) by the factor 2, the implicit form for the considered line becomes

$$\tilde{F}(x, y) = 2 \cdot dy \cdot x - dx \cdot 2 \cdot y + 2 \cdot C = 0. \qquad (3.6)$$

---

[2] Note that (x_0, y_0) and (x_1, y_1) are assumed to be pixels, so that x_0, x_1, y_0 and y_1 must be integer values.

When the midpoint $M = (x_M, y_M)$ is inserted into this equation, the computations can be reduced to integer arithmetic. Instead of inserting the value y_M with 0.5 as the value after the decimal point directly, the term $2 \cdot y_M$ can be replaced by the integer value $2 \cdot y_M^{(0)} + 1$.

In this way, the computations for drawing lines can be reduced completely to integer arithmetic. Nevertheless, equation (3.6) is not used directly for drawing lines since it still contains multiplications that are more expensive in terms of computational costs than additions or subtractions. The multiplications can be avoided by an incremental computation scheme. Instead of calculating the value (3.6) for the midpoint M in each step directly, only the value for the first midpoint is computed and afterwards the change of (3.6) in each step is added to the previously computed value.

Instead of equation (3.6) the form (3.5) is used for the derivation of the incremental computation scheme. In each step, the decision variable

$$d = F(x_M, y_M) = dy \cdot x_M - dx \cdot y_M + C$$

determines whether the pixel above or below the midpoint $M = (x_M, y_M)$ should be drawn. The upper pixel NE must be chosen for $d > 0$, the lower pixel E in the case of $d < 0$. How does d change in each step, when going from one pixel to the next? Assuming that the pixel (x_p, y_p) has been drawn correctly in terms of rounding the y-value, how does d change, when the pixel (x_{p+1}, y_{p+1}) has been drawn and the next midpoint is inserted to determine the pixel (x_{p+2}, y_{p+2})? Two cases must be distinguished here that are illustrated in figure 3.4.

Case 1: E, i.e., $(x_{p+1}, y_{p+1}) = (x_p + 1, y_p)$ was the pixel to be drawn after (x_p, y_p). This case corresponds to the left situation in figure 3.4. Therefore, the midpoint M_{new} to be considered for drawing the pixel (x_{p+2}, y_{p+2}) has the coordinates $\left(x_p + 2, y_p + \frac{1}{2}\right)$. Inserting this point into equation (3.5) yields the following value for the decision variable d:

$$d_{\text{new}} = F\left(x_p + 2, y_p + \frac{1}{2}\right) = dy \cdot (x_p + 2) - dx \cdot \left(y_p + \frac{1}{2}\right) + C.$$

In the previous step for determining the pixel (x_{p+1}, y_{p+1}), the midpoint $\left(x_p + 1, y_p + \frac{1}{2}\right)$ had to be inserted into equation (3.5), so that the decision variable took the value

$$d_{\text{old}} = F\left(x_p + 1, y_p + \frac{1}{2}\right) = dy \cdot (x_p + 1) - dx \cdot \left(y_p + \frac{1}{2}\right) + C.$$

Thus, the change of the decision variable is in this case given by

$$\Delta_E = d_{\text{new}} - d_{\text{old}} = dy.$$

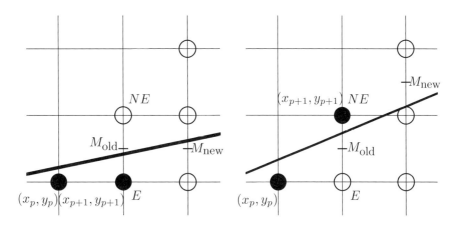

Figure 3.4 The new midpoint depending on whether the previously drawn pixel was E or NE

Case 2: NE, i.e., $(x_{p+1}, y_{p+1}) = (x_p+1, y_p+1)$ was the pixel to be drawn after (x_p, y_p). This case corresponds to the right situation in figure 3.4. So here the midpoint $M_{new} = (x_p + 2, y_p + \frac{3}{2})$ must be considered for finding the pixel (x_{p+2}, y_{p+2}). Thus, the value for the decision variable is

$$d_{new} = F\left(x_p + 2, y_p + \frac{3}{2}\right) = dy \cdot (x_p + 2) - dx \cdot \left(y_p + \frac{3}{2}\right) + C.$$

The previous value of the decision variable d is the same as in the first case of the pixel E, resulting in the change of the decision variable given by

$$\Delta_{NE} = d_{new} - d_{old} = dy - dx.$$

Combining the two cases together, the change of the decision variable is

$$\Delta = \begin{cases} dy & \text{if } E \text{ was chosen,} \\ dy - dx & \text{if } NE \text{ was chosen.} \end{cases}$$

This means

$$\Delta = \begin{cases} dy & \text{if } d_{old} < 0, \\ dy - dx & \text{if } d_{old} > 0. \end{cases}$$

Δ is always an integer value, so that the decision variable d will only be changed by integer values.

In order to be able to compute the value of the decision variable d in each step, in addition to its change the initial value of d is also needed. The initial

value is obtained by inserting the first midpoint into equation (3.5). The first
pixel to be drawn for the line has the coordinates (x_0, y_0). Therefore, the first
midpoint to be considered is $(x_0 + 1, y_0 + \frac{1}{2})$, so that the initial value of the
decision variable becomes

$$
\begin{aligned}
d_{\text{init}} &= F\left(x_0 + 1, y_0 + \frac{1}{2}\right) \\
&= dy \cdot (x_0 + 1) - dx \cdot \left(y_0 + \frac{1}{2}\right) + C \\
&= dy \cdot x_0 - dx \cdot y_0 + C + dy - \frac{dx}{2} \\
&= F(x_0, y_0) + dy - \frac{dx}{2} \\
&= dy - \frac{dx}{2}.
\end{aligned}
$$

The value $F(x_0, y_0)$ is zero since the initial point (x_0, y_0) lies by definition on
the line to be drawn.

Unfortunately, the initial value d_{init} is not an integer value, except when
dx happens to be even. Since the change dx of d is always integer-valued, this
problem can be avoided by considering the new decision variable $D = 2 \cdot d$.
This corresponds to replacing the implicit form (3.5) of the line to be drawn
by the implicit form

$$
D = \hat{F}(x, y) = 2 \cdot F(x, y) = 2 \cdot dy \cdot x - 2 \cdot dx \cdot y + 2 \cdot C = 0.
$$

For determining the pixel to be drawn, it does not matter whether the decision
variable d or $D = 2 \cdot d$ is used, since only the sign of D is relevant for the choice
of the pixel.

Putting everything together leads to the following equations for initialising
and updating the decision variable D.

$$
D_{\text{init}} = 2 \cdot dy - dx, \tag{3.7}
$$

$$
D_{\text{new}} = D_{\text{old}} + \Delta \quad \text{where}
$$

$$
\Delta = \begin{cases} 2 \cdot dy & \text{if } D_{\text{old}} < 0, \\ 2 \cdot (dy - dx) & \text{if } D_{\text{old}} > 0. \end{cases} \tag{3.8}
$$

The decision variable can only take integer values. For the initialisation of
D one multiplication and one subtraction is required. The two values for Δ
should also be computed only once in the beginning. This needs two more
multiplications and one subtraction. The iterative update of Δ in each step
can then be accomplished by a single addition.

$$
\begin{array}{rcll}
dx & = & 10 - 2 & = & 8 \\
dy & = & 6 - 3 & = & 3 \\
\Delta_E & = & 2 \cdot dy & = & 6 \\
\Delta_{NE} & = & 2 \cdot (dy - dx) & = & -10 \\[4pt]
D_{\text{init}} & = & 2 \cdot dy - dx & = & -2 \quad (E) \\
D_{\text{init}+1} & = & D_{\text{init}} + \Delta_E & = & 4 \quad (NE) \\
D_{\text{init}+2} & = & D_{\text{init}+1} + \Delta_{NE} & = & -6 \quad (E) \\
D_{\text{init}+3} & = & D_{\text{init}+2} + \Delta_E & = & 0 \quad (E?) \\
D_{\text{init}+4} & = & D_{\text{init}+3} + \Delta_E & = & 6 \quad (NE) \\
D_{\text{init}+5} & = & D_{\text{init}+4} + \Delta_{NE} & = & -4 \quad (E) \\
D_{\text{init}+6} & = & D_{\text{init}+7} + \Delta_E & = & 2 \quad (NE) \\
D_{\text{init}+7} & = & D_{\text{init}+6} + \Delta_{NE} & = & -8 \quad (E) \\
D_{\text{init}+8} & = & D_{\text{init}+7} + \Delta_E & = & -2 \\
\end{array}
$$

Table 3.1 Steps required for the calculation of the line connecting the points (2,3) and (10,6) using the midpoint algorithm

The problem of drawing a line connecting the points (2,3) and (10,6) shall illustrate the principle of this algorithm, also called *midpoint algorithm* or named after its inventor *Bresenham algorithm*. The resulting values for the initialisation and for the decision variable are given step by step in Table 3.1.

After setting the start pixel (2,3), the initial decision variable D_{init} results in the negative value of -2, so that the next pixel to be drawn is the one "east" or right of the start pixel. The decision variable must be changed by $\Delta_E = 6$. This makes the new decision variable positive, meaning that the next pixel to be drawn should be "northeast" or right above the previous pixel and that the decision variable should be changed by the value Δ_{NE}. This results in a zero-value for the decision variable in the next step. In other words, the line passes exactly through the midpoint between the two candidates for the next pixel to be drawn. Here, the convention is assumed to prefer the "eastern" pixel in such cases. The remaining values can be calculated analogously. Figure 3.5 shows the resulting pixel line.

The precondition for the application of the midpoint algorithm is that the line to be drawn has a slope between 0 and 1. It was already mentioned that the roles of the x- and the y-axis can be exchanged for drawing lines with an absolute slope greater than 1. In this case, the y-values are incremented step by step and the decision variable D is used for the computation of the corresponding x-value. By exchanging the roles of the coordinate axes if necessary, it can always be guaranteed that the slope of the line to be drawn is between -1 and

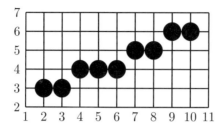

Figure 3.5 Drawing a line with the Bresenham algorithm

1. The above-described midpoint algorithm can only take care of lines with a slope between 0 and 1. In a completely analogous way, an algorithm for lines with a slope between -1 and 0 can be derived. Instead of the "northeastern" pixel, the "southeastern" pixel has to be considered for the midpoint algorithm for lines with slope between -1 and 0.

A crucial prerequisite for the midpoint algorithm is the assumption that the line to be drawn connects two pixels. This restricts the endpoints of the line to integer coordinates. For a line that was modelled in a vector graphics framework, it is not guaranteed at all that the endpoints fulfil this requirement. In this case, the line connecting the endpoints with rounded coordinates is drawn. This might lead to a small deviation of the pixel line obtained from rounding the y-coordinates compared to the ideal line. However, the deviation is at most one pixel and can therefore be tolerated for the higher computational efficiency.

3.3 Structural algorithms

The midpoint algorithm requires in addition to the computations for the initialisation n operations to draw a line of n pixels, so that its computational complexity is linear. *Structural algorithms* try to reduce this complexity further by analysing repeated patterns that occur when a line is drawn on a pixel raster. Figure 3.6 illustrates such a repeated pattern with an overall length of five pixels. In order to better identify the repeated pattern, the pixels within one pattern are marked differently. The basic pattern in figure 3.6 consists of a first pixel (filled circle), two neighbouring pixels right above the first pixel (simple circles), followed by two other neighbouring pixels (double circles) right above the previous ones. Let D denote a diagonal step (drawing a "northeastern" pixel) and H a horizontal step (drawing an "eastern" pixel). Then drawing the pixel line can be described by a repetition of the basic pattern $DHDHD$.

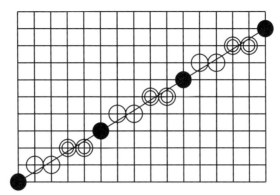

Figure 3.6 A repeated pixel pattern for drawing a line on pixel raster

If the line in figure 3.5 on page 60 would not end at the point (10,6), the corresponding pattern $HDHHDHDHD$ would be repeated again. This can also be seen from the calculations of the midpoint algorithm in Table 3.1 on page 59. The initial value D_{init} of the decision variable is equal to the last value $D_{\text{init}+8}$ in the table. Continuing the calculations of the midpoint algorithm would therefore lead to the same results as shown in the table.

Since it was assumed that the endpoints (x_0, y_0) and (x_1, y_1) of the line to be drawn lie on the pixel raster, the numbers x_0, y_0, x_1, y_1 must be integers and therefore also the values $dx = x_1 - x_0$ and $dy = y_1 - y_0$. The line has a rational slope of $\frac{dy}{dx}$. For drawing the line, the y-values

$$\frac{dy}{dx} \cdot x + b \tag{3.9}$$

with a rational constant b and integer values x have to be rounded, no matter whether this calculation is carried out explicitly as in the naïve line drawing algorithm or implicitly as in the midpoint algorithm. It is obvious that only a finite number of different remainders is possible for the computation of the y-values (3.9). Therefore, any pixel line connecting two endpoints on the pixel raster must be based on a repeated pattern, although the pattern might be quite long. In the worst case the repetition of the pattern would only start again when the final endpoint of the line is reached.

Structural algorithms make use of this fact for drawing lines and determine the underlying basic pattern that defines the line. This can lead to a reduction for line drawing to a logarithmic complexity, but with the price of more complex integer operations than simple additions.

For the same reasons as in the context of the midpoint algorithm, the considerations for structural algorithms will also be restricted to lines with a slope between zero and one. A structural algorithm constructs the repeated pattern for drawing the pixels as a sequence of horizontal (H) and diagonal steps (D), based on the following principles.

Given the two endpoints (x_0, y_0) and (x_1, y_1) of a line with slope between zero and one, the values $dx = x_1 - x_0$ and $dy = y_1 - y_0$ are computed. In addition to the initial pixel dx more pixels have to be drawn. For these dx pixels dy diagonal steps are required. The remaining $(dx - dy)$ must be horizontal steps. The problem to be solved consists of finding the correct order of the diagonal and horizontal steps. The sequence[3] $H^{dx-dy}D^{dy}$, containing the correct number of horizontal and diagonal steps but probably in the wrong order, is used as a first approximation for the drawing pattern of the line. A suitable permutation of this initial sequence will yield the correct sequence for drawing the line.

Brons' algorithm constructs the correct permutation of the initial sequence $H^{dx-dy}D^{dy}$ in the following way [7, 8].

- If dx and dy (and therefore also $(dx - dy)$) have a common divisor greater than one, i.e., $g = \gcd(dx, dy) > 1$, then the pixel line can be drawn by g repetitions of a sequence of length dx/g.

- Therefore, it can be assumed without loss of generality that dx and dy have no common divisor.

- Let P and Q be two words (sequences) over the alphabet $\{D, H\}$.

- From a starting sequence P^pQ^q with frequencies p and q having no common divisor and assuming without loss of generality $1 < q < p$, the integer division

$$p = k \cdot q + r, \quad 0 < r < q$$

  leads to the permutated sequence

$$(P^kQ)^{q-r}(P^{k+1}Q)^r \quad \text{if } (q - r) > r,$$
$$(P^{k+1}Q)^r(P^kQ)^{q-r} \quad \text{if } r > (q - r).$$

- Apply the same procedure in a recursive manner to the subsequences of length r and $(q - r)$, respectively, until $r = 1$ or $(q - r) = 1$ holds.

As an example how to apply this procedure, drawing a line from the point $(x_0, y_0) = (0, 0)$ to the point $(x_1, y_1) = (82, 34)$ is considered. Obviously, $dx = 82$, $dy = 34$ and therefore $\gcd(dx, dy) = 2$ holds. The line has a slope of $dy/dx = 17/41$. Starting from the initial pixel (x_0, y_0) that is located on the ideal line, the

---

[3] $H^{dx-dy}D^{dy}$ means $(dx - dy)$ letters H followed by dy letters D.

next pixel on the ideal line is reached after 41 pixels. Therefore, it is sufficient to construct a sequence for drawing the first half of the line up to the pixel $(41, 17)$ and to repeat this sequence for drawing the remaining pixels. Therefore, the values $\widetilde{dx} = dx/2 = 41$ and $\widetilde{dy} = dy/2 = 17$ are considered. So the initial sequence is $H^{24}D^{17}$ and the corresponding integer division with $p = 24$ and $q = 17$ yields $24 = 1 \cdot 17 + 7$. This leads to the sequence $(HD)^{10}(H^2D)^7$ with $p = 10$ and $q = 7$. Integer division for this sequence produces $10 = 1 \cdot 7 + 3$, resulting in the sequence $(HDH^2D)^4((HD)^2H^2D)^3$. Here $p = 4$ and $q = 3$ holds and the final integer division yields $4 = 1 \cdot 3 + 1$. The corrected sequence of intermediate steps is therefore

$$(HDH^2D(HD)^2H^2D)^2((HDH^2D)^2(HD)^2((HD)^2H^2D))^1.$$

This sequence has to be applied twice for drawing the pixel line connecting the points (0,0) and (82,34).

3.4 Pixel densities and line styles

Drawing lines in a raster graphics framework causes various undesired effects. The pixel grid leads to jaggies or staircasing instead of straight lines. This so-called aliasing effect and how to avoid it will be discussed in section 3.8 in more detail. So far it was assumed that the width of a line should be one pixel, resulting in very thin lines. Drawing thicker lines will be the topic of section 3.9. The density of thin lines where one pixel is set per step in the x- or y-direction depends on the slope of the line. Figure 3.7 illustrates this effect. The highest pixel density is achieved for horizontal lines. An increasing slope leads to thinner lines and the lowest density is reached at a slope of one. Since lines with a larger absolute slope than one are drawn by exchanging the roles of the coordinate axes, the pixel density increases again for lines with a slope greater than one. The same applies to lines with negative slopes.

Analysing the example of a line connecting the points $(0, 0)$ and (n, m) with $m \leq n$ will provide a better understanding of the influence of the slope of a line on its pixel density. No matter how m, i.e., the slope, is chosen, the line will always contain n pixels, not counting the first pixel at $(0, 0)$. The pixel densities depending on the choice of m are listed in Table 3.2. The last line of the table contains the general formula for arbitrary values $m \leq n$.

The horizontal line, having a length of n and containing n pixels, has the highest pixel density. The pixel density of a diagonal line with slope one reduces to $1/\sqrt{2} \approx 0.7$, roughly 70% of the density of a horizontal line. If not only black and white, but also grey pixels with different intensities can be drawn, one can

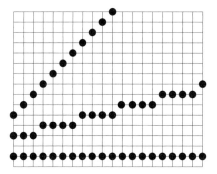

Figure 3.7 Different pixel densities depending on the slope of a line

m	Slope	Length of the line	Pixel density
0	0	n	1
$\dfrac{n}{4}$	$\dfrac{1}{4}$	$n \cdot \sqrt{1 + \dfrac{1}{16}}$	$\dfrac{1}{\sqrt{1 + \frac{1}{16}}}$
n	1	$n \cdot \sqrt{2}$	$\dfrac{1}{\sqrt{2}}$
m	$\dfrac{m}{n}$	$n \cdot \sqrt{1 + \left(\dfrac{m}{n}\right)^2}$	$\dfrac{1}{\sqrt{1 + \left(\frac{m}{n}\right)^2}}$

Table 3.2 Pixel densities for lines with different slopes

try to compensate this effect by using the maximum intensity only for diagonal lines and drawing horizontal and vertical lines with only 70% intensity of the diagonal lines. However, this compensation strategy will reduce the overall intensity, since only lines with the lowest pixel density obtain full intensity. The intensity for all other lines will be reduced, so that they look more palish.

The slope of a line not only can influence how thick it occurs on a pixel raster, but it can also have similar effects when lines are drawn with different line styles. A *line style* determines the way a line is drawn. So far it was always assumed that the two endpoints of a line had to be connected by a solid line. This corresponds to the default or standard line style. Other common line styles include dotted or dashed lines.

Bitmasks offer a simple way for defining different line styles. A bitmask is a finite sequence of zeros and ones. The repeated bitmask is mapped to the pixels of the line. Only those pixels are drawn where a one occurs in the bitmask. Pixels where the bitmask has a zero are skipped.

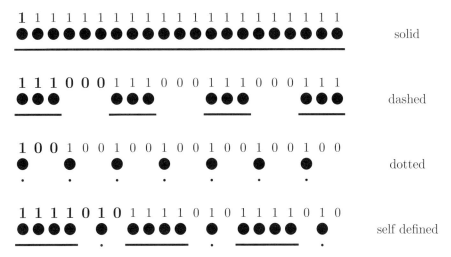

Figure 3.8 Different line styles

Figure 3.8 illustrates how bitmasks determine which pixels have to be drawn and how the resulting line looks, when a specific bitmask is chosen for a line style. For each line, the underlying bitmask is shown once in the beginning in slightly enlarged boldface digits, afterwards the repetitions of the bitmask are shown in the normal font. Below the bitmask the corresponding sequence of pixels is drawn in a magnified manner. Below the pixels it is illustrated how the corresponding line style should look. The first bitmask for drawing a solid line consists of a single 1. For a dashed line one could use, for instance, the bitmask 111000 with three pixels drawn and three pixels skipped, alternatingly.

Since a bitmask determines the pixels to be drawn based on the way the line is traversed, i.e., the corresponding coordinate axis, similar effects occur as they have already been discussed for pixel densities in connection with the slope of the line. For instance, for a dashed line the length of the dashes based on a bitmask depends on the slope of the line. If the bitmask $1^n 0^n$ is used, i.e., n pixels are drawn and n pixels are skipped alternatingly, the length of a single dash varies with the slope of the line. For vertical and horizontal lines the length of a single dash is n, whereas a line with a slope of $45°$ will have dashes with a length of $n \cdot \sqrt{2}$. This means that diagonal lines have dashes that are 40% longer than those of horizontal or vertical lines. Figure 3.9 illustrates how the slope of a line influences the length of the dashes, when a simple bitmask is used.

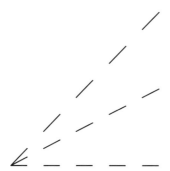

Figure 3.9 Different dash lengths for the same bitmask

3.4.1 Different line styles with Java 2D

Java 2D provides the class `BasicStroke` not only for defining different line styles, but also for controlling the thickness of lines as well as the shape of line endings and joins between lines in a polyline. The default thickness of a line is 1.0 pixel in Java 2D and since such lines tend to be very thin on high-resolution output devices, it is recommended to choose a larger value for the line thickness. This can be achieved in the following way.

```
BasicStroke bsThickLine = new BasicStroke(3.0f);
g2d.setStroke(bsThickLine);
```

In this case the chosen line thickness is specified as 3.0 pixels.

For defining dash patterns, the constructor

```
BasicStroke bsDash =
  new BasicStroke(thickness,
                  BasicStroke.CAP_BUTT,
                  BasicStroke.JOIN_BEVEL,
                  2.0f,
                  dashPattern,dashPhase);
```

can be used. The `float`-value `thickness` specifies the thickness of the line to be drawn. The three following parameters determine how the endings of lines should look and how joins in polylines should be drawn. The corresponding effects and choices will be explained in section 3.9. The `float`-array `dashPattern` defines the desired dash pattern. For drawing a dashed line, whose dashes are 20 pixels long with gaps in between with a length of 10 pixels, the array `dashPattern` must have two entries, the corresponding values 20 and 10.

```
float[] dashPattern = new float[]{20,10};
```

The `float`-value `dashPhase` determines at which position in the dash pattern drawing should begin.

Figure 3.10 shows a selection of lines for which different dash patterns were defined. For the left line, only the simple constructor `new BasicStroke(3.0f)` was used to make it a little bit thicker. The three rightmost lines were drawn with the above-given dash pattern `dashPattern`. The two rightmost lines have an offset of `dashPhase=0`, whereas the offset was set to 10 for the line in the middle. Comparing the two rightmost lines shows that Java 2D does not work with a simple bitmask which is applied to pixels. Java 2D computes the dash pattern in such a way that the dash length is kept independent of the slope of the line.

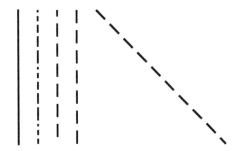

Figure 3.10 Examples for different line styles

The second line to the left is based on a `dashPattern` with the values 4,5,8,5,12,5,16,5,20,5, so that the gaps between the dashes have a constant length of 5, whereas the lengths of the dashes increase from 4 to 20.

Figure 3.10 was generated by the program `StrokingExample.java`.

3.5 Line clipping

When objects of a more complex "world" are modelled in terms of vector graphics, it is necessary to specify which section of the world—the scene—is chosen for display. Then it must be decided for each object whether it belongs completely or at least partially to the section of the world to be displayed. The task of deciding whether objects belong to the scene to be displayed or whether they can be neglected for the specific scene is called *clipping*. The part of the world to be displayed is the *clipping area* or *clipping region*. This section focusses on specific algorithms for clipping lines.

In the case of *line clipping*, four different cases, as illustrated in figure 3.11, are possible.

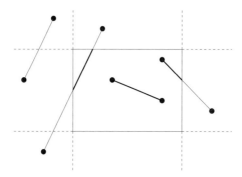

Figure 3.11 Different cases for line clipping

– Both endpoints of the line lie within the clipping area. This means the line is included completely in the clipping area, so that the whole line must be drawn.

– One endpoint of the line lies within, the other outside the clipping area. It is necessary to determine the intersection point of the line with the bounding rectangle of the clipping area. Only a part of the line should be drawn.

– Both endpoints are located outside the clipping area and the line does not intersect the clipping area. In this case, the line lies completely outside the clipping area and can be neglected for the scene.

– Both endpoints are located outside the clipping area and the line intersects the clipping area. The two intersection points of the line with the clipping area must be determined. Only the part of the line between these two intersection points should be drawn.

A straightforward way to implement line clipping would be to compute all intersection points of the line with the bounding rectangle of the clipping area. It should be noted that this problem is more difficult than determining the intersection points of infinite lines. The line to be drawn has limited extension bounded by its two endpoints. For the clipping procedure it is important to know whether an intersection point lies between or outside the two endpoints of the line segment. The same applies to the four edges of the bounding rectangle of the clipping area. The edges have also limited extension. Intersection points outside the edges or outside the endpoints of the considered line have no influence on drawing the line. For the computation of the intersection points it is useful to represent the line segment between the two endpoints (x_0, y_0) and (x_1, y_1) as a convex combination of these two points.

$$\mathbf{g}(t) = \begin{pmatrix} x(t) \\ y(t) \end{pmatrix} = (1-t) \cdot \begin{pmatrix} x_0 \\ y_0 \end{pmatrix} + t \cdot \begin{pmatrix} x_1 \\ y_1 \end{pmatrix} \qquad (0 \le t \le 1). \ (3.10)$$

Let $(x_{\min}, y_{\min})$ and $(x_{\max}, y_{\max})$ be the lower left and the upper right corner, respectively, of the rectangle defining the clipping area. As an example for the necessary computations for clipping, the calculation of a possible intersection point of the line with the lower edge of the clipping rectangle is described in the following. For determining a possible intersection point the formulae for the two lines, the line segment (3.10) and the lower edge, must be equal.

$$(1-t_1) \cdot \begin{pmatrix} x_0 \\ y_0 \end{pmatrix} + t_1 \cdot \begin{pmatrix} x_1 \\ y_1 \end{pmatrix} = (1-t_2) \cdot \begin{pmatrix} x_{\min} \\ y_{\min} \end{pmatrix} + t_2 \cdot \begin{pmatrix} x_{\max} \\ y_{\min} \end{pmatrix}. \ (3.11)$$

Two equations for t_1 and t_2 result from considering the x- and y-component of equation (3.11). If this system of two linear equations does not have a unique solution, the two lines are parallel, so that the lower edge of the clipping rectangle would not be important for clipping the line. If the system of equations has a unique solution, the following cases must be distinguished.

- $t_1 < 0$ and $t_2 < 0$: The intersection point lies not between the endpoints of the line segment and lies before $x_{\min}$.

- $0 \le t_1 \le 1$ and $t_2 < 0$: The line segment intersects the extension of the lower edge before $x_{\min}$.

- $t_1 > 1$ and $t_2 < 0$: The intersection point lies not between the endpoints of the line segment and lies before $x_{\min}$.

- $t_1 < 0$ and $0 \le t_2 \le 1$: The intersection point of the line with the lower edge lies before (x_0, y_0).

- $0 \le t_1 \le 1$ and $0 \le t_2 \le 1$: The line segment intersects the lower edge.

- $t_1 > 1$ and $0 \le t_2 \le 1$: The intersection point of the line with the lower edge lies behind (x_1, y_1).

- $t_1 < 0$ and $t_2 > 1$: The intersection point lies not between the endpoints of the line segment and lies behind $x_{\max}$.

- $0 \le t_1 \le 1$ and $t_2 > 1$: The line segment intersects the extension of the lower edge behind $x_{\max}$.

- $t_1 > 1$ and $t_2 > 1$: The intersection point lies not between the endpoints of the line segment and lies behind $x_{\max}$.

Similar considerations can be carried out for the other edges of the clipping rectangle. Combining the results for the single edges will provide the necessary information as to which part of the line should be drawn.

The *Cohen-Sutherland line clipping algorithm* (see for instance [18]) tries to avoid the complex computations of intersection points for lines. To simplify the calculations, the plane is divided into nine areas described by a 4-bit code. The bit code $b_1^{(P)}b_2^{(P)}b_3^{(P)}b_4^{(P)} \in \{0,1\}^4$ is assigned to the point according to the following rules.

$$
\begin{aligned}
b_1^{(P)} = 1 &\iff x_p < x_{\min}, \\
b_2^{(P)} = 1 &\iff x_p > x_{\max}, \\
b_3^{(P)} = 1 &\iff y_p < \cdot y_{\min}, \\
b_4^{(P)} = 1 &\iff y_p > y_{\max}
\end{aligned}
$$

Figure 3.12 shows the nine areas and their corresponding bit codes.

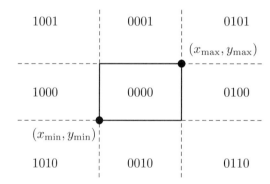

Figure 3.12 Bit code for Cohen-Sutherland clipping

Clipping should be applied to a line connecting the two endpoints P and Q. The corresponding bit code $b^{(P)}$ and $b^{(Q)}$ of P and Q, respectively, can be determined by simple comparisons of numbers. For drawing the correct part of the line, three cases must be distinguished. The part of the line that has to be drawn is determined in an iterative procedure. The first two cases terminate the calculations. In the third case, the line segment is further subdivided.

Case 1· The bitwise logical disjunction of the bit codes of the two points yields $b^{(P)} \lor b^{(Q)} = 0000$.

Then both points lie within the clipping rectangle, the whole line $\overline{PQ}$ must be drawn, and no further clipping is needed for this line.

Case 2: The bitwise logical conjunction of the bit codes of the two points yields $b^{(P)} \wedge b^{(Q)} \neq 0000$.

This means that the two bit codes must share the entry one in at least one position. If the common one of the two bit codes is at the first position, then the whole line is left of the clipping rectangle. If the common one is at the second position, the whole line lies right of the clipping rectangle. Analogously, a common one at the third or fourth position indicates that the line lies completely below or completely above the clipping rectangle. In all these cases no further clipping is required for the line.

Case 3: Neither the first nor the second case apply.

Then $b^{(P)} \neq 0000$ and $b^{(Q)} = 0000$ must be true.

Without loss of generality, it can be assumed that $b^{(P)} \neq 0000$. Otherwise the points P and Q are simply exchanged. Note that $b^{(P)} = 0000 = b^{(Q)}$ is impossible, since this would lead to case 1. Since the bit code of P must contain a value one, P cannot lie within the clipping rectangle. The bit code of P cannot contain a one at more than two positions. From the definition of the bit code it is clear that it is impossible to have a one simultaneously at the first two positions, since the point cannot lie left and right of the clipping rectangle at the same time. The same applies to the last position. Now it is necessary to compute possible intersection points of the line with edges of the clipping rectangle. Starting from point P the line can enter the clipping rectangle only via an edge that is associated with a one in the bit code of P. If the first component of the bit code is one, this means that P lies left of the clipping rectangle and the line might enter the clipping rectangle via its left edge. The same holds for the other edges and the corresponding position of the one in the bitcode. So there can be one or at most two possible edges by which the line might enter the clipping area.

If there is only one possible edge as a candidate for the intersection with the line, the intersection point of the line with the prolongation of the corresponding edge is determined and the point P is replaced by this intersection point. If there are two candidate edges, the intersection of the line with the prolongation of one of the edges is determined and the point P is replaced by this intersection point. In both cases, the algorithm starts again with the updated point P. In this way, the line is shortened and the shortened line is treated in the same way as the original one until one of the first two cases of the algorithm applies.

Figure 3.13 illustrates how the Cohen-Sutherland line clipping algorithm works. The line $\overline{PQ}$ is reduced stepwise to the lines $\overline{S_1Q}$, $\overline{S_2Q}$, $\overline{S_2S_3}$ and finally to $\overline{S_2S_4}$. The last line lies completely within the clipping rectangle and can be drawn immediately.

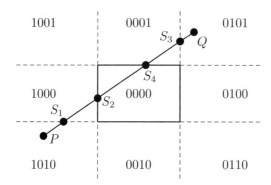

Figure 3.13   Cohen-Sutherland line clipping

The *Cyrus-Beck line clipping algorithm* [14] uses normals of the edges of the clipping rectangle to determine the part of the line which should be drawn. The line is represented in a parametric form in terms of a convex combination of its endpoints $\mathbf{p}_0$ and $\mathbf{p}_1$ as introduced in equation (3.10) on page 69.

$$\mathbf{g}(t) \;=\; (1-t)\cdot\mathbf{p}_0 + t\cdot\mathbf{p}_1 \;=\; \mathbf{p}_0 + (\mathbf{p}_1 - \mathbf{p}_0)\cdot t \qquad (t \in [0,1]).$$

For each of the four edges of the clipping rectangle, a normal vector is determined in such way that it points outwards of the rectangle. The corresponding normal vector for the left edge is therefore $(-1,0)^\top$, for the lower edge it is $(0,-1)^\top$, and for the upper and the right edge the normal vectors $(0,1)^\top$ and $(1,0)^\top$ are obtained, respectively.

Figure 3.14 illustrates the principle of the Cyrus-Beck line clipping algorithm for the left edge of the clipping rectangle. In addition to the normal vector $\mathbf{n}$ a point on the corresponding edge is also chosen. For the left edge this point is denoted by $\mathbf{p}_E$ in figure 3.14.

The vector connecting the point $\mathbf{p}_E$ with a point on the line defined by the points $\mathbf{p}_0$ and $\mathbf{p}_1$ can be written in the following form.

$$\mathbf{p}_0 + (\mathbf{p}_1 - \mathbf{p}_0)t - \mathbf{p}_E.$$

For the intersection point of the line with the corresponding edge of the clipping rectangle

$$0 \;=\; \mathbf{n}_E^\top\cdot(\mathbf{p}_0 + (\mathbf{p}_1 - \mathbf{p}_0)t - \mathbf{p}_E) \;=\; \mathbf{n}_E^\top\cdot(\mathbf{p}_0 - \mathbf{p}_E) + \mathbf{n}_E^\top\cdot(\mathbf{p}_1 - \mathbf{p}_0)t$$

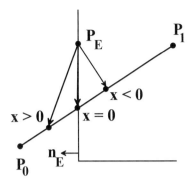

Figure 3.14 Cyrus-Beck line clipping

must hold. This equation requires that the vector connecting $\mathbf{p}_E$ with the intersection point must be orthogonal to the normal vector $\mathbf{n}_E$, since the connection vector must be parallel to the left edge of the clipping rectangle. Solving for t yields

$$t = -\frac{\mathbf{n}_E^\top \cdot (\mathbf{p}_0 - \mathbf{p}_E)}{\mathbf{n}_E^\top \cdot (\mathbf{p}_1 - \mathbf{p}_0)}. \tag{3.12}$$

The denominator can only be zero, if either $\mathbf{p}_0 = \mathbf{p}_1$ holds, meaning that the line to be clipped consists only of a single point, or if the line is orthogonal to the normal vector $\mathbf{n}_E$. The latter case implies that the line is parallel to the edge E, so that no intersection point with this edge has to be computed.

The value t is determined for each of the four edges of the clipping rectangle in order to determine whether the line to be drawn intersects the corresponding edge. A value of t outside the interval $[0, 1]$ indicates that the line does not intersect the corresponding edge of the clipping rectangle. The dot products in the numerator and the denominator of equation (3.12) are simplified to choosing the x- or the y-component of $(\mathbf{p}_0 - \mathbf{p}_E)$ and $(\mathbf{p}_1 - \mathbf{p}_0)$ and a possible change of the sign since the normal vectors $\mathbf{n}_E$ are all of the form $\pm(1, 0)^\top$ or $\pm(0, 1)^\top$.

A t-value between zero and one in equation (3.12) means that the line to be drawn either intersects the corresponding edge itself or the prolongation of the edge. Therefore, only those intersection points for t-values between zero and one are potential points where the line enters or leaves the clipping rectangle. These points are marked as possible entering (PE) and possible leaving points (PL). All of them lie between the endpoints of the line, but not necessarily on an edge of the clipping rectangle. Figure 3.15 illustrates the situation.

The angle between the line $\overline{\mathbf{p}_0\mathbf{p}_1}$ and the normal vector $\mathbf{n}$ of the corresponding edge of the clipping rectangle determines whether a point should be marked PE or PL.

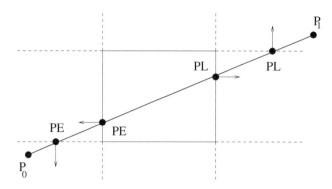

Figure 3.15 Potential intersection points with the clipping rectangle

– If the angle is larger than $90°$, the intersection point should be marked PE.

– If the angle is less than $90°$, the intersection point should be marked PL.

For the decision PE or PL it is sufficient to determine the sign of the dot product

$$\mathbf{n}^\top \cdot (\mathbf{p}_1 - \mathbf{p}_0).$$

In the case of PE, the sign will be negative. PA will lead to a positive sign. Since only one of the components of the normal vector $\mathbf{n}$ is nonzero, the sign of the dot product is obtained by considering only the signs of the corresponding component of the vector $\mathbf{p}_1 - \mathbf{p}_0$ and the nonzero component of the normal vector.

In order to determine which part of the line lies within the clipping rectangle, the largest value t_E for PE-points and the smallest value t_L for possible PL-points must be computed. If $t_E \leq t_L$ holds, then the part of the line between the points $\mathbf{p}_0 + (\mathbf{p}_1 - \mathbf{p}_0)t_E$ and $\mathbf{p}_0 + (\mathbf{p}_1 - \mathbf{p}_0)t_L$ must be drawn. In case of $t_E > t_L$ the line lies out of the clipping rectangle and nothing has to be drawn.

Apart from determining which part of a line should be drawn for a given clipping area, computing the first pixel of the line inside the clipping rectangle is another problem. In general, it is not sufficient to calculate the rounded coordinates of the intersection point of the line with the corresponding edge of the clipping rectangle where the line enters the clipping area. Figure 3.16 shows an example where this procedure would lead to an incorrect result. The left or "eastern" edge of the clipping rectangle is marked with "left," the lower or "southern" edge with "lower." In this example, the first pixel would be missed if rounding the coordinates of the intersection point of the line with the lower edge was applied. For lines with a smaller slope, the procedure could miss many

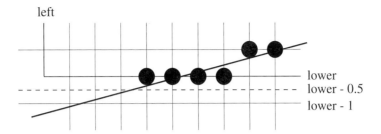

Figure 3.16 Finding the pixel where a line enters the clipping rectangle

more pixels. Therefore, instead of the intersection of the line with the edge, its intersection point with the edge shifted 0.5 unit downwards is computed. The rounded x-value of this intersection point gives the correct position where drawing of the line should start. The other edges are treated analogously.

3.6 The midpoint algorithm for circles

In section 3.2 an efficient line drawing algorithm based solely on integer arithmetic was introduced. This midpoint algorithm can be generalised to drawing circles and also various other curves under certain restrictions. The main constraint for circles is that the centre or midpoint (x_m, y_m) of the circle must be located on a pixel, i.e., x_m and y_m must be integer values. In this case, it is sufficient to develop an algorithm for drawing circles centred around the origin of the coordinate system. For circles with midpoint (x_m, y_m) the same algorithm can be applied as for circles with midpoint $(0, 0)$, but all points are drawn with an offset of (x_m, y_m).

In order to determine the pixels to be drawn for a circle centred around the origin of the coordinate system, the calculations are only carried out for an eighth part of the circle. The other pixels can be derived directly by symmetry arguments as figure 3.17 shows. If the pixel (x, y) has to be drawn within the considered hatched eighth part of the circle, then the pixels $(\pm x, \pm y)$ and $(\pm y, \pm x)$ have to be drawn in the other parts of the circle.

For the generalisation of the *midpoint* or *Bresenham algorithm* to circles [6], another constraint is introduced. It is assumed that the radius R is integer-valued. In the considered eighth part of the circle, the slope of the circle line decreases from 0 to -1. Analogously to the case of drawing lines with a slope between zero and one, the number of candidates for the next pixel to be drawn can be reduced to two. If the pixel (x_p, y_p) has been drawn in one step, the

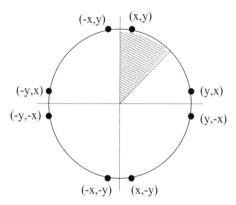

Figure 3.17 Exploiting symmetry for drawing circles

next pixel can only be the pixel E with coordinates $(x_p + 1, y_p)$ or SE with coordinates $(x_p + 1, y_p - 1)$ as is illustrated in figure 3.18.

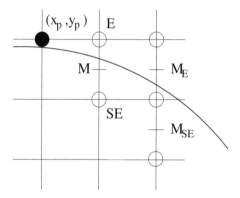

Figure 3.18 Midpoint algorithm for circles

In the same way as in the case of the midpoint algorithm for lines, the decision which pixel is the correct one to be drawn in the next step is based on a decision variable involving the midpoint between the two pixel candidates. For this purpose, the equation for the circle $x^2 + y^2 = R^2$ is rewritten in the form

$$d = F(x,y) = x^2 + y^2 - R^2 = 0 \tag{3.13}$$

For this implicit equation and a point (x, y) the following statements are obvious.

– $F(x, y) = 0 \Leftrightarrow (x, y)$ lies on the circle.

– $F(x, y) > 0 \Leftrightarrow (x, y)$ lies outside the circle.

– $F(x, y) < 0 \Leftrightarrow (x, y)$ lies inside the circle.

In order to decide whether pixel E or SE is the next pixel to be drawn, the midpoint M is inserted into equation (3.13) leading to the following decisions.

– If $d > 0$ holds, then SE must be drawn.

– If $d < 0$ holds, then E must be drawn.

As in the case of the midpoint algorithm, the value of the decision variable d is not computed in each step by inserting the midpoint M directly. Instead, only the change of d is calculated in each step. Starting with pixel (x_p, y_p) which is assumed to be drawn correctly, the change of d is calculated for the transition from pixel (x_{p+1}, y_{p+1}) to (x_{p+2}, y_{p+2}). Two cases must be distinguished here.

Case 1: E, i.e., $(x_{p+1}, y_{p+1}) = (x_p + 1, y_p)$ was the pixel drawn after (x_p, y_p). This corresponds to the case shown in figure 3.18. The midpoint M_E to be considered for drawing the pixel (x_{p+2}, y_{p+2}) has the coordinates $\left(x_p + 2, y_p - \frac{1}{2}\right)$. Inserting this midpoint into equation (3.13) yields the following value for the decision variable d.

$$d_{\text{new}} = F\left(x_p + 2, y_p - \frac{1}{2}\right) = (x_p + 2)^2 + \left(y_p - \frac{1}{2}\right)^2 - R^2.$$

In the previous step for determining the pixel (x_{p+1}, y_{p+1}), the midpoint $\left(x_p + 1, y_p + \frac{1}{2}\right)$ was considered. Inserting this midpoint into equation (3.13) gives

$$d_{\text{old}} = F\left(x_p + 1, y_p - \frac{1}{2}\right) = (x_p + 1)^2 + \left(y_p - \frac{1}{2}\right)^2 - R^2$$

as the previous value for the decision variable d. The change of the decision variable is in this case

$$\Delta_E = d_{\text{new}} - d_{\text{old}} = 2x_p + 3.$$

Case 2: SE, i.e., $(x_{p+1}, y_{p+1}) = (x_p + 1, y_p - 1)$ was the pixel drawn after (x_p, y_p). In this case, the next midpoint to be considered is $M_{SO} = \left(x_p + 2, y_p - \frac{3}{2}\right)$ (see figure 3.18). Then the value for the decision variable is

$$d_{\text{new}} = F\left(x_p + 2, y_p - \frac{3}{2}\right) = (x_p + 2)^2 + \left(y_p - \frac{3}{2}\right)^2 - R^2.$$

The previous value of d is the same as in the case of the pixel E, so that the change of the decision variable is given by

$$\Delta_{SE} = d_{\text{new}} - d_{\text{old}} = 2x_p - 2y_p + 5.$$

Taking these two cases together, the change of the decision variable is

$$\Delta = \begin{cases} 2x_p + 3 & \text{if } E \text{ was chosen,} \\ 2x_p - 2y_p + 5 & \text{if } SE \text{ was chosen.} \end{cases}$$

This means

$$\Delta = \begin{cases} 2x_p + 3 & \text{if } d_{\text{old}} < 0, \\ 2x_p - 2y_p + 5 & \text{if } d_{\text{old}} > 0, \end{cases}$$

so that the change Δ of the decision variable d is always an integer value.

In order to compute the decision variable d in each step, in addition to its change the initial value is also needed. The first pixel to be drawn has the coordinates $(0, R)$, so that $\left(1, R - \frac{1}{2}\right)$ is the first midpoint to be considered. The initial value for d is therefore

$$F\left(1, R - \frac{1}{2}\right) = \frac{5}{4} - R. \tag{3.14}$$

As in the case of lines, the change of the decision variable is always integer-valued, but the initial value is not. The same principle as for lines could be applied to circles. Using the modified decision variable $D = 4 \cdot d$ would resolve the problem of the initial floating point value. A simpler solution is, however, to simply ignore the resulting digits after the decimal dot in equation (3.14) for the initialisation of d. The reason why this does not lead to any mistakes for the drawing of the circle is very simple. In each step, it is only of interest whether d has a positive or a negative value. Since d will always be changed by an integer value, the sign of d is the same with or without the digits after the decimal dot.

For the derivation of the midpoint algorithms for drawing circles it was assumed that the centre of the circle is in the origin of the coordinate system or at least a point on the pixel raster. In addition, the constraint that the radius must have an integer value was introduced. The midpoint algorithm can be extended easily to circles with an arbitrary, not necessarily integer-valued radius. Since the radius does not occur in the update equations for the decision variable d, the radius must only be considered for the initialisation of d. For a floating point radius R the first pixel to be drawn is $(0, \text{round}(R))$, leading to $\left(1, \text{round}(R) - \frac{1}{2}\right)$ as the first midpoint that must be considered. Therefore, d must be initialised with the value

$$F\left(1, \text{round}(R) - \frac{1}{2}\right) = \frac{5}{4} - \text{round}(R).$$

For the same reasons as for circles with an integer-valued radius, the digits after the decimal dots can be ignored. This makes the initialisation of d integer-valued and the change of d remains integer-valued independent of the radius.

3.7 Drawing arbitrary curves

The midpoint algorithm can be generalised not only to circles, but also to other curves, for instance ellipses [26, 35, 47]. A very restrictive requirement of the midpoint algorithm is that the slope of the curve to be drawn must lie between 0 and 1 or between 0 and -1. For drawing arbitrary curves, or at least continuous curves, the plot of the graph is based on piecewise approximations of the curve by short lines. For drawing the continuous function $y = f(x)$ it is not sufficient to iterate stepwise through the x-values and draw the corresponding pixel with the rounded y-coordinate. Whenever the function has an absolute slope larger than one, the same problem of pixel gaps occurs as already happened with the naïve line drawing algorithm in figure 3.2 on page 50. Lines have a constant slope that can be determined easily. Therefore, the problem of pixel gaps can be avoided for lines by simply exchanging the roles of the coordinate axes for drawing a line with an absolute slope greater than one. This means that in this case the inverse function of the line is drawn along the y-axis. Arbitrary functions have neither a constant slope, nor can the slope or the inverse function be calculated easily for arbitrary functions. For this reason, drawing arbitrary curves is carried out by stepwise iterating through the desired range on the x-axis and computing the corresponding rounded y-values. However, not only these pixels are drawn, but also the connecting line between pixels with neighbouring x-values is drawn based on the midpoint algorithm for lines.

Figure 3.19 illustrates the principle for drawing a continuous function $y = f(x)$ in the interval $[x_0, x_1]$ with $x_0, x_1 \in \mathbb{N}$. The filled circles are the pixels of the form $(x, \text{round}(f(x)))$ for integer-valued x-coordinates. The empty circles correspond to the pixels that are drawn when two of the computed pixels with neighbouring x-coordinates shown as full circles are connected by a line. Drawing a curve in this way might not lead to exactly the same pixels that would result if always the closest pixel to the curve was chosen. However, the deviation is at most one pixel.

```
int yRound1, yRound2;
yRound1 = round(f(x0))
for (int x=x0; x<x1; x++)
{
    yRound2 = round(f(x+1));
    drawLine(x,yRound1,x+1,yRound2);
    yRound1 = yRound2;
}
```

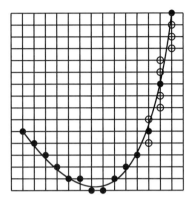

Figure 3.19 Drawing arbitrary curves

3.8 Antialiasing

The term *aliasing effect* originates from the field of signal processing and refers to phenomena that occur when a continuous signal is sampled in a discrete manner with a constant rate. Drawing a line or curve is a similar procedure. The ideal line or curve as a continuous function is sampled by the pixel raster. The most common aliasing effects in computer graphics are the staircasing effects that occur when continuous curves or objects with smooth boundaries are mapped to a pixel raster. Assuming that lines must have a width of only one pixel and pixels can only be black or white, nothing can be done to avoid aliasing effects.

For grey-scale images or images that allow colour intensities, aliasing effects can be reduced. The basic idea of reducing staircasing effects for drawing lines and curves is to soften the boundaries of the line by decreasing the intensity. This technique is called *antialiasing*, for which various approaches are available. Some of these approaches are outlined in the following, explaining their principles for drawing lines.

Unweighted area sampling interprets a line as a long, but very thin rectangle. A pixel is not understood as a point, but as a small square that can be filled with colour. The intensity of the pixel is chosen proportionally to the area of the pixel's square that is covered by the rectangle that represents the line. Figure 3.20 illustrates this concept.

The main disadvantage of this method is that for each pixel's square the intersection with a rectangle representing the line must be determined and the area of this intersection must be computed, requiring high computational costs. A simple heuristic approach to estimate the proportion of the pixel's square

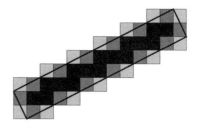

Figure 3.20   Unweighted area sampling

that is covered by the line rectangle uses an imaginary refined pixel grid on each pixel's square. The proportion of refined pixels in the square that also lie in the line rectangle gives a good estimation for the desired intensity of the pixel. In this way, the pixel whose refined 5×5 pixel grid is shown in figure 3.21 would obtain an intensity equal to 11/25.

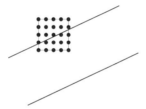

Figure 3.21   Estimation of the area by sampling with refined pixels

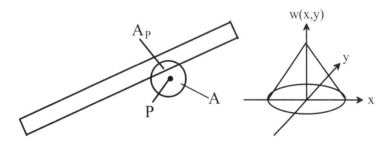

Figure 3.22   Weighted area sampling

Weighted area sampling does not only consider the area of the pixel's square that is covered by the line rectangle, but takes also a weighting function $w(x, y)$ into account. $w(x, y)$ has the highest value in the centre of the pixel and decreases with increasing distance. A typical weighting function is shown in figure 3.22. The weighting function is defined on a circle A around pixel P as can be seen in the left part of the figure. The intensity for the pixel is given by

$$\frac{\int_{A_P} w(x,y)dx\,dy}{\int_A w(x,y)dx\,dy}$$

where A_P is the intersection of the circle with the line rectangle. Although this formula might appear complicated and computationally inefficient, since integrals are involved, the intensity of the pixel depends only on its distance to the ideal line, at least when a weighting function is used as illustrated in the right part of figure 3.22. The intensity can be written as a function $I(d_P)$ where d_P stands for the distance of pixel P to the line. The number of displayable intensity values is usually limited, for computer screens by 256. Instead of considering the real function $I : [0,\infty) \rightarrow [0,1]$, it is sufficient to restrict to a discrete version $\hat{I} : [0,\infty) \rightarrow \{0,...,i_{\max}\}$ of the function, when the available levels of intensities are $0,...,i_{\max}$. Scanning the pixel raster in the neighbourhood of the line in order to determine the intensity for each pixel, means that for each pixel a corresponding value of $\hat{I}$ must be computed. This task is related to the problem of drawing a line or curve $y = f(x)$ on a pixel raster. For drawing a line, the procedure scans the pixel raster step by step—in this case only along one of the coordinate axes—and determines the corresponding rounded value of the function $\mathtt{round}(f(x))$. The differences versus antialiasing are that the pixel raster is not only scanned along a coordinate axis, but in the neighbourhood of a line and that the discrete value $\hat{I}$ to be determined is not the y-value of the pixel to be drawn, but the corresponding discretised intensity value. Based on this analogy, the concept of the midpoint algorithm was also extended to antialiasing, requiring only integer arithmetic to determine the discrete intensity value. Examples for such antialiasing techniques are Gupta-Sproull antialiasing [22] and the algorithm of Pitteway and Watkinson [36]. For a detailed description of these algorithms the reader is referred to the original work [22, 36] or to [18, 25].

3.8.1 Antialiasing with Java 2D

In Java 2D the method

```
g2d.setRenderingHint(RenderingHints.KEY_ANTIALIASING,
                     RenderingHints.VALUE_ANTIALIAS_ON);
```

will make sure that all Shape and area objects, i.e., all objects that do not represent text, are drawn using antialiasing.

To apply antialiasing to drawing text, the method must be called with the following parameters.

```
g2d.setRenderingHint(RenderingHints.KEY_TEXT_ANTIALIASING,
                    RenderingHints.VALUE_TEXT_ANTIALIAS_ON);
```

3.9 Drawing thick lines

Today's output devices have a high resolution that leads to very thin lines, when lines are rendered with only one pixel as their width. Various techniques for drawing thick lines with a thickness of more than one pixel are available. The simplest approach is *pixel replication*. For drawing a curve with a slope between -1 and 1, with each pixel the n pixels below and above are also drawn, so that the curve has a thickness of $2n + 1$ pixels in the y-direction. The same effect that lines with larger slope look thinner as was demonstrated in section 3.4 occurs here as well. It was mentioned in section 3.1 that for drawing lines with an absolute slope larger than one the roles of the coordinate axes should be exchanged. Even for drawing arbitrary curves, this technique will be applied as was explained in section 3.7. This is the reason why only lines with slope between -1 and 1 are considered here. The principle of pixel replication is illustrated in the left-hand side of figure 3.23. The right part of the figure shows the *moving pen* technique. For drawing a pixel a thick pen with a tip of for instance 5×5 pixels is used, so that in addition to the pixel in the centre all other pixels belonging to the tip of the pen are also drawn.

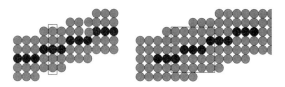

Figure 3.23 Pixel replication and the moving pen technique

Pixel replication can be viewed as a special case of the moving pen technique where the tip has a rectangular shape with a width of one pixel in one direction. As in the case of pixel replication, a line with higher slope up to an absolute slope of one will look thinner when a squared tip is used for the moving pen technique.

In order to avoid drawing the same pixel multiple times in the case of the moving pen technique, the shape of the tip should be taken into account. For the tip in figure 3.23 consisting of 5×5 pixels and a line with a slope between zero and one, all 25 pixels have to be drawn in the first step. In the following steps, only the five pixels to the right, in case the right (eastern) pixel is the next pixel for the line, or nine pixels must be drawn, when the northeastern pixel is the next pixel of the line.

Another strategy for drawing thick lines considers the lines as thin rectangles or, more generally, as polygons that have to be filled. Techniques for filling polygons will be the topic of the next chapter.

When thick lines are drawn, line endings and joins in polylines can be modelled in different ways. Simple pixel replication results in lines whose endings are always parallel to one of the coordinate axes. This problem can be solved when the lines are considered as filled rectangles. But this leads to other problems at the joins for polylines. Figure 3.24 shows different ways line endings and joins between thick lines could be drawn. The thickness of the lines is exaggerated in the figure in order to display the effects clearly. In the leftmost part of the figure lines are considered as rectangles leading to an undesired effect where two lines meet. For the other three cases in the figure this bad effect is amended in three different ways. A prolongation of the outer lines of the rectangles until they meet as in the second case in figure 3.24 produces a sharp tip. For the next image, the join was cut off and the last image on the right uses the segment of a circle to join the lines.

Figure 3.24 Different line endings and joins

3.9.1 Drawing thick lines with Java 2D

The way line endings and joins should be drawn can be controlled by the class BasicStroke within Java 2D. This class was introduced in section 3.4.1 for drawing dashed and thicker lines. The constructor

```
new BasicStroke(thickness,ending,join);
```

defines the thickness of line as the `float`-value `thickness`. The value `ending` determines how line endings should be drawn. The following values are available.

– `BasicStroke.CAP_BUTT`: The endings are cut off straight, orthogonal to the direction of the line. (Figure 3.24, second image from the left)

– `BasicStroke.CAP_ROUND`: A half circle is attached to each line ending. (Figure 3.24, second image from the right)

– `BasicStroke.CAP_SQUARE`: A rectangle is appended to the line ending, so that the line is prolongated by half of its thickness. (Figure 3.24, right image)

The variable `join`, defining how lines in a polyline should be joined, allows the following values.

– `BasicStroke.JOIN_MITER`: The outer edges of the line rectangles are prolonged until they meet, leading to a join with a sharp tip (figure 3.24, second image from the left). For acute angles of the lines, the tip can be extremely long. To avoid this effect, another `float`-value can be specified, defining the maximum length of the tip. If the tip exceeds this length, then the following join mode is used.

– `BasicStroke.JOIN_BEVEL`: The join is a straight cut-off, orthogonal to the middle line between the two lines to be connected. (Figure 3.24, second image from the right)

– `BasicStroke.JOIN_ROUND`: The line endings are cut off at the join and a circle segment similar to the style `BasicStroke.JOIN_BEVEL` for line endings is attached to the join. The angle of the circle segment is chosen such that the lines form the tangents at the circle segment. (Figure 3.24, right image).

Figure 3.24 was generated by the program `LineEndings.java`.

3.10 Exercises

Exercise 3.1

Derive the midpoint algorithm for drawing lines with a slope between -1 and 0.

Exercise 3.2

Apply the structural algorithm in section 3.3 to draw the line in figure 3.6.

Exercise 3.3

Extend the program `GeneralPathCar.java` for drawing the car of figure 2.10. Show the control points for the quadratic and cubic curves and connect the endings of the curves with their corresponding control points by dashed lines.

Exercise 3.4

The midpoint algorithm shall be applied to drawing a part of the graph of the function $y = -a\sqrt{x} + b\ (a, b \in \mathbb{N}^+)$.

(a) For which x-values is the slope between -1 and 0?

(b) Rewrite the function in a suitable implicit form $F(x, y) = 0$. Use $d = F(x, y)$ as a decision variable to develop the midpoint algorithm. How does d change depending on whether the eastern (E) or the southeastern (SE) point was drawn in the previous step of the midpoint algorithm?

(c) How should the initial value d_{init} for d be chosen, if $(x_0, y_0) = (a^2, -a^2 + b)$ is the first point of the curve to be drawn?

(d) How can the rational values for the decision variable be avoided?

4

Areas, text and colours

Filling areas is applied in the context of drawing thick lines where thick lines are considered as long rectangles. But filling areas and polygons is also a general technique of computer graphics that is also needed as a drawing mode. This chapter contains in addition to techniques for filling areas also basic models for colours and a short introduction to handling text in images.

4.1 Filling areas

Areas are usually bounded by polygons or closed sequences of curves. In order to fill a polygon, points inside the polygon must be distinguished from exterior ones. For polygons whose edges do not intersect, it is obvious which points should be considered as inner and outer points. For polygons with intersecting edges it is not immediately clear what its inner parts are. The *odd parity rule* provides a definition of inner and outer points based on the following considerations.

If one starts to move along a line from an inner point of a polygon in one direction, then a bounding edge of the polygon must be reached at some point on the line. If the polygon is not convex, then it might happen that other edges are met, when the movement along the line is continued. Since the movement along the line was started at an inner point, one changes from the inner to the outer part of the polygon when the first polygon edge is met. After the second intersection point along the line with an edge, the polygon is entered again. So each time, when the line meets an edge, a change from the inside to the outside of the polygon or vice versa takes place. Since the polygon is bounded, the last edge that is met along the line must correspond to a change from the inside to the outside of the polygon. Because the starting point was assumed to be an inner point of the polygon, the intersection point with the first edge must also represent a change from inside to outside.

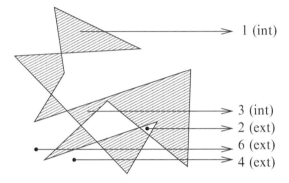

Figure 4.1 Odd parity rule

Figure 4.1 illustrates the application of the odd parity rule to selected points inside and outside a polygon. For each point a line is drawn and the number of intersection points of the line with edges of the polygon is given in the figure. If the number is odd, then the point is an interior ("int") point of the polygon, otherwise it is an exterior ("ext") point.

The odd parity rule is a useful mathematical definition of interior and exterior points of a polygon, but it is not suited for implementation, since the computational costs would be unacceptable if the rule is applied separately to each pixel. Instead, a *scan line technique* is applied. Scan line techniques are very common in computer graphics. They carry out computations along a line, the scan line, usually along lines parallel to one of the coordinate axes. For each pixel row, the corresponding line is considered, and the intersection points of the line with polygon edges are determined. These intersection points are sorted in ascending order with respect to their x-coordinates. Let $x_1 < \ldots < x_n$ be the x-coordinates of the intersection points. This means the scan line enters the polygon at x_1, leaves the polygon at x_2, enters it again at x_3 until it finally leaves the polygon at x_n. Therefore, exactly the pixels between x_1 and x_2, between x_3 and x_4, etc. and between x_{n-1} and x_n must be drawn for filling the polygon. The number n of intersection points must be even including the possible value zero. Figure 4.2 illustrates the principle of this scan line technique.

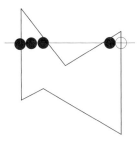

Figure 4.2 Scan line technique for filling polygons

For the implementation of the scan line technique, some specific problems need extra attention. One of these problems is clipping. It is necessary to compute all intersection points of the scan line with the polygon. But only those pixels need to be drawn that lie within the clipping area. Therefore, drawing might not start at the first intersection point x_1. Another problem occurs when the scan line intersects vertices of the polygon. These cases need special treatment. In figure 4.3, the scan line intersects two vertices of the polygon. At the first vertex a change from the exterior to the interior part of the polygon takes place. At the second vertex, the scan line remains outside the polygon. The treatment of vertices as intersection points requires considering the angles between the scan line and the edges that are attached to the corresponding vertices. Horizontal edges also need a special treatment.

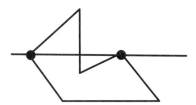

Figure 4.3 A scan line intersecting two vertices of a polygon

Filling and drawing the outlines of polygons are usually viewed as two different drawing modes. There might be pixels that belong to the interior as well as to the boundary of the polygon at the same time, especially when the polygon is drawn with thick lines. Antialiasing can also lead to points that belong to the interior and the boundary of the polygon. In order to avoid gaps at the boundary when a polygon should be filled and its boundary should be drawn as well, antialiasing must be applied to the outer part of the edges but not to their inner parts. Polygons with long acute-angled edges might introduce new aliasing effects when they are filled. The connected interior of the polygon might be represented as a disconnected set of pixels as the example in figure 4.4 demonstrates.

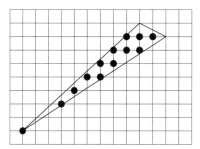

Figure 4.4 Filling a polygon can lead to aliasing effects

Instead of filling an area with one colour, a *texture* can also be used for filling. A texture can be an arbitrary image. Very often, textures are patterns, for instance in the form of grains of wood. Before an area can be filled with a texture, the position where the texture should start must be defined. Filling then means to draw the texture and to apply clipping with respect to the area that should be filled. Since areas can have an arbitrary shape, clipping might have to be applied to a nonrectangular region. Sometimes the image defining the texture is too small to fill the complete area. In this case, the texture must be used repeatedly like tiles to fill the whole area. Here it is also necessary to apply clipping with respect to the area to be filled, and also an *anchor* must be specified. The anchor defines a starting point from which the texture is laid like tiles. The brick pattern texture on the left of figure 4.5 is used to fill the rectangle on the right. The black circle marks the anchor.

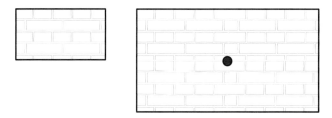

Figure 4.5 Filling an area with a texture

When a texture is used repeatedly for filling an area, fissures might be visible at the places where the texture is repeated. This effect can also be seen in figure 4.5. The horizontal fissure is more articulated than the vertical one. This effect can be avoided when a texture is used where the left and right as well as the upper and lower edges fit together perfectly. There are also techniques to modify a texture in such a way that fissures will not occur. The best modification strongly depends on the type of texture. For textures with a very regular geometric pattern like the bricks in figure 4.5, it might be necessary to modify the whole geometric pattern. For textures with unstructured patterns like marble, it is very often sufficient to apply colour interpolation techniques at the edges as they are described in section 4.7.

4.2 Buffered images in Java 2D

The class `BufferedImage` in Java 2D is very useful for various purposes in connection with images. This section demonstrates how images can be loaded, how they can be used as textures and how images can be saved directly without the need of screen dumps. The previously mentioned double buffering technique is also introduced.

A `BufferedImage`, a subclass of `Image`, is an image in the memory of the computer. The usual drawing and filling commands are available for a `BufferedImage`, but a `BufferedImage` can also be drawn on an object of the class `Image`. In this way, a `BufferedImage` can be drawn on another `BufferedImage` or on a window on the computer screen.

The constructor

```
BufferedImage bi = new BufferedImage(width,height,
                              BufferedImage.TYPE_INT_RGB);
```

generates a `BufferedImage`, whose width and height in pixels are given by the integer values `width` and `height`. The constant `BufferedImage.TYPE_INT_RGB` refers to the fact that the standard colour model is used for the `BufferedImage`. The method `createGraphics()` generates a `Graphics2D` object for the `BufferedImage`.

```
Graphics2D g2dbi = bi.createGraphics();
```

The `Graphics2D` object `g2dbi` can be used in the same way as the `Graphics2D` object `g2d` in the context of drawing on a window on the computer screen. Methods like `g2dbi.draw(...)` or `g2dbi.fill(...)` will draw on the `BufferedImage` bi instead of the window on the computer screen. Since bi is only a virtual image in the memory, the results from calling these methods are not visible directly. The method[1]

---

[1] The last parameter of this method is set to `null` here. It is an `ImageObserver`

```
g2d.drawImage(bi,xpos,ypos,null);
```

allows `bi` to show in the window on the computer screen. `bi` will be drawn
within the rectangle defined by the two opposing corners (`xpos,ypos`) and
(`xpos+width,ypos+height`). It is also possible to draw `bi` onto another
`BufferedImage`. In this case, the `Graphics2D` object `g2d` has to be replaced by
the `Graphics2D` object of the corresponding `BufferedImage`.

4.2.1 Double buffering in Java 2D

It was mentioned in section 2.9 that it is not recommended to carry out all computations needed for drawing within the `paint` method. At least for animated
graphics, it is better to exclude the computations from the `paint` method and
to draw the desired image first on a `BufferedImage` outside the `paint` method.
In the `paint` method only the updated `BufferedImage` will be drawn on the
screen. In this case, the `paint` method should be called by the `repaint` method
in each step.

For the implementation of the double buffering technique, it is necessary
to modify the class that was used so far for drawing images on the screen.
The computations that were so far carried out within the `paint` method will
be transferred to a new class. The old class for the window on the computer
screen is extended by the following two attributes.

```
public BufferedImage bi;
public Graphics2D g2dbi;
```

These two attributes are the `BufferedImage` which has to be drawn within
the `paint` method and its corresponding `Graphics2D` object. The constructor
should make sure that they are initialised with the corresponding instances.
Since the `repaint` method calls the `update` method of the window which overwrites the complete window, and because this can lead to flickering effects, the
`update` method should be overwritten and the corresponding `BufferedImage`
`bi` should be drawn in the `update` method. When the window is drawn the
first time, the `paint` method is called, so that the `update` method should be
called there as well. Altogether, the `paint` and the `update` method should be
overwritten in the following way.

---

which would be needed if the `BufferedImage` `bi` to be drawn is not completely
available when the method `drawImage` is called. This could, for instance, happen
when `bi` is a larger image that is downloaded from the Internet. Such cases will
not be considered here.

```
public void paint(Graphics g)
{
  update(g);
}

public void update(Graphics g)
{
  g2d = (Graphics2D) g;
  g2d.drawImage(bi,0,0,null);
}
```

Because the update method is called repeatedly for animations, its Graphics2D
object g2d is defined as an attribute of the class, so that it is not necessary to
generate it each time. This implementation and further details can be found
in the file BufferedImageDrawer.java, which can be used as a generic class
for the double buffering technique. The image sequence to be drawn is computed outside this class. The clock, already known from section 2.10, will serve
as an example. All calculations for drawing the clock now take place in the
class DoubleBufferingClockExample.java. Since the paint method of the
BufferedImageDrawer will be called in short time intervals again and again,
this class is implemented as an extension of the Java class TimerTask. Any subclass of TimerTask must have a run method. This method is called repeatedly
with fixed time intervals in between. The run method contains the same commands that are already known from the for-loop of the old paint method of
the class NonSynchronizedClock for the clock without double buffering. Only
the following changes are necessary.

- Instead of the Graphics2D object of the paint method of the window, the
  Graphics2D object of the corresponding BufferedImage bi is used.

- Instead of overwriting the image, i.e., the BufferedImage bi, by a white
  rectangle each time, before the image is updated, another BufferedImage
  is used as a background image. Therefore, this background image is drawn
  each time on bi, before the updated clock itself is drawn. The background
  image also contains a fixed rectangular frame around the whole scene that
  will not change during the animation.

- At the end of the run method the repaint method of the
  BufferedImageDrawer is called.

The initialisations take place in the main method and in the constructor of
DoubleBufferingClockExample. The run method, which computes the image
sequence and initiates the drawing of the updated image on the screen each
time, is called repeatedly by

```
Timer t = new Timer();
t.scheduleAtFixedRate(dbce,0,delay);
```

dbce is an instance of the class DoubleBufferingClockExample and delay specifies after how many milliseconds the image should be updated. The second value defines the waiting time until the run method is called the first time, i.e., the time until the animation is started.

4.2.2 Loading and saving of images with Java 2D

For loading an image in JPEG format, only the method

```
Image theImage =
          new javax.swing.ImageIcon("file.jpg").getImage();
```

is required. The loaded image can then be drawn on the window on the computer screen or on another BufferedImage by the method drawImage that was already explained for the class BufferedImage. The file ImageLoadingExample.java demonstrates how a JPEG image can be loaded and displayed in a window.

In order to save an image in JPEG format which was generated using Java 2D, the following steps are needed. First, a BufferedImage is generated and the desired image is drawn on this BufferedImage. After drawing is completed, the image can be saved by the commands within the try section of the following code excerpt.

```
theImage = new BufferedImage(width,height,
                             BufferedImage.TYPE_INT_RGB);
Graphics2D g2dImage = theImage.createGraphics();
//Drawing the desired image
g2dImage.draw(...);
...
//Saving the image
try
{
  FileOutputStream fos = new FileOutputStream("file.jpg");
  JPEGImageEncoder jie = JPEGCodec.createJPEGEncoder(fos);
  jie.encode(theImage);
}
catch (Exception e)
{
  System.out.println(e);
}
```

A complete example for saving a self-generated image can be found in the file
ImageSavingExample.java.

4.2.3 Textures in Java 2D

Images in the form of JPEG files can be loaded and directly drawn in the
corresponding window. But they can also be used as textures to fill areas or
shapes. For filling an area by a texture in Java 2D without repetition of the
texture, clipping can be applied with respect to the corresponding Shape. First,
the JPEG image must be loaded into an instance theImage of the class Image
and a Shape s has to be defined which should be filled with the texture. It is
recommended to first remember the old clipping area which can be obtained
by the method getClip. Then the method setClip can be used to define the
corresponding Shape as the new clipping area. After the texture has been drawn
with the drawImage method, the old clipping area should be reactivated with
the setClip method.

```
Shape clipShape = g2d.getClip();
g2d.setClip(s);
g2d.drawImage(theImage,50,50,null);
g2d.setClip(clipShape);
```

If the texture is too small or positioned wrongly, it might not fill the area
defined by the Shape s completely.

In order to fill an area repeatedly with a texture, the class TexturePaint
can be used. The texture must be available as a BufferedImage buffImage. A
rectangle in the constructor of TexturePaint defines the position and the size
of a single copy of the texture. So this rectangle defines how the texture is laid
like tiles on the plane. The texture will become visible when a given Shape s
is filled with it. This corresponds to opening a window with the corresponding
shape through which the texture tiles can be seen.

```
TexturePaint tp =
  new TexturePaint(buffImage,
                  new Rectangle(0,0,buffImage.getWidth(),
                                      buffImage.getHeight())));
g2d.setPaint(tp);
g2d.fill(s);
```

The file Texture2DExample.java demonstrates the use of the two techniques
for displaying textures.

4.3 Displaying text

Printing and displaying text is a field with a long tradition with roots in typography and printing technology. The details of letter and text representation cannot be covered within this book, so that the following two sections discuss only a very small selection of problems within this complex topic. General information about letter fonts and their representation can, for instance, be found in [30].

For displaying text, a *font* must be chosen which will be used for the symbols and characters to be printed. The size of a font is given in the unit pt (points) with 1 pt $\approx$ 0.3515 mm. A font contains more than just the specification of its size and the descriptions of the shapes of its letters or symbols. For each symbol it is necessary to specify the baseline. Not all letters are above the baseline. Letters like "g" or "p" reach below the baseline. Even this information is not sufficient, since symbols in the font can also have different widths. In this case, the font is called *proportional font*. In a proportional font each symbol or letter has its own width and even the distance between letters is not constant but varies with the combination of the letters. Certain pairs of letters are printed closer together than others. *Kerning*[2] refers to this concept. *Ligatures* even construct a new connected symbol for certain pairs of letters. Double-f as in "coffee" or the combination "fi" as in "first" are subject to ligatures.[3] Kerning and ligatures depend on the chosen font.

Another important aspect of fonts are modifications like **boldface** or *italic* fonts.

Fonts can be stored in terms of raster or vector graphics. The advantage of raster graphics is that no additional rendering is needed when symbols of the font have to be drawn. The corresponding pixels are directly given by the defined raster image of the symbol. The disadvantage of storing fonts in terms of raster graphics is that individual raster graphics are needed for different sizes of the same font and for the different styles (normal, boldface, italic). As already mentioned in section 2.1, it is not recommended to try to generate fonts in different sizes by applying scaling to the raster graphics images. There are techniques for deriving raster graphics from a normal font for the boldface and the italic style of the font. For the italic style, pixel lines are shifted to the right. The higher the pixel line in the symbol, the more it is shifted to the right. For boldface printing, the whole symbol is copied and shifted one pixel to the right. Figure 4.6 illustrates this technique. The letter on the left is defined in a relatively rough pixel raster. The letter in the middle is the resulting italic

---

[2] Compare the word "Van"—"Van" with and without kerning.

[3] Compare the following words printed with and without ligature: coffee—coffee, first—first.

version, the letter on the right the boldface printing.

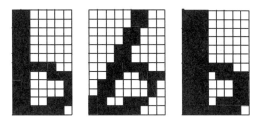

Figure 4.6 Italic and boldface printing for letters given in raster graphics

These techniques for italic and boldface fonts and scaling of fonts for different sizes lead to unacceptable results, so that fonts are usually stored in terms of vector graphics. Nevertheless, rendering fonts in an optimal way remains a nontrivial problem [31].

4.4 Text in Java 2D

The method

```
g2d.drawString("text",posx,posy);
```

in Java 2D draws a string—here the string "text"—at the position (xpos,ypos). A default font is used to draw the string. Java 2D offers a variety of methods to choose and modify fonts. Since the focus of this book is not on text representation, only very few methods will be introduced here. A new font can be chosen by the command

```
Font f = new Font("type",Font.STYLE,size);
```

The name of the font is specified by the string "**type**". A list of fonts available on the specific computer is obtained with the following lines of code.

```
Font[] fl =
GraphicsEnvironment.getLocalGraphicsEnvironment(
                                    ).getAllFonts();
for (int i=0; i<fl.length; i++)
{
  System.out.println(fl[i].getName());
}
```

All names appearing in this list can be used for `type`. `Arial, Times New Roman, sansserif` are typical standard fonts. Possible values `STYLE` for style are `PLAIN` (*normal*), `ITALIC` (*italic*), `BOLD` (**boldface**) and `ITALIC | BOLD` (*italic* and **boldface**). The integer value `size` specifies the size of the font in the unit pt, not in pixels. After calling the method `g2d.setFont(f)`, `drawString` will use the font `f`.

In addition to the above-mentioned parameters, a font can also be modified in Java 2D by applying transformations to the font.

```
Font transformedFont = f.deriveFont(affTrans);
```

`f` is an arbitrary `Font` and `affTrans` is an affine transformation of the class `AffineTransform`. This technique can be applied in connection with the transformation `yUp` from section 2.8. `yUp` was used to make the y-axis of a window pointing upwards. This involves a reflection which is applied to all drawn objects, unfortunately also to strings. As a result, the `drawString` method will produce text which is written upside down. This problem can be solved by transforming the desired font in such a way that its letters would occur upside down. Drawing the upside down symbols again upside down, will let them occur in normal readable fashion. The suitable transformation `affTrans` to be applied to the font should carry out a reflection with respect to the x-axis and afterwards a translation in the y-direction by the height of the font. Otherwise all letters would occur below instead of above their intended line. This technique was, for instance, applied in the file `RotationExample.java` to make sure that the shown coordinate system has the correct orientation.

It is also possible to apply transformations to single symbols of a font only. One can define a `String s` that contains the symbols to be transformed. Then a `GlyphVector` is derived from the string.

```
FontRenderContext frc = g2d.getFontRenderContext();
GlyphVector gv = f.createGlyphVector(frc,s);
```

The `GlyphVector` contains the characters of the `String s`. `f` is the `Font` to be used for the symbols in `s`. The method `gv.getNumGlyphs()` returns the number of characters in the `GlyphVector` and in the `String`.

```
Point2D p = gv.getGlyphPosition(i);
```

yields the coordinates of the ith character. The method

```
Shape glyph = gv.getGlyphOutline(i);
```

transforms the ith character into a `Shape` object. The desired `AffineTransform` `at` can then be applied to this `Shape` object to modify and to position it.

```
Shape transGlyph = at.createTransformedShape(glyph);
```

Finally, the transformed character `transfGlyph` can be drawn by the method `g2d.fill(transfGlyph)`. The file `TextExample.java` demonstrates the use of these methods.

4.5 Grey images and intensities

So far it was always assumed that a pixel is coloured black or white. The only exception was made in the context of antialiasing techniques for drawing smooth boundaries of curves to reduce the staircasing effect. The human perception of light intensities is mainly a relative one. A 60-watt light bulb is much brighter in comparison to a 20-watt light bulb than a 100-watt light bulb in comparison to a 60-watt light bulb. In both cases the difference is 40 watts. Nevertheless, the 60 watts is three times as bright as 20 watts, whereas 100 watts is not even twice as bright as 60 watts.

For grey-scale and colour images only a finite number of intensity levels can be used. The intensity levels should be chosen according to the human perception. This means the intensity levels should not increase linearly, but exponentially. Starting from the lowest intensity (black for grey-values) I_0, the intensities should be chosen according to the rule

$$I_0 = I_0, \quad I_1 = rI_0, \quad I_2 = rI_1 = r^2 I_0, \quad \ldots$$

up to a maximum intensity $I_n = r^n I_0$ where $r > 1$ is a constant. The average human vision system is able to distinguish between grey-levels when they differ by at least 1%, i.e., if $r > 1.01$ holds [50]. Choosing $R = 1.01$ and assuming a normalised maximum intensity of $I_n = 1$ and minimum intensity I_0 for a specific output device, from $1.01^n I_0 \leq 1$ it follows that

$$n \leq \frac{\ln\left(\frac{1}{I_0}\right)}{\ln(1.01)}$$

grey-levels are sufficient for the representation on the corresponding output device. A finer resolution of the intensity levels would not make a visible difference. Based on these considerations, Table 4.1 contains the maximum number of intensity levels for different output media.

If an output device allows only binary pixels, for instance a black-and-white laser printer, different intensity levels can be represented for the price of a lower resolution. The technique is called *halftoning* and it combines binary pixels to larger pixels. For instance, if 2×2 smaller pixels form a larger pixel, five intensity levels are expressible. Combining 3×3 smaller pixels to form a larger pixel allows 10 different intensity levels and the combination of $n \times n$ pixels leads

Medium	I_0 (ca.)	Max. no. of grey-levels
monitor	0.005-0.025	372-533
newspaper	0.1	232
photo	0.01	464
slide	0.001	695

Table 4.1 Intensity levels for different output media (according to [10])

to $n^2 + 1$ possible intensity levels. Of course, the resolution is getting worse, the larger the combined pixels are chosen. The coarsened resolution must still be high enough so that the pixel raster is not immediately visible.

The different intensity levels are achieved by drawing a different number of smaller pixels in the corresponding combined larger pixel. If a larger pixel should be drawn with intensity $\frac{k}{n^2}$, k out of the $n \times n$ smaller pixels will be drawn. The k pixels should be chosen in such a way that they are neighbouring pixels and they do not form a regular pattern like a line. Otherwise, this might introduce new visual artifacts like stripes in an area of identical intensity values.

Figure 4.7 shows the representation of five grey-levels by a matrix of 2×2 pixels and below the representation of ten grey-levels based on a 3×3 pixel matrix.

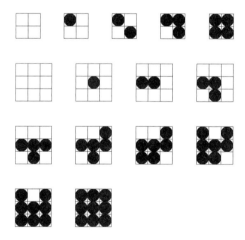

Figure 4.7 Grey-level representation based on halftoning for a 2×2 (top line) and on 3×3 pixel matrices (3 bottom lines)

Dither matrices provide a simple way to define which pixels in an $n \times n$ matrix should be set to represent different intensity levels. For the intensity level $\frac{k}{n^2}$, those pixels should be chosen whose corresponding entries in the dither matrix are greater than k. The five pixel matrices from the first line in figure 4.7 are encoded by the dither matrix D_2, the ten 3×3 pixel matrices by the dither matrix D_3 where

$$D_2 = \begin{pmatrix} 0 & 2 \\ 3 & 1 \end{pmatrix}, \qquad D_3 = \begin{pmatrix} 6 & 8 & 4 \\ 1 & 0 & 3 \\ 5 & 2 & 7 \end{pmatrix}.$$

Halftoning can also be applied to nonbinary intensity levels in order to refine the intensity levels further. For instance, using 2×2 pixel matrices where each pixel can have four different intensity levels yields 13 possible intensity levels:

$$\begin{pmatrix} 0 & 0 \\ 0 & 0 \end{pmatrix}, \begin{pmatrix} 1 & 0 \\ 0 & 0 \end{pmatrix}, \begin{pmatrix} 1 & 0 \\ 0 & 1 \end{pmatrix}, \begin{pmatrix} 1 & 1 \\ 0 & 1 \end{pmatrix}, \begin{pmatrix} 1 & 1 \\ 1 & 1 \end{pmatrix},$$

$$\begin{pmatrix} 2 & 1 \\ 1 & 1 \end{pmatrix}, \begin{pmatrix} 2 & 1 \\ 1 & 2 \end{pmatrix}, \begin{pmatrix} 2 & 2 \\ 1 & 2 \end{pmatrix}, \begin{pmatrix} 2 & 2 \\ 2 & 2 \end{pmatrix}, \begin{pmatrix} 3 & 2 \\ 2 & 2 \end{pmatrix},$$

$$\begin{pmatrix} 3 & 2 \\ 2 & 3 \end{pmatrix}, \begin{pmatrix} 3 & 3 \\ 2 & 3 \end{pmatrix}, \begin{pmatrix} 3 & 3 \\ 3 & 3 \end{pmatrix}.$$

For instance, the first matrix in the second line represents the fifth intensity level.[4] For this intensity level, one of the four pixels should be drawn with the grey-level 2, the other three with the grey-level 1.

4.6 Colour models

The human eye can see light starting with a wavelength of about 300-400 nm (violet) up to roughly 700-800 nm (red). From the theoretical point of view, a colour is defined by the distribution of the intensities over the visible spectrum of the light. For colour perception, the human eye has three different types of receptors. Each receptor type is more sensitive to a certain smaller range of the spectrum. They are called red-, green- and blue-receptors. The blue-receptors are in general less sensitive than the other two. The main characteristics of a colour for human perception are the following ones.

---

[4] The lowest intensity level is 0.

– hue corresponding to the dominant wavelength in the spectrum of the colour,

– saturation or purity which is high when the spectrum consists of a narrow peak at the dominant wavelength, and which is low for a flatter spectrum, and

– intensity or *lightness* depending on the energy of the spectrum. The higher the energy of the single frequencies, the higher is the intensity.

Figure 4.8 shows the distribution of energies for the frequencies or wavelengths for a spectrum with a high and a low saturation. The perceived intensity depends on the average height of the spectrum.

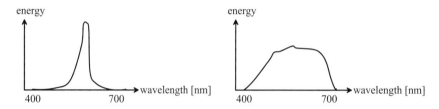

Figure 4.8 Distribution of the energies over the wavelengths for high (left) and low (right) saturation

Perception of colours is based on three components or receptors in the human eye, and also the intuitive understanding of colours is based on three components, hue, saturation and lightness. Therefore, most colour models in computer graphics also use three components to represent colours leading to a three-dimensional colour space.

There are *additive* and *subtractive colour models*. In additive colour models the colour is determined by a superposition of light of different colours. Colours are aggregated in an additive fashion, when the background itself is black or dark. A computer monitor is a typical example where additive colour models are used. The addition of all colours yields white. The situation is different for printers. Colours are applied to a white background (paper). Mixing all colours will yield black in this case.

The most common colour model in computer graphics is the *RGB model*. Most of the monitors also work with the RGB model. The RGB model is an additive model and each colour is composed of the three primary colours red, green and blue. Therefore, three values $R, G, B \in [0, 1]$ are sufficient to specify a colour. The minimum intensity is zero, one is the maximum intensity for each of the primary colours. $(0, 0, 0)$ corresponds to black, $(1, 1, 1)$ is white, (x, x, x) defines a lighter or darker grey, depending on the choice of x, $(1, 0, 0)$ encodes red, $(0, 1, 0)$ green and $(0, 0, 1)$ blue. Usually, for the coding of the intensity of a colour, one byte is used, so that each of the primary colours has 256 different levels of intensity. Instead of three floating point values between zero and one, it is therefore also very common to specify three integer values between 0 and 255 for the intensities in order to define a colour.

Not every colour can be represented exactly as an additive combination of the three primary colours red, green and blue. For this reason, the Commission Internationale de l'Éclairage (CIE) introduced a model with three artificial colours X, Y and Z which can represent any other colour. However, finding suitable combinations of the three artificial colours to model a desired colour is not very intuitive, so that the *CIEXYZ model* is seldom used.

The subtractive *CMY model* is the dual to the RGB model and is used for printers and plotters. The primary colours are cyan, magenta and yellow. The transformation from an RGB colour to its CMY representation is given by the equation

$$\begin{pmatrix} C \\ M \\ Y \end{pmatrix} = 1 - \begin{pmatrix} R \\ G \\ B \end{pmatrix}.$$

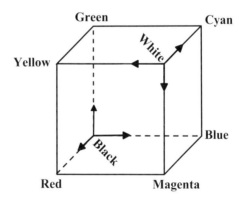

Figure 4.9 RGB and CMY model

Figure 4.9 shows the colour cube. Each vertex represents a specific colour. For the RGB model, the origin of the coordinate system is the lower left rear vertex at the colour black. The origin of the coordinate system for the CMY model is in the upper right front vertex at the colour white. The diagonal between these vertices contains all greytones.

Today, most printers do not use the CMY model. They are based on four-colour printing with the *CMYK model* where the fourth additional colour K is black.[5] In this direct way, black is better represented than by mixing the three other colours. The transformation from the CMY model to the CMYK model is given by the following equations.

$$
\begin{aligned}
K &:= \min\{C, M, Y\}, \\
C &:= C - K, \\
M &:= M - K, \\
Y &:= Y - K.
\end{aligned}
$$

With these equations, at least one of the four values C, Y, M, K will always be equal to zero.

The *YIQ model* is not based on three primary colours as in the RGB and the CMY model, but it uses the three components luminance Y and two values I and Q characterising the chromaticity, the type of colour. This colour model is also used in the American NTSC television norm. When a coloured representation has to be transformed into a grey-scale representation, for instance for black-and-white TV, the Y-component alone defines the corresponding grey-scale intensity. The transformation from the RGB model to the YIQ model is given by the following matrix.

$$
\begin{pmatrix} Y \\ I \\ Q \end{pmatrix} = \begin{pmatrix} 0.299 & 0.587 & 0.114 \\ 0.596 & -0.275 & -0.321 \\ 0.212 & -0.523 & 0.311 \end{pmatrix} \cdot \begin{pmatrix} R \\ G \\ B \end{pmatrix}.
$$

The property that the value Y determines the luminance or intensity directly is also helpful when computer monitors with different brightness should be adjusted, so that the colours they show are more or less the same for identical RGB values. It is much easier to adjust only the Y-value of the YIQ model than to adjust the three values R, G and B at the same time.

Like the YIQ model, the *HSV model* is not based on three elementary colours, but on the three parameters hue, saturation and value (intensity). The HSV model represents the colour space as a pyramid standing on its tip. The tip corresponds to the colour black. The hue H is given by an angle around the vertical axis. Principal colours are represented by angles, starting with red at $0°$, having yellow at $60°$, green at $120°$, blue at $240°$ and purple at $300°$. The saturation S of a colour ranges from zero along the V-axis to one at the sides. The value V encodes lightness. The higher V is, the lighter the colour. Figure 4.10 illustrates the HSV model.

The *HLS model* is based on similar ideas as the HSV model. The hue is defined in the same way as in the HSV model. The lightness is defined by a

---

[5] Since the letter B is already used for blue in the RGB model, K is used for black, standing for key colour.

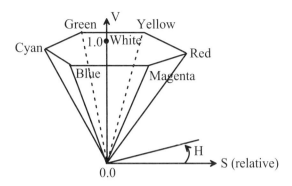

Figure 4.10   HSV model

value between zero and one. The saturation depends on the distance to the middle axis representing the grey-values. The saturation is also between zero and one. Figure 4.11 shows two versions of the HLS model. Sometimes, the HLS model is interpreted as a cylinder as in the left-hand side of the figure. But sometimes the double cone on the right is preferred for the HLS model. The double cone reflects the fact that it does not make sense to speak of saturation for the colours black and white, when grey-values are already characterised by the luminance value.

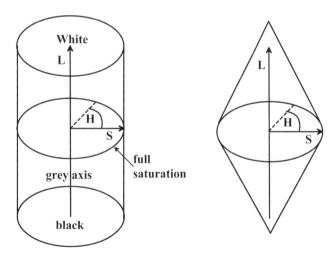

Figure 4.11   HLS model

Algorithms to transform colours from the HSV and the HLS model to the RGB model and back can be found in [18]. The HSV and the HLS model count as *perception-oriented colour models* since they reflect the intuitive perception of colours better. Specifying the parameters of a desired colour is easier with perception-oriented models than with models like RGB or CMY. For the latter models, graphic programs very often support the specification of colours by providing a colour palette.

Like the HSV and the HLS model, the *CNS model* is another perception-oriented colour model based on the specification of the type of the colour, its saturation and its lightness. The CNS model does not use numbers for these parameters but words. For the type of the colour, values like purple, red, orange, brown, yellow, green, blue are available including mixtures like yellowish green, green-yellow or greenish yellow. The lightness can be defined as one of the values very dark, dark, medium, light and very light. The saturation can be greyish, moderate, strong or vivid. The number of possible combinations of these expressions is much smaller than the number of colours expressible with the RGB model. But the description of the colour is much more intuitive.

4.6.1 Colours in Java 2D

With the exception of the CNS model, Java 2D supports all colour models mentioned in the previous section. Because most applications are based on the RGB model, within this book only this model will be used. The class `Color` allows to define colours based on RGB values using the constructor

```
Color col = new Color(r,g,b);
```

The values `r,g,b` are either `float`-values between zero and one, specifying the red, green and blue intensity, respectively, or they can be integer values between 0 and 255, defining the corresponding intensity levels for the colours. The class `Color` also provides some constants for standard colours, for instance `Color.red` or `Color.yellow`. Another constructor needs only a single integer parameter. From the byte coding of these integer values the corresponding byte values, yielding numbers between 0 and 255, for the three colours red, green and blue are derived. Integers are coded by four bytes. Colours can also use the fourth byte as the so-called alpha-value which defines how transparent the colour is.

When the method

```
g2d.setPaint(col);
```

is called, everything drawn with methods of the `Graphics2D` object `g2d` will be drawn in the colour `col` until `setPaint` is called again with another colour.

4.7 Colour interpolation

Most of the colour models are based on a three-dimensional colour space in which colours are defined by three components. Within the RGB model a colour can be associated with a vector $(r, g, b) \in [0, 1]^3$. This interpretation of colours also allows the definition of convex combinations of colours. One application of such convex combinations are colour gradients. If an area should not be filled with a homogeneous colour but with changing colour, this can be achieved by a colour gradient. Two colours (r_0, g_0, b_0) and (r_1, g_1, b_1) must be defined for two points $\mathbf{p}_0$ and $\mathbf{p}_1$. The colour (r_0, g_0, b_0) is used in the point $\mathbf{p}_0$, the colour (r_1, g_1, b_1) in the point $\mathbf{p}_1$. For points on the connecting line between $\mathbf{p}_0$ and $\mathbf{p}_1$, the corresponding convex combination of the colours is used. For the point $\mathbf{p} = (1-\alpha)\mathbf{p}_1 + \alpha\mathbf{p}_0$ (where $\alpha \in [0, 1]$) the colour $(1-\alpha) \cdot (r_0, g_0, b_0) + \alpha \cdot (r_1, g_1, b_1)$ is used.

Colour interpolation can also help to amend textures that are used repeatedly to fill an area. As mentioned in section 4.1, fissures as in a tile pattern might occur at the boundaries of the texture. Image processing techniques include *smoothing operators* [46] to let edges appear less sharp. Simple smoothing operators are characterised by a weight matrix that defines how the colour values of pixels should be modified. For instance, the weight matrix

0.1	0.1	0.1
0.1	0.2	0.1
0.1	0.1	0.1

means that the smoothing operator assigns a new colour to a pixel in the following way. The new colour is the weighted sum of the pixel's colour with weight 0.2 and the colours of its eight neighbour pixels, each one with a weight of 0.1. The smoothing operator is applied to each pixel. Depending on how strong the smoothing effect should be, the weights can be changed, for instance all weights could have the same value $1/9$ to achieve a stronger smoothing effect. The weight matrix can also be enlarged to take not only the colours of the direct neighbours of a pixel into account. For smooth transitions at the boundaries of a texture, the smoothing operator must be applied to pixels at the edges of the texture. For this purpose, the pixels on the right edge should be considered as left neighbours of the pixels at the left edge and vice versa. The same applies to the pixels at the lower and upper edge.

Interpolators were already discussed in section 2.11 in the context of continuous movements of objects. These interpolators were based on geometric transformations. One application for such animated graphics was the transformation of one geometric object into another one by convex combinations of transformations. Another interesting example is the transformation of one

image to another which will be discussed here in more detail. The simplest way
to transform two images of the same size into each other is to apply convex combinations of the intensity values of the corresponding intensities for red, green
and blue at every pixel. This will lead to a continuous blending of the two images. While one image fades away, the other one appears. More realistic effects
can be achieved, when also the geometric shapes in the two images are transformed properly into each other. In this case, geometric transformations are
also needed in addition to colour interpolation. A common technique that does
more than just blending the two images is based on a *triangulation* of the two
images. A triangulation is a partition using triangles. The two triangulations
must use the same number of vertices and the triangles in the triangulations
must be chosen accordingly. This means that if the points $\mathbf{p}_i$, $\mathbf{p}_j$ and $\mathbf{p}_k$ form
a triangle of the triangulation in the first image, then the corresponding points
in the second image must also form a triangle of the triangulation of the second
image. It is not necessary that points which correspond to each other in the
two images have the same coordinates.

Figure 4.12 Compatible triangulations of two images

Each triangle of a triangulation determines a section of the corresponding
image. Such a section has a corresponding section in the other image although
the two triangles might be different in size and shape. Figure 4.12 illustrates this
situation. On the left-hand side, two faces are shown that should be transformed
into each other. The right part of the figure shows compatible triangulations of
the two images. Each triangle is responsible for a certain section in the images.
For instance, the upper triangle includes the forehead of the corresponding face,
the lower triangle the chin. It should be noted that the number of points for
the triangulation is identical for both images, but the points do not have the
same positions.

In order to transform one image into the other step by step with intermediate images, first the triangulation of the corresponding intermediate image
must be determined. The points for the triangulation result from convex combinations of the associated points in the two images. The triangles for the

intermediate image are defined in the same way as for the other two images. If the points $\mathbf{p}_i$, $\mathbf{p}_j$ and $\mathbf{p}_k$ form a triangle in the first image and the associated points $\mathbf{p}'_i$, $\mathbf{p}'_j$ and $\mathbf{p}'_k$ form a triangle in the second image, then the points

$$(1 - \alpha)\mathbf{p}_\ell + \alpha\mathbf{p}'_\ell, \qquad \ell \in \{i, j, k\}$$

form a triangle in the intermediate image.

Within one triangle, the colour for the pixels is determined by colour interpolation. Before the colour of a pixel in the intermediate image can be computed, the triangle in which the pixel lies must be determined. If the pixel belongs to more than one triangle, in case it lies on an edge or a vertex of a triangle, then any of these triangles can be chosen. The task is to find out whether a pixel $\mathbf{q}$ lies within a triangle defined by the points $\mathbf{p}_1, \mathbf{p}_2, \mathbf{p}_3$. As long as the triangle is not degenerated to a line or a point, there is exactly one representation of $\mathbf{q}$ in the form

$$\mathbf{q} = \alpha_1 \cdot \mathbf{p}_1 + \alpha_2 \cdot \mathbf{p}_2 + \alpha_3 \cdot \mathbf{p}_3 \qquad (4.1)$$

where

$$\alpha_1 + \alpha_2 + \alpha_3 = 1. \qquad (4.2)$$

This is a system of linear equations with three variables $\alpha_1, \alpha_2, \alpha_3$ and three equations. The vector equation (4.1) contributes two equations, one for the x- and one for the y-coordinate. The third equation is the constraint (4.2). The point $\mathbf{q}$ lies within the triangle defined by the points $\mathbf{p}_1, \mathbf{p}_2, \mathbf{p}_3$ if and only if $0 \leq \alpha_1, \alpha_2, \alpha_3 \leq 1$ holds, i.e., if $\mathbf{q}$ can be written as a convex combination of $\mathbf{p}_1, \mathbf{p}_2, \mathbf{p}_3$.

After the triangle in which the considered pixel lies and the corresponding values $\alpha_1, \alpha_2, \alpha_3$ have been determined, the colour of the pixel is calculated as a convex combination of the colours of the corresponding pixels in the first and the second image. The triangle in the intermediate image is associated to one triangle in the first and the second image. For each of these two triangles the convex combination of its vertices with weights $\alpha_1, \alpha_2, \alpha_3$ specifies the point corresponding to the considered pixel in the intermediate image. Rounding might be required to obtain a pixel from the point coordinates. The colour of the pixel in the intermediate image is a convex combination of the colours of these two pixels in the first and the second image.

Figure 4.13 illustrates this principle. The triangle in the middle belongs to the intermediate image in which the pixel lies for which the colour should be determined. The left and right triangle are the corresponding triangles in the first and the second image. The pixels in the three triangles originate from the same convex combination of the vertices in the corresponding triangle.

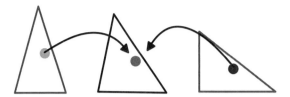

Figure 4.13 Computation of the interpolated colour of a pixel

4.8 Colour interpolation with Java 2D

The Java 2D class `GradientPaint` provides a simple way for colour interpolation or colour gradients. A colour gradient between the two points (x0,y0) and (x1,y1) can be defined by

```
GradientPaint gradPaint =
    new GradientPaint(x0,y0,colour0,x1,y1,colour1, repeat);
```

which is activated by

```
g2d.setPaint(gradPaint);
```

The coordinates of the points should be `float` values. The `colour0` is used in the point (x0,y0), the colour `colour1` in point (x1,y1). Points on the line connecting these two points obtain their colour from the corresponding convex combination of `colour0` and `colour1`. The same colour gradient is applied to lines parallel to the connecting line between (x0,y0) and (x1,y1). The Boolean value `repeat` specifies whether the colour gradient should be repeated before (x0,y0) and after (x1,y1). If `false` is chosen for `repeat`, then pixels before (x0,y0) are drawn with the colour `colour0` and pixels behind (x1,y1) are drawn with the colour `colour1`. In case of `true`, the colour gradient is repeated again and again. Behind the point (x1,y1) the interpolation is continued from colour `colour1` back to colour `colour0`, then again to `colour1` etc. The point (x0,y0) is treated analogously. The file `GradientPaintExample.java` demonstrates the use of `GradientPaint`.

Methods for colour gradients are provided in the class `GradientPaint`, but more general colour interpolation techniques as described at the end of section 4.7 cannot be implemented by a simple `GradientPaint`. For these colour interpolation techniques, it is necessary to read and set the colour of pixels in an image. For this purpose, the following methods are available in Java 2D. The colour of the pixel with coordinates (x, y) in the `BufferedImage bi` can be obtained by

```
int rgbValue = bi.getRGB(x,y);
Color pixelColour = new Color(rgbValue);
```

The method `getRGB(x,y)` returns the colour as a single integer value in which each colour of the primary colours red, green and blue is encoded by one byte. In order to access the corresponding values red, green and blue directly, a new colour instance of the `Color` is generated from which the RGB-values can be obtained by

```
int red   = pixelColour.getRed();
int green = pixelColour.getGreen();
int blue  = pixelColour.getBlue();
```

as integer values in the range from 0 to 255.

For interpolating or mixing the colours of a set of pixels, the colour of each pixel must be determined as described above. Then the corresponding values for red, green and blue can be combined as a suitable convex combination, depending on how the pixel colours should be interpolated or mixed. If `rMix`, `gMix` and `bMix` denote the interpolated values for the three colours, then the pixel with coordinates (x, y) in the `BufferedImage mixedBi` obtains this colour by

```
Color mixedColour = new Color(rMix, gMix, bMix);
mixedBi.setRGB(x,y,pixelColour.getRGB());
```

The method `setRGB` requires the colour encoded in the form of an integer value, not as an instance of the class `Color`.

The class `MorphingCandS.java` uses this technique for colour interpolation in order to transform one image into another one step by step. For both images suitable compatible triangulations must be defined in advance. The interpolation between the two images, as described at the end of section 4.7 and as illustrated in figure 4.13 on page 110, is carried out in the class `TriangulatedImage.java`.

4.9 Exercises

Exercise 4.1

Mark the interior of the polygon shown below according to the odd parity rule.

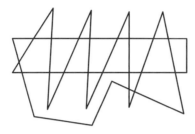

Exercise 4.2

Rewrite the program `ConvexCombTransforms.java` by applying double buffering.

Exercise 4.3

Create an image with Java 2D and store it as a JPEG file. Use the stored image as a texture for filling an ellipse.

Exercise 4.4

Define an algorithm for filling an annulus with a nonlinear colour gradient. Assume that two colours at $0°$ and $180°$ are specified and the interpolation between these two colours shall take place along the arc of the circle. Use polar coordinates to describe the points in the annulus. Implement your algorithm for this colour interpolation technique in Java 2D.

5

Basic principles of three-dimensional graphics

This chapter and all following ones are devoted to methods and problems in connection with the representation of three-dimensional scenes. Before the topics are discussed in more detail, the following section provides a short overview on which tasks and problems occur on the way from the real world or an abstract 3D model to the representation on the computer screen or another output device.

5.1 From a 3D world to a model

Before anything can be drawn on the computer screen, a three-dimensional virtual world of objects must be defined and stored in the computer. The same principle applies even to two-dimensional virtual worlds. Geometric objects like rectangles, circles or polygons must be specified before they can be drawn. The three-dimensional virtual world can contain much more than what will be displayed in one moment on the computer screen. The virtual world might consist of a building or even a city, perhaps a larger landscape, but the viewer will only see a small part of this virtual world, for instance only a single room in a building. Of course, the viewer can move around in the virtual world and explore it. But in the above examples he will never see the whole virtual world in one single image.

The first step consists in modelling the objects of the virtual world. The description of a three-dimensional object must contain information about its geometry but also properties of its surface. What is the object's colour? Is the surface shiny or dull?

There are two different approaches for modelling the geometry of objects. In many applications of computer graphics, the objects do not have existing counterparts in reality. This is the case for fantasy worlds of computer games as well as for models of concept cars or possible future buildings that have not been built yet and might or might not be built in the future. In these cases, the designer or programmer of the virtual world needs methods for constructing and modelling three-dimensional virtual objects. Even if existing objects are to be modelled, such construction and modelling techniques might be necessary. For existing buildings or furniture some principal measurements like height or width might be available. But such information is by far not enough to generate a realistic representation of the objects. The objects might, for instance, have rounded corners.

In other cases, detailed measurements of the geometric structure of objects might be available. 3D laser scanners provide detailed information about an object's surface geometry. However, the raw data coming from 3D laser scanners are not suitable for a direct use in virtual worlds of computer graphics. They are usually processed further automatically with additional manual corrections to yield simpler surface models. The same applies to techniques for measuring inner geometric structures. Steel girders in buildings or bridges are an example where such techniques are applied. Another important and quickly developing application field in this context is medical informatics. X-ray, ultrasonic and tomography techniques provide information about skeletal and tissue structures from which 3D models of bones and organs can be derived.

The first step in computer graphics is therefore the creation of a computer model of the virtual world, either manually by a designer or programmer, or automatically derived from measurements. To represent a specific part of this virtual world, the viewer's position and direction of view in the virtual world must be defined. This also includes his field of view, the viewing angle and the distance he can see. In this way, a three-dimensional clipping region is defined so that only objects within the region need to be considered for rendering.

However, so far the image will remain black when no lights are added to the virtual world. The sources of light, their locations as well as their characteristics must be defined. Characteristics are for instance the colour of the light or whether the light shines only in one direction like a spotlight. Only with this information is it possible to compute how much light a single object receives, whether it is in the shadow or in the bright light.

Determining which objects are visible and which objects are hidden by others within the clipping region is another problem.

Finally, additional special effects might be needed in the scene like fog, smoke or reflections.

5.2 Geometric transformations

As in the two-dimensional case, geometric transformations also play a crucial role in three-dimensional computer graphics.

Three-dimensional coordinates in this book will always refer to a *right-handed coordinate system*. Using the thumb of the right hand for the x-axis, the forefinger for the y-axis and the middle finger for the z-axis, one obtains the correct orientation of the coordinate system. In a right-handed coordinate system the x-axis is mapped to the y-axis by a positive, i.e., anticlockwise, rotation of $90°$ around the z-axis. The y-axis is mapped by a positive rotation of $90°$ around the x-axis to the z-axis and the z-axis is transformed to the x-axis by a positive rotation of $90°$ around the y-axis to the x-axis. Figure 5.1 illustrates a right-handed coordinate system.

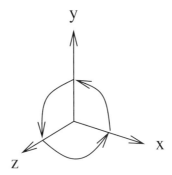

Figure 5.1   A right-handed coordinate system

A rotation by a positive angle around an oriented axis in the three-dimensional space refers to an anticlockwise rotation for a viewer to whom the axis points. This definition of positive rotations is consistent with rotations in the two-dimensional x/y-plane around the origin of the coordinate system when it is interpreted as a rotation around the z-axis. In order to determine whether a rotation is positive or negative, one can also apply the *right-hand rule*. When the thumb of the right hand points in the same direction as the rotation axis and the other fingers form a fist, then the bent fingers indicate the direction of positive rotation.

In section 2.6 homogeneous coordinates were introduced in order to be able to express all affine transformations in the plane in terms of matrix multiplications. The same principle of extending the coordinates by an additional dimension is also applied in the case of points and affine transformations in the three-dimensional space. A point in the three-dimensional space $\mathbb{R}^3$ is represented by four coordinates $(\tilde{x}, \tilde{y}, \tilde{z}, w)$ where $w \neq 0$. The point $(\tilde{x}, \tilde{y}, \tilde{z}, w)$ in homogeneous coordinates stands for the point $\left(\frac{\tilde{x}}{w}, \frac{\tilde{y}}{w}, \frac{\tilde{z}}{w}\right) \in \mathbb{R}^3$ in Cartesian coordinates. The point $(x, y, z) \in \mathbb{R}^3$ can be represented in homogeneous coordinates in the form $(x, y, z, 1)$. This is, however, not the only way. Any representation in the form $(x \cdot w, y \cdot w, z \cdot w, w)$ with $w \neq 0$ encodes the same point as well.

A *translation* by the vector $(d_x, d_y, d_z)^\top$ can be written as a matrix multiplication in homogeneous coordinates in the following way.

$$\begin{pmatrix} x' \\ y' \\ z' \\ 1 \end{pmatrix} = \begin{pmatrix} 1 & 0 & 0 & d_x \\ 0 & 1 & 0 & d_y \\ 0 & 0 & 1 & d_z \\ 0 & 0 & 0 & 1 \end{pmatrix} \cdot \begin{pmatrix} x \\ y \\ z \\ 1 \end{pmatrix} = \begin{pmatrix} x + d_x \\ y + d_y \\ z + d_z \\ 1 \end{pmatrix}.$$

The translation matrix is

$$T(d_x, d_y, d_z) = \begin{pmatrix} 1 & 0 & 0 & d_x \\ 0 & 1 & 0 & d_y \\ 0 & 0 & 1 & d_z \\ 0 & 0 & 0 & 1 \end{pmatrix}.$$

A *scaling* by the factors s_x, s_y, s_z is given by

$$\begin{pmatrix} x' \\ y' \\ z' \\ 1 \end{pmatrix} = \begin{pmatrix} s_x & 0 & 0 & 0 \\ 0 & s_y & 0 & 0 \\ 0 & 0 & s_z & 0 \\ 0 & 0 & 0 & 1 \end{pmatrix} \cdot \begin{pmatrix} x \\ y \\ z \\ 1 \end{pmatrix} = \begin{pmatrix} s_x \cdot x \\ s_y \cdot y \\ s_z \cdot z \\ 1 \end{pmatrix}$$

with

$$S(s_x, s_y, s_z) = \begin{pmatrix} s_x & 0 & 0 & 0 \\ 0 & s_y & 0 & 0 \\ 0 & 0 & s_z & 0 \\ 0 & 0 & 0 & 1 \end{pmatrix}$$

as scaling matrix.

In the two-dimensional case, it was sufficient to consider rotations around the origin of the coordinate system. By applying suitable transformations in addition, rotations around arbitrary points can be defined. In the three-dimensional case, instead of a centre point a rotation axis must be specified. The three elementary *rotations* in the three-dimensional space are the rotations around the coordinate axes. A rotation around the z-axis by the angle θ in homogeneous coordinates is given by

$$\begin{pmatrix} x' \\ y' \\ z' \\ 1 \end{pmatrix} = \begin{pmatrix} \cos\theta & -\sin\theta & 0 & 0 \\ \sin\theta & \cos\theta & 0 & 0 \\ 0 & 0 & 1 & 0 \\ 0 & 0 & 0 & 1 \end{pmatrix} \cdot \begin{pmatrix} x \\ y \\ z \\ 1 \end{pmatrix}$$

with the rotation matrix

$$R_z(\theta) = \begin{pmatrix} \cos\theta & -\sin\theta & 0 & 0 \\ \sin\theta & \cos\theta & 0 & 0 \\ 0 & 0 & 1 & 0 \\ 0 & 0 & 0 & 1 \end{pmatrix}.$$

This rotation matrix corresponds to the one already known from the two-dimensional case. It is only extended by the z-dimension. A rotation around the z-axis leaves the z-coordinates of a point unchanged. The matrices for rotations around the x- and the y-axis can be obtained from the above matrix by exchanging the roles of the corresponding axes so that a rotation around the x-axis by the angle θ is described by the matrix

$$R_x(\theta) = \begin{pmatrix} 1 & 0 & 0 & 0 \\ 0 & \cos\theta & -\sin\theta & 0 \\ 0 & \sin\theta & \cos\theta & 0 \\ 0 & 0 & 0 & 1 \end{pmatrix}$$

and a rotation around the y-axis by the angle θ by the matrix

$$R_y(\theta) = \begin{pmatrix} \cos\theta & 0 & \sin\theta & 0 \\ 0 & 1 & 0 & 0 \\ -\sin\theta & 0 & \cos\theta & 0 \\ 0 & 0 & 0 & 1 \end{pmatrix}.$$

By combining these three elementary rotations around the coordinate axes with suitable translations, a rotation around an arbitrary axis and an arbitrary angle can be realised. Given an arbitrary rotation axis and a rotation angle, the first step is to apply a translation $T(d_x, d_y, d_z)$, shifting the rotation's axis in such a way that it passes through the origin of the coordinate system. Afterwards, a rotation around the z-axis is carried out, mapping the translated rotation axis to the y/z-plane. Then this axis can be transformed into the

z-axis by a rotation around the x-axis. Now the original rotation can be carried out as a rotation around the z-axis by the angle θ. Finally, all previous transformations have to be reversed again. Altogether, the transformation

$$T(-d_x,-d_y,-d_z)\cdot R_z(-\theta_z)\cdot R_x(-\theta_x)\cdot R_z(\theta)\cdot R_x(\theta_x)\cdot R_z(\theta_z)\cdot T(d_x,d_y,d_z)$$

is obtained. It should be noted that the transformations are carried out like matrix multiplications from right to left.

In all above-mentioned transformation matrices the last row is $(0,0,0,1)$. Applying matrix multiplication to such matrices preserves this property.

In the two-dimensional case there is exactly one transformation matrix that maps three noncollinear[1] points to three other noncollinear points. Correspondingly, in the three-dimensional case there exists exactly one transformation matrix that maps four noncoplanar[2] points to four other noncoplanar points. Given four noncoplanar points $\mathbf{p}_1,\mathbf{p}_2,\mathbf{p}_3,\mathbf{p}_4\in\mathbb{R}^3$ and the target points $\mathbf{p}_1',\mathbf{p}_2',\mathbf{p}_3',\mathbf{p}_4'$, the transformation matrix is obtained by solving the system of linear equations

$$\mathbf{p}_i' = M\cdot\mathbf{p}_i \qquad (i=1,2,3,4). \tag{5.1}$$

The matrix

$$M = \begin{pmatrix} a & b & c & d \\ e & f & g & h \\ i & j & k & l \\ 0 & 0 & 0 & 1 \end{pmatrix}$$

in homogeneous coordinates must be derived from the four vector equations (5.1), each of them representing three[3] equations, one for the x-, the y- and the z-component, from which the twelve parameters of the matrix M can be calculated.

In this sense, transformations can be interpreted as changing from one coordinate system to another. This property will be used later on, for instance to view the same scene from different perspectives.

5.2.1 Java 3D

Unlike Java 2D, Java 3D does not belong to the standard Java framework and needs to be installed separately. Information about where Java 3D can be downloaded freely and how to install it can be found at the end of this book and on the web page of the book.

---

[1] Points not lying on the same line.
[2] Points not lying on the same plane.
[3] Since the vectors are given in homogeneous coordinates, there are actually four equations, but the fourth one is always of the form $0\cdot p_x+0\cdot p_y+0\cdot p_z+1\cdot 1=1$.

It is not the intention of this book to provide a complete introduction and overview on Java 3D. The main goal is to demonstrate how the computer graphics concepts introduced in this book can be used in practical examples in a quick and easy way. Some of the introduced concepts go even further than Java 3D at its present state to outline further perspectives. Nevertheless, the small selection of Java 3D classes and methods explained in this book will equip the reader with enough knowledge to get started with Java 3D and to write animated 3D graphics programs with interaction. Readers who would like to learn Java 3D in further detail are referred to books like [9, 33, 41, 42, 48], the Java 3D API documentation and the Java 3D tutorial. Special topics, like the design of 3D user interfaces with Java 3D, can be found in [1].

5.2.2 Geometric transformations in Java 3D

Instances of the class `Transform3D` store three-dimensional transformations as matrices in homogeneous coordinates similarly to the class `AffineTransform` for two-dimensional affine transformations. The constructor

```
Transform3D tf = new Transform3D();
```

generates the identity transformation corresponding to the unit matrix. The method

```
tf.rotX(theta);
```

defines `tf` as a rotation by the angle `theta` around the x-axis. Correspondingly, the methods `rotY` and `rotZ` specify rotations around the y- and the z-axis, respectively. Using

```
tf.set(new AxisAngle4d(x,y,z,theta));
```

a rotation by the angle `theta` around the axis in the direction of the `float`-vector $(x, y, z)^{\top}$ is defined.

A translation by the `float`-vector $(x, y, z)^{\top}$ is specified by

```
tf.setTranslation(new Vector3f(x,y,z));
```

The method

```
tf.setScale(new Vector3f(x,y,z));
```

leads to the scaling $S(x, y, z)$.

The method `tf.setScale(factor)` defines a scaling with the same scaling factor `factor` for the x-, y- and z-direction.

An arbitrary transformation can be specified by `tf.set(matrix)` where `matrix` is a one-dimensional `double`-array with 16 values specifying the entries in the matrix. It should be noted that the last row of the matrix can also be defined. Usually, the last row should be $(0, 0, 0, 1)$. `tf.get(matrix)` stores the matrix associated with the transformation `tf` in the (one-dimensional) `double`-array `matrix`.

The composition of transformations in the sense of matrix multiplication can be realised by `tf.mul(tf1,tf2)` or `tf1.mul(tf2)`. In the first case, the transformation resulting from the composition of the transformations `tf1` and `tf2` is stored in the transformation `tf`, in the latter case in the transformation `tf1`. Since the composition of transformations is carried out in Java 3D in the same way as matrix multiplications are computed, the rightmost transformation will be applied first. This means that the resulting transformation corresponds to first applying the transformation `tf2` and then `tf1`.

Figure 5.2 A chair constructed with elementary geometric objects

5.3 The scenegraph

For modelling a three-dimensional scene, geometric objects have to be defined and positioned in the scene. Techniques for constructing and modelling geometric objects are discussed in chapter 6. In addition to defining elementary objects like boxes, spheres, cylinders or cones, there are more sophisticated techniques for modelling complex objects. Complex objects are usually composed of simpler smaller objects. The chair in figure 5.2 is an object that is composed of elementary geometric objects. The legs and the seat are boxes, the backrest is a cylinder.

In order to model the chair, the corresponding elementary geometric objects must be defined with the intended admeasurements and then these objects have to be positioned correctly. To position an object correctly, suitable transformations need to be applied to it. If the whole chair should occur at another position in the scene, for instance farther to the right, then a corresponding transformation must be applied to all its parts. For an object designer or a programmer, it would be a quite tedious task to ensure explicitly that this transformation is applied to every single part, especially when much more complicated objects than the simple chair are considered. Therefore, instead of thinking of each particular geometric object as an independent instance, a *scenegraph* is defined in which the objects are grouped in a hierarchy of *transformation groups*. In the case of the chair, the chair itself would be a transformation group on its own, combining the legs, the seat and the backrest into one group. A transformation applied to the transformation group of the chair will automatically be applied to all members of the transformation group. In this way, the whole chair can be positioned anywhere in the scene by an arbitrary transformation without the need to state explicitly that this transformation should be applied to all parts of the chair.

To explain the concept of scenegraphs better, a slightly more complex example than the simple chair is considered. The scene contains a very simplified helicopter positioned on a cubical platform. A simplified tree also belongs also to the scene that is shown in figure 5.3.

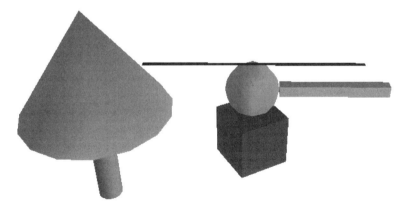

Figure 5.3 A scene composed of various elementary objects

A possible scenegraph of this scene is shown in figure 5.4. The root of the scenegraph has two child nodes. Both are transformation groups. Elementary geometric objects, other transformation groups or transformations can be assigned to a transformation group as child nodes. The transformation groups tgHeliPlat and tgTree represent the helicopter including the platform and the tree, respectively. Both of these transformation groups have a transformation as a direct child node. The transformation tfHeliPlat positions the helicopter together with the platform at the desired place in the scene, the transformation tfTree does the same for the tree.

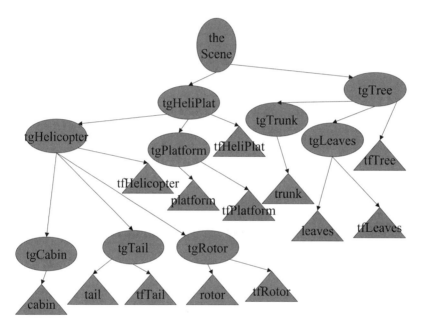

Figure 5.4 The scenegraph for figure 5.3

The transformation group tfTree also has two transformation groups as child nodes. tgTrunk stands for the trunk of the tree and tgLeaves for the treetop. The transformation group has only one child node in the form of an elementary geometric object tgTrunk, a cylinder that is generated in the origin of the coordinate system. The transformation group tgLeaves consists of the elementary geometric object leaves in the form of a cylinder and a transformation tfLeaves. This transformation moves the treetop which was also generated in the origin of the coordinate system to the top of the tree trunk.

The transformation group tgHeliPlat for the helicopter and the platform is built in a similar way. It contains a transformation for positioning the platform together with the helicopter correctly in the scene, and there are two other child nodes, the individual transformation groups tgHelicopter and tgPlatform for the helicopter and the platform, respectively. The helicopter transformation group itself has a transformation tfHelicopter to position the helicopter on top of the platform and three other transformation groups containing elementary geometric objects. The cockpit of the helicopter is a sphere, the tail and the rotor blade are boxes. The transformations tfTail and tfRotor are needed to position the tail at the end and the rotor blade on top of the cockpit.

5.4 Elementary geometric objects in Java 3D

To be able to show objects of a three-dimensional scene, it is not sufficient to outline their geometry only. It is also necessary to specify what the surface of the object looks like. A colour or a texture must be assigned to the surface. Even this is not sufficient for more realistic images. Reflection properties of the surface, e.g., how shiny it is, are also needed. The appearance of the surface of an object is defined in the class `Appearance` in Java 3D. More details of the class `Appearance` will be explained in connection with illumination in chapter 8. Here, the focus is on basic geometry and transformations. Therefore, a simplified default appearance is used until chapter 8. A simple instance of `Appearance` is generated in the following way.

```
Appearance myApp = new Appearance();
setToMyDefaultAppearance(myApp,new Color3f(r,g,b));
```

The method `setToMyDefaultAppearance` is not a standard method of Java 3D. It was written for the purpose of this book. The method can be found in some of the example programs, for instance in the class `StaticSceneExample.java`. The method assigns a desired colour given by an instance of the class `Color3f` to the `Appearance myApp`. The colour is defined by the three `float`-values r,g,b∈ [0, 1] specifying the intensities for red, blue and green.

After an `Appearance myApp` has been created, the following elementary geometric objects can be defined within Java 3D. In the following, all floating point values are of the type `float`, unless otherwise stated.

A box is generated by

```
Box xyzBox = new Box(x,y,z,myApp);
```

The box has the size $(2x) \times (2y) \times (2z)$ and is centred in the origin of the coordinate system. Unless specific transformations are applied or the viewpoint of the viewer in the scene is changed, the x-axis in Java 3D points to the right, the y-axis upwards and the z-axis in the direction forward to the viewer.

```
Sphere rSphere = new Sphere(r,myApp);
```

defines a sphere with radius **r** and midpoint in the origin of the coordinate system. A cylinder with radius **r** and height **h** whose centre point is again in the origin of the coordinate system is generated by

```
Cylinder rhCylinder = new Cylinder(r,h,myApp);
```

The cylinder is positioned in such a way that the axis along its height coincides with the y-axis. This means the cylinder extends **h**/2 units above and below the x/z-plane.

In the same way a cone with radius **r** and height **h** is constructed by

```
Cone rhCone = new Cone(r,h,myApp);
```

The cone is positioned in the same way as the cylinder centred around the y-axis with its tip **h**/2 units above the x/z-plane.

5.5 The scenegraph in Java 3D

Java 3D offers a complex scenegraph with a variety of different structures. Most of the programs in this book are based on a division into three branches. One branch is for modelling the objects within the scene, their positions and possible animated movements. Another branch is responsible for illumination, providing one or more light sources. The third branch takes care of the view of the scene. The position of the viewer and the direction of his view belong to this branch. Information about his field of view, like the angle or how far he can see, is also found in this branch. Even options like 3D-viewing with a head-mounted display providing different images for the left and right eye could be incorporated in this branch. The class `SimpleUniverse` in Java 3D simplifies the definition of this branch, the so-called *view platform*. The parameters are set to default values and the programmer is freed from providing detailed definitions. There are also methods to modify the default parameter settings, which will be introduced later on. For the purpose of this book, the options provided by the class `SimpleUniverse` are sufficient. In later sections, more details about the parameter settings in `SimpleUniverse` and their modifications will be explained. Since this section is only concerned with modelling of geometric objects, the default settings of `SimpleUniverse` are simply taken as they are. Figure 5.5 shows the general scenegraph for Java 3D and the role of the class `SimpleUniverse`, making the programming task a little easier.

All Java 3D classes in this book have the same basic structure, except for small modifications for specific applications. As a first step, some standard Java

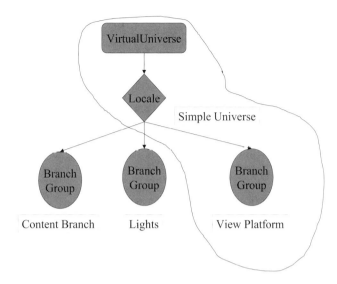

Figure 5.5 The overall scenegraph for Java 3D

and Java 3D packages need to be imported. This is usually done by

```
import javax.vecmath.*;
import com.sun.j3d.utils.geometry.*;
import com.sun.j3d.utils.universe.*;
import javax.media.j3d.*;
import com.sun.j3d.utils.behaviors.vp.*;
import javax.swing.JFrame;
```

In special cases additional classes or packages are required. For the representation on the computer screen an instance of the Java class JFrame is used. The corresponding class with the Java 3D program must therefore extend the class JFrame.

```
public class MyJava3DClass extends JFrame
```

The class with the Java 3D program will also need an instance of the class Canvas3D as one of its attributes.

```
public Canvas3D myCanvas3D;
```

The constructor of the class has the following structure.

```
public MyJava3DClass()
{
  this.setDefaultCloseOperation(JFrame.EXIT_ON_CLOSE);

  myCanvas3D = new Canvas3D(
                 SimpleUniverse.getPreferredConfiguration());
  SimpleUniverse simpUniv = new SimpleUniverse(myCanvas3D);
  simpUniv.getViewingPlatform().setNominalViewingTransform();

  createSceneGraph(simpUniv);

  addLight(simpUniv);

  setTitle("Title");
  setSize(700,700);
  getContentPane().add("Center", myCanvas3D);
  setVisible(true);
}
```

The first method `setDefaultCloseOperation` has nothing to do with Java 3D.
It is only for closing the display window in which the virtual scene will be shown
and for terminating the program. Afterwards the `SimpleUniverse` is built with
its default settings. The method `createSceneGraph` must be implemented individually for each program or scene. All geometric objects, information about
their surfaces and dynamic changes can be incorporated in this method, representing the content branch in figure 5.5. Further details about the content
branch will be provided later on in this section. The method `addLight` defines
the illumination of the scene and it can also be implemented differently for
each virtual scene, depending on whether the scene is an open air scenario with
sunlight or located in a room with artificial light. The details of this method
and illumination are explained in chapter 8. The last four lines of the constructor are again concerned with the display window, not with Java 3D specific
tasks. They determine the title of the window, its size as well as its layout, and
display the window.

It is very useful to include the following three lines of code after the method
`addLight` is called.

```
OrbitBehavior ob = new OrbitBehavior(myCanvas3D);
ob.setSchedulingBounds(new BoundingSphere(
              new Point3d(0.0,0.0,0.0),Double.MAX_VALUE));
simpUniv.getViewingPlatform().setViewPlatformBehavior(ob);
```

These three lines enable navigation through the scene using the mouse. Moving the mouse while pressing its left button, the scene is rotated. The right mouse button is for moving through the scene. Zooming can be achieved by pressing the ALT-key together with the left mouse button and moving the mouse. How this is actually realised from the computer graphics point of view will be described in section 5.8.

Once the methods `createSceneGraph` and `addLight` have been implemented, all that has to be done is to call the constructor of the corresponding created class in the `main` method.

```
public static void main(String[] args)
{
    MyJava3DClass myJava3D = new MyJava3DClass();
}
```

How to implement the method `createSceneGraph`, depending on the specific scene to be modelled, shall be demonstrated with the example in figure 5.3 on page 121. The associated scenegraph is shown in figure 5.4 on page 122. Only the construction of the tree will be explained in detail here. The helicopter together with the platform is built in the same way. The complete program code can be found in the class `StaticSceneExample.java`.

As a first step the tree trunk is created. Before an instance of the corresponding geometric object can be defined, it is necessary to specify a suitable `Appearance` with a brown colour for the tree trunk.

```
Appearance brownApp = new Appearance();
setToMyDefaultAppearance(brownApp,
                         new Color3f(0.5f,0.2f,0.2f));
```

Then the tree trunk can be defined as a cylinder with height 0.4 and radius 0.05, centred in the origin of the coordinate system.

```
float trunkHeight = 0.4f;
Cylinder trunk = new Cylinder(0.05f,trunkHeight,brownApp);
```

Afterwards, an instance `tgTrunk` of the class `TransformGroup` is generated and the tree trunk is assigned to this transformation group by the method `addChild`.

```
TransformGroup tgTrunk = new TransformGroup();
tgTrunk.addChild(trunk);
```

After the transformation group has been created for the tree trunk, the treetop can be handled in a similar manner. Since the treetop should have a green instead of a brown colour, a new instance `greenApp` of the class `Appearance` has to be generated. In the example program, this `Appearance` has already

been created for the cockpit of the helicopter. The treetop is generated as a
cone centred in the origin of the coordinate system.

```
float leavesHeight = 0.4f;
Cone leaves = new Cone(0.3f,leavesHeight,greenApp);
```

The treetop should be positioned on top of the trunk. This means, it must be
lifted by half the height of the tree trunk plus half of the height of the treetop.
It is only half the height for both objects since the corresponding cylinder
and cone are centred in the origin of the coordinate system. The following
transformation is defined for this purpose.

```
Transform3D tfLeaves = new Transform3D();
tfLeaves.setTranslation(
            new Vector3f(0.0f,
                        (trunkHeight+leavesHeight)/2,
                        0.0f));
```

Now a transformation group can be generated for the treetop. Since this transformation group has to incorporate the above translation, it is not sufficient to
use the default constructor without parameters as in the case of the tree trunk.
Otherwise both the trunk and the treetop would remain centred around the
origin of the coordinate system. The corresponding constructor for the transformation group tfLeaves will be called with the previously defined translation
as its argument. Then the treetop can be assigned to the transformation group
by the method addChild.

```
TransformGroup tgLeaves = new TransformGroup(tfLeaves);
tgLeaves.addChild(leaves);
```

So far, the tree has been constructed correctly, but its trunk is centred around
the origin of the coordinate system. This might not be the desired position in
the scene. In order to position the whole tree, another transformation group
has to be defined. As a first step, a suitable transformation must be defined,
then the transformation group can be created with this transformation, and
finally the single transformation groups tgTrunk and tgLeaves for the trunk
and the treetop can by assigned to the transformation group for the whole tree.

```
Transform3D tfTree = new Transform3D();
tfTree.setTranslation(new Vector3f(-0.6f,0.0f,0.0f));

TransformGroup tgTree = new TransformGroup(tfTree);
tgTree.addChild(tgTrunk);
tgTree.addChild(tgLeaves);
```

The advantage of this hierarchical structure becomes obvious here. Once the tree has been constructed, i.e., once the treetop is positioned correctly on top of the trunk, the whole tree can be positioned anywhere in the scene without worrying about the fact that the corresponding transformation has to be applied to all single parts of the tree. With this hierarchical structure, the two transformations—one for positioning the treetop on top of the trunk and one for positioning the tree itself—are automatically applied correctly to the tree-top. Especially, more complex objects built from more than just two elementary geometric objects can be handled and controlled in a very comfortable way in a scenegraph. When the scene is displayed, the underlying rule for the calculations is very simple. The scenegraph has to be traversed and all transformations along a path to a geometric object have to be applied to this object.

It is also possible to use the same object, for instance the tree, more than just once in the same scene. The class Link is required for this, which will be explained in section 9.2.

The helicopter and the platform are built in the same way based on the hierarchical structure shown in the scenegraph in figure 5.4 on page 122. In this case, not only translations are applied to position the objects, but also a rotation in addition to the platform in order to turn it slightly. In principle, any transformation defined directly by a corresponding method or matrix, or specified as a composition of elementary transformations can be assigned to a transformation group. For the purpose of positioning an object, combinations of translations and rotations are sufficient. When objects should be enlarged or made smaller, scalings are required.

After all transformation groups for a scene have been created and organised in a suitable hierarchical structure, the transformation groups on the top of the hierarchical structure must be assigned to the scene itself. In the example of the helicopter scene, there are only two top transformation groups: tgTree for the tree and tgHeliPlat for the helicopter together with the platform. For the details of the construction of the transformation group tgHeliPlat the reader is referred again to the program StaticSceneExample.java.

The BranchGroup, containing the scene, can now be generated. The transformation groups tgTree and tgHeliPlat are assigned to the BranchGroup by the method addChild. Afterwards the BranchGroup should be compiled by the method compile and assigned to the SimpleUniverse by calling the method addBranchGraph.

```
BranchGroup theScene = new BranchGroup();
theScene.addChild(tgHeliPlat);
theScene.addChild(tgTree);
theScene.compile();
su.addBranchGraph(theScene);
```

Figure   5.3   on   page   121   was   generated   with   the   class
`StaticSceneExample.java`. For better viewing purposes, the scene was slightly
tilted by mouse movements. Also a white background instead of the default
black background in Java 3D was added to the scene. How to change the background colour or add a background image will be explained in more detail in
chapter 8.

5.6 Animation and moving objects

So far, only static three-dimensional scenes were considered. For dynamic
scenes, similar techniques as described in section 2.9 for the two-dimensional
case are applied. Movements can be implemented as piecewise interpolations
or convex combinations between positions or states. The same applies to other
transitions, for instance a slow change from one colour to another or the transition from bright light to the dark. In the two-dimensional case, complex or combined movements, as for instance in the example of the moving clock with rotating hand, were modelled by explicit compositions of single transformations. A
scenegraph also simplifies modelling and handling complex or combined movements. Each transformation group can have its own movement which is then
applied to all objects that are located below the corresponding transformation
group in the hierarchy of the scenegraph. For the example of the moving clock,
the hand would be assigned to a transformation group with a rotation and this
transformation group could be a child of another transformation group with
the frame of the clock and the movement of the whole clock. In this way, the
rotation and the linear movement of the clock would be applied automatically
to the hand. The principle is the same as for static transformations to position
objects. The transformations in a transformation group in the upper part of
the scenegraph are applied to all nodes below the corresponding transformation
group.

To illustrate the principle of modelling animations, the helicopter scene in
figure 5.3 on page 121 is considered again. The helicopter is supposed to start
the rotor blade and should then take off from the platform in a slightly tilted
upwards direction. This means that the rotor blade itself will carry out a helix-
like movement, composed of the rotation of the blade and the linear movement
of the helicopter. Based on a suitable scenegraph, the complex movement can be
described and handled in a very simple manner. The rotor blade is generated in
the origin of the coordinate system and a rotation around the y-axis is assigned
to the transformation group of the rotor blade. Then the whole transformation
group of the rotor blade including its rotation is assigned to another transfor-

mation group that positions the rotor blade on top of the cockpit. This will have
the effect that the blade no longer rotates in the origin of the coordinate system but on top of the cockpit. When the whole helicopter is positioned on the
platform and also when the platform together with the helicopter is positioned
somewhere in the scene, the blade including its rotation will be transformed in
the correct way. A linear movement for the take-off of the helicopter from the
platform will be assigned to the transformation group of the helicopter. Again,
this movement will also be applied to the blade including the rotation.

For dynamic scenes, it is not only possible to assign objects, other transformation groups and transformations for positioning objects to a transformation
group. Interpolators for the description of the dynamic changes can also be assigned to transformation groups. Figure 5.6 shows an excerpt of the extended
scenegraph for the helicopter in which the rotation of the rotor blade and the
take-off of the helicopter can be described. The names of those transformation groups that contain dynamic movements, i.e., interpolators, start with the
letters tgm for Transformation Group with Movement.

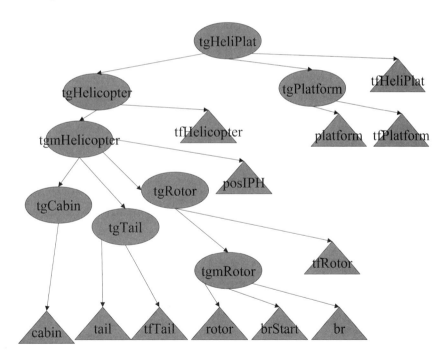

Figure 5.6 Excerpt of the scenegraph with dynamic transformations

The transformation group tgmRotor contains the rotor blade constructed as a box centred in the origin of the coordinate system and two dynamic rotations br and brStart around the y-axis. These two movements are carried out one after the other. The first one starts the rotor blade slowly and then the second one takes over to model the accelerated rotation of the blade. Only after the accelerated rotation has started, the helicopter should take off. The linear movement of the helicopter for the take-off is implemented in the transformation group tgmHelicopter.

It is important to separate positioning from dynamic movements within the transformation groups. It should be avoided to have static and dynamic transformations in the same transformation group. In this case, it is not clear whether the static or the dynamic transformations should be carried out first. Therefore, such a transformation group should be split into two transformation groups, one for the static and one for the dynamic part. One of the transformation groups should be the child of the other one. Which one should be the parent and which one the child depends on how the movement is intended. In the example of the helicopter, the rotor blade is first rotated in the origin of the coordinate system. This happens in the transformation group tgmRotor. Then this transformation group becomes a child of the transformation group tgRotor which positions the rotor together with its rotation on top of the cockpit.

The same applies to the linear movement of the helicopter. The take-off of the helicopter is described in the transformation group tgmHelicopter relative to the origin of the coordinate system. Afterwards, the helicopter together with its movement is positioned on the platform in the parent transformation group tgHelicopter so that the take-off takes place from the top of the platform. It would also be possible to exchange the order of these two transformation groups in the scenegraph. The way the movement was modelled here, corresponds to the following principle. The helicopter should take off from the platform and ascend for h units, measured from the platform. The height of the platform itself is of no importance for the ascend. The helicopter will fly exactly h units. However, if the helicopter should ascent from the platform until it has reached a fixed height, measured from the ground, the duration of the flight depends on the height of the platform. In this case, it might make sense to exchange the two transformation groups for the movement and the positioning of the helicopter. Nevertheless, the movement of the helicopter in the transformation group tgmHelicopter would have to be defined in a different way, since it starts from another point.

5.7 Animation in Java 3D

For animated scenes Java 3D provides the abstract class `Interpolator` with a number of subclasses. There, Java 3D extends the basic principle which was introduced in section 2.11. For modelling a continuous change within an animation, an initial and a final state are needed. For example, the animation could be a linear movement of an object between two points along a line in the form of a translation or a circular movement along an orbit in the form of a rotation. It could also be the transition from one colour to another one. The initial state is associated with the value zero, the final state with one. Intermediate states correspond to values between zero and one. The interpretation of the initial and the final state and the computation of intermediate states depends on the type of interpolation, whether a linear movement between two positions, a circular orbit or the change between two colours is desired. There are certain basic parameters that are required for an interpolator, independent of the precise interpretation of the states. For example, the following specifications are always needed for an interpolator.

- When should the interpolation start?

- Should the interpolation only go from state zero to state one or should it also be reversed?

- How long should the transition from state zero to state one take?

- Should the transition between the two states zero and one be carried out with constant speed or should it accelerate slowly in the beginning at state zero until a maximum speed is reached and then slow down again to have a smooth stop in state one?

- Should the interpolation be carried out just once or should it be repeated?

In Java 3D, these properties are specified within the class `Alpha`. An `Alpha` object must be associated with every interpolator. To generate an instance of the class `Alpha`, the following constructor can be used.

```
Alpha a = new Alpha(lc,id,tt,pdd,iad,iard,aa1d,dad,dard,aa0d);
```

Figure 5.7 illustrates the meaning of the main parameters of `Alpha`, which will be explained in the following in detail. For a better understanding of the single parameters, the example of the helicopter is used again. The corresponding `Alpha` object shall be used to describe the timing of the linear movement of the helicopter. The state zero corresponds to the initial position of the helicopter at the ground. In state one the helicopter is at its highest point.

The integer value `lc` specifies the attribute `loopCount` which determines how often the interpolator should be repeated. For instance, the helicopter

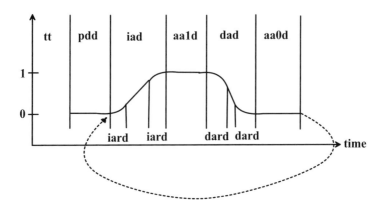

Figure 5.7 Progression of the Alpha-values

could ascent and descend three times. In this case, one would choose `lc=3`. Setting `lc=-1` implies that the interpolator is repeated without end. This means that the helicopter would never stop the alternating scheme of ascending and descending. The second parameter `id` for the attribute `mode` defines in which direction the interpolator should be carried out. There are three possibilities.

– `id=Alpha.INCREASING_ENABLE`: Only the interpolation from state zero to state one is carried out. If `lc>1` is chosen, it will be carried out more than once. In this case, the helicopter would only ascend and jump back to its initial position instead of flying back after the ascend is finished.

– `id=Alpha.DECREASING_ENABLE`: Only the interpolation from state one to state zero is carried out so that the helicopter could only descend for landing. Instead of a slow take-off it would jump to the highest position.

– `id=Alpha.INCREASING_ENABLE+Alpha.DECREASING_ENABLE`: Here, the interpolator alternates between the transition from state zero to state one and the reverse transition. This is the correct solution for the helicopter. The helicopter could alternate between ascending and descending. However, for modelling the movement of the rotor blade, one would only define `id=Alpha.INCREASING_ENABLE`, since the blade should rotate only in one direction and not backwards as well.

All other parameters in the above-mentioned constructor for `Alpha` are of the type `long`. They are integer values specifying times or time intervals in milliseconds.

The attribute `triggerTime` of `Alpha` is given by the value `tt`. `tt` determines after how many milliseconds after the start of the program `Alpha` should deliver the first values. `pdd` determines the value of the attribute `phaseDelayDuration`.

`Alpha` remains in the state zero for `phaseDelayDuration` milliseconds after the `triggerTime` has passed. In all programs presented here, it is sufficient to use only one of the two values `triggerTime` or `phaseDelayDuration`. The example programs will always assume `phaseDelayDuration`=0 and the start of the animation will be controlled by `triggerTime` alone. In the example of the helicopter, `triggerTime` should be chosen in such a way that the take-off of the helicopter starts after the slow blade rotation is finished and the fast blade rotation has begun.

The parameter `iad` defines how long the transition time `increasingAlphaDuration` from the state zero to the state one should take. For the helicopter, this is the time it should take from take-off to reach the highest point. The next parameter `iard` determines the value of the attribute `increasingAlphaRampDuration`. In the case of the helicopter and in many other applications, it is not realistic that the object remains in the initial position until the `triggerTime` has passed and then suddenly moves without continuous acceleration from state zero to state one. `iard` specifies the duration of the linear acceleration phase until the constant maximum speed is reached. The value `iard` is also used for slowing down the movement, before state one is reached, so that the object comes to a smooth and not a sudden stop. The speed is decreased linearly. The appropriate continuous accelerations and the appropriate constant maximum speed are calculated by Java 3D automatically.

After the transition from state zero to state one is completed, `aa1d` determines the value `alphaAtOneDuration`, i.e., how long state one should be kept. For the helicopter, this would correspond to the time it would spend hovering in the air at its top position.

The values `dad` and `dard` are used for the attributes `decreasingAlphaDuration` and `decreasingAlphaRampDuration`, respectively. They have the same meaning as `increasingAlphaDuration` and `increasingAlphaRampDuration`, respectively. However, they do not refer to the transition from state zero to state one but to the reverse transition from state one to state zero. Therefore, in the helicopter example, `dad` determines how long the descending flight of the helicopter should take. Accordingly, `dard` specifies how long the phase of acceleration and slowing down should be.

Finally, `aa0d` is for the attribute `alphaAtZeroDuration`, i.e., how long to stay in the state zero after a cycle from state zero to state one and back has been completed. This value is only of importance when the movement or transition should be repeated, i.e., when the parameter `lc` for `loopCount` was either greater than 1 or −1. If a repetition is desired, the sequence consisting of

- increasingAlphaDuration,

- alphaAtOneDuration,

- decreasingAlphaDuration and

- alphaAtZeroDuration

is iterated, taking into account the values for increasingAlphaRampDuration and decreasingAlphaRampDuration for the acceleration and braking time.

The specified durations increasingAlphaDuration and increasingAlphaRampDuration are only relevant when Alpha.INCREASING_ENABLE was set within the parameters id. Analogously, the durations decreasingAlphaDuration and decreasingAlphaRampDuration are only taken into account when Alpha.DECREASING_ENABLE was set.

The class Alpha serves as a description of the timing of a movement or, more generally, of an interpolator. The interpolator itself to which the Alpha object is associated determines what the state changes look like. The Alpha object calculates the appropriate value between zero and one for the state at any time. Java 3D provides a number of standard interpolators. Some selected interpolators will be explained here in more detail.

The PositionInterpolator is responsible for movements between two points along a straight line.

```
PositionInterpolator pi =
   new PositionInterpolator(alpha,transformgroup,axis,
                            startingPoint,endPoint);
```

The first argument of this constructor is an instance of the class Alpha to describe the timing of the movement along the straight line. The second argument specifies the transformation group in which the interpolator should be applied. The instance axis of the class Transform3D determines the axis or the line along which the movement should take place. This axis should be created before the constructor of the interpolator is called.

```
Transform3D axis = new Transform3D();
```

In this way, the identical transformation is generated. If this transformation is used directly in the constructor of the interpolator, then the axis for the movement will be the x-axis. If a movement along another axis should take place, the transformation axis must be defined in such a way that it maps the x-axis onto the desired axis. For instance, a movement along the y-axis is achieved by a rotation around the z-axis by 90° since this transformation maps the x-axis to the y-axis. In this case, one would add the line

```
axis.rotZ(Math.PI/2);
```

before calling the constructor for the `PositionInterpolator`.

The values `startingPoint` and `endPoint` determine the states zero and one, i.e., the starting and the endpoint of the linear movement along the specified axis. The starting point should be located at the same position as the object or transformation group to which the position interpolator is applied. For instance, if one generated an object centred in the origin of the coordinate system to be moved along the x-axis, the choice of `startingPoint=1` would lead to a sudden jump of the object to the starting point $(1, 0, 0)$ when the movement is initiated. Vice versa, if the object has been shifted to some other point than the origin of the coordinate system and a position interpolator along the x-axis with `startingPoint=0` is defined for the corresponding transformation group, then the object would jump back to the origin of the coordinate system at the start of the movement.

For the definition of an interpolator further specifications are needed. A bounding region must be assigned to interpolators and a number of other concepts in Java 3D. This bounding region determines whether the corresponding concept should be taken into account for rendering or not, depending on the viewer's position. When the bounding region does not contain the viewer or a part of the clipping region, the corresponding concept is not applied. For instance, in an office building with a large number of rooms, each room might have a clock hanging on the wall. If the viewer is inside one of the offices, it is not necessary to compute the movement of the hands of the clocks in the other rooms since the viewer will not be able to see them, as long as he stays in his office. Therefore, the movement of the clock hands would be restricted to the bounding region coinciding with the office in which the clock is located. The avoidance of calculating unnoticed changes and movement can save a significant amount of computation time for larger virtual worlds. The interpolator is reactivated, once the viewer enters its bounding region again. The interpolator is not started at the same point where it was frozen when the viewer had left the room. Based on the `Alpha` object associated with the interpolator and the current time, the actual state of the interpolator can be computed exactly, even though the intermediate states have not been calculated while the viewer was outside the bounding region. In the example of the office building with the clocks, the clock would stop its movement, once the viewer has left the room. But when the viewer enters the room again, the clock will simply jump to the current time and continue its movement so that the viewer will not notice that intermediate states were not calculated.

The class `BoundingSphere` with the constructor

```
BoundingSphere bs = new BoundingSphere(new Point3d(x,y,z),r);
```

can be used to define a bounding region. In this way, a spherical bounding region
with radius r and centre point (x, y, z) is specified. For an unlimited bounding
region, one can choose r=Double.MAX_VALUE. The class BoundingBox allows
the definition of bounding regions in the form of a box.

After the definition of a suitable bounding region bs, this bounding region
has to be assigned to the interpolator pi by

```
pi.setSchedulingBounds(bs);
```

For static objects which will not be changed or moved in a scene, certain
rendering properties can be calculated in advance for efficiency reasons in Java
3D. Therefore, it is necessary to state explicitly by

```
transformationgroup.setCapability(
                    TransformGroup.ALLOW_TRANSFORM_WRITE);
```

that the corresponding transformation group transformationgroup can be
changed by transformations during the animation. Finally, the interpolator pi
has to be assigned to its transformation group by

```
transformationgroup.addChild(pi);
```

The class RotationInterpolator can be used to model rotations in the
same way as position interpolators are used for linear movements. In the constructor

```
RotationInterpolator ri =
  new RotationInterpolator(alpha,transformgroup,axis,
                        startAngle,endAngle);
```

the parameters alpha and transformgroup have the same meaning as in the
case of position interpolators. The rotation axis is specified by the instance
axis of the class Transform3D. If axis is the identity, i.e., it was created by the
default constructor of Transform3D without further modifications, then the y-
axis will become the rotation axis. For another rotation axis, the transformation
axis must be defined in such a way that the y-axis is mapped onto the desired
rotation axis. For instance,

```
Transform3D axis = new Transform3D();
axis.rotX(Math.PI/2);
```

defines a rotation around the z-axis. The parameters startAngle and endAngle
specify the starting and the final angle of the rotation in radians. It should be
noted that negative angles and angles larger than 2π are mapped to the interval
$[0, 2\pi]$. For instance, choosing π as the starting and 4π as the final angle, will
only lead to a rotation starting at π and ending at 2π, but not to 1.5 full
rotations.

For rotation interpolators the same lines of code concerning the bounding region and the associated transformation group are required as in the case of position interpolators.

In the same way, scalings can be defined based on the class `ScaleInterpolator` with the constructor

```
ScaleInterpolator si =
  new ScaleInterpolator(alpha,transformgroup,axis,
                        startScale,endScale);
```

If the scaling should not be carried out with respect to the origin of the co-ordinate system, the `Transform3D axis` should be defined in such a way that it maps the origin to the desired fixed point of the scaling. The parameters `startScale` and `endScale` determine the scaling factors for the states zero and one, respectively. Usually, `startScale=1` will be chosen. Otherwise, the object will first be scaled to the value of `startScale` in a sudden jump, before the continuous scaling of the interpolator is started, unless the object has been scaled before. For instance, to let an object grow to double its size, one would define `startScale=1` and `endScale=2`.

Examples for the use of position and rotation interpolators can be found in the example programs `SimpleAnimation3d.java` of the helicopter, where a position interpolator models the flight and rotation interpolators are responsible for rotations of the rotor blade. A scaling interpolator can be found in the example program `InteractionExample.java`, which will be described in chapter 9.

5.8 Projections

So far, transformations were used to position objects in a scene or to move them in animations. For the representation of a three-dimensional scene on a flat computer screen a *projection* to the two-dimensional plane is required. Such projections can also be described in terms of geometric transformations.

For the representation of a three-dimensional scene, the viewer's position and the projection plane need to be defined. The viewer looks in the direction of the *projection plane*, which can be interpreted as a kind of window behind which the virtual world lies. The projection of an object onto this plane is obtained by connecting the points of the object with the *centre of projection* and computing the intersection points of these lines, called *projectors*, with the projection plane. This method is illustrated on the left-hand side of figure 5.8. It is called *perspective projection*.

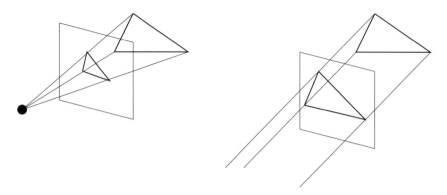

Figure 5.8 Perspective and parallel projection

When the centre of projection is moved farther and farther away from the projection plane and finally moved to infinity, the projectors become parallel lines. In this case, it is not necessary to specify a centre of projection, only the direction of the projection is needed. For such a *parallel projection*, the projectors are all parallel to this direction. Usually it is assumed that the direction of projection is perpendicular to the projection plane. A parallel projection is shown on the right-hand side of figure 5.8.

Before considering arbitrary projections, the special case of a parallel projection with a projection plane $z = z_0$, a plane parallel to the x/y-plane, is described by an affine transformation in more detail. This parallel projection maps the point (x, y, z) to the point (x, y, z_0). In homogeneous coordinates, this mapping can be written as a matrix multiplication in the following form.

$$\begin{pmatrix} x \\ y \\ z_0 \\ 1 \end{pmatrix} = \begin{pmatrix} 1 & 0 & 0 & 0 \\ 0 & 1 & 0 & 0 \\ 0 & 0 & 0 & z_0 \\ 0 & 0 & 0 & 1 \end{pmatrix} \cdot \begin{pmatrix} x \\ y \\ z \\ 1 \end{pmatrix}. \tag{5.2}$$

Based on this representation, now any parallel projection can be described in the form of matrix multiplication in homogeneous coordinates. If the projection plane is not parallel to the x/y-plane, another transformation has to be carried out before the matrix in equation (5.2) is applied. This transformation maps the projection plane to the x/y-plane. This can always be achieved by a rotation around the y-axis, followed by a rotation around the x-axis as illustrated in figure 5.9.

Therefore, it is sufficient for the understanding of parallel projections to examine only parallel projections to the x/y-plane. For other parallel projections, the above-described transformation is applied to the whole scene first

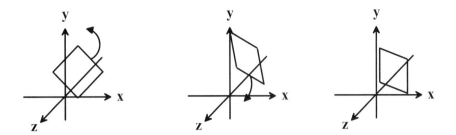

Figure 5.9   Mapping an arbitrary plane to a plane parallel to the x/y-plane

and then a parallel projection to a plane parallel to the x/y-plane is carried out. It is even sufficient to consider only parallel projections to the x/y-plane since a suitable translation along the z-axis can map any plane parallel to the x/y-plane itself.

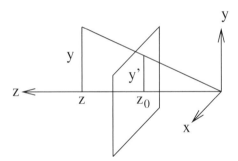

Figure 5.10   Derivation of the matrix for the perspective projection

Perspective projections can also be represented in the form of a matrix multiplication in homogeneous coordinates. As in the case of parallel projections, a specific perspective projection is considered first. It is assumed that the centre of projection lies in the origin of the coordinate system and that the projection plane is a plane parallel to the x/y-plane in the form $z = z_0$. As can be seen from figure 5.10, one can apply one of the intercept theorems to derive the equations

$$\frac{x'}{x} = \frac{z_0}{z} \qquad \text{and} \qquad \frac{y'}{y} = \frac{z_0}{z}$$

and therefore

$$x' = \frac{z_0}{z} \cdot x \qquad \text{and} \qquad y' = \frac{z_0}{z} \cdot y.$$

This means the perspective projection maps the point (x, y, z) to the point

$$(x', y', z_0) = \left(\frac{z_0}{z} \cdot x, \frac{z_0}{z} \cdot y, z_0 \right). \tag{5.3}$$

This mapping can be written in homogeneous coordinates in the following way.

$$\begin{pmatrix} x \\ y \\ z \\ \frac{z}{z_0} \end{pmatrix} = \begin{pmatrix} 1 & 0 & 0 & 0 \\ 0 & 1 & 0 & 0 \\ 0 & 0 & 1 & 0 \\ 0 & 0 & \frac{1}{z_0} & 0 \end{pmatrix} \cdot \begin{pmatrix} x \\ y \\ z \\ 1 \end{pmatrix}. \tag{5.4}$$

When the resulting point $\left(x, y, z, \frac{z}{z_0} \right)$ is transformed back to Cartesian coordinates by dividing the first three components by the last one, the desired point in equation (5.3) is obtained.

The matrix for the perspective projection in equation (5.4) does not have the property of all previous matrices in homogeneous coordinates that the last row is $(0, 0, 0, 1)$. Therefore, the resulting point is not obtained in normalised homogeneous coordinates with 1 as its fourth component.

In a similar way as for parallel projections, the specific choice of a perspective projection with the origin of the coordinate system as its centre of projection and a projection plane parallel to the x/y-plane is not restrictive at all. Any perspective projection can be reduced to this specific projection when suitable transformations are applied in advance. First the centre of projection of the considered perspective projection is translated into the origin of the coordinate system. Then the same transformations as in the case of the parallel projection as shown in figure 5.9 are applied in order to make the projection plane parallel to the x/y-plane.

Another special case of a perspective projection shall be considered here. Instead of having the centre of projection in the origin of the coordinate system, the centre is shifted along the z-axis by the translation $(0, 0, -z_0)^\top$ so that the projection plane becomes the x/y-plane. Applying the same considerations based on the intercept theorem as in figure 5.10 to compute the perspective projection of the point (x, y, z) to the point $(x', y', 0)$, one obtains

$$x' = \frac{z_0}{z_0 + z} \cdot x = \frac{x}{1 + \frac{z}{z_0}} \quad \text{and} \quad y' = \frac{z_0}{z_0 + z} \cdot y = \frac{y}{1 + \frac{z}{z_0}}. \tag{5.5}$$

This mapping can be written in matrix form in homogeneous coordinates in the following way.

$$\begin{pmatrix} x \\ y \\ 0 \\ 1 + \frac{z}{z_0} \end{pmatrix} = \begin{pmatrix} 1 & 0 & 0 & 0 \\ 0 & 1 & 0 & 0 \\ 0 & 0 & 0 & 0 \\ 0 & 0 & \frac{1}{z_0} & 1 \end{pmatrix} \cdot \begin{pmatrix} x \\ y \\ z \\ 1 \end{pmatrix}. \tag{5.6}$$

Again, the resulting point $\left(x, y, 0, 1 + \frac{z}{z_0}\right)$ in homogeneous coordinates corresponds to the projected point in Cartesian coordinates in equation (5.5).

It was already demonstrated that, with a suitable transformation, any perspective projection can be reduced to a perspective projection with the centre of projection in the origin of the coordinate system and a projection plane parallel to the x/y-plane. This specific perspective projection can be reduced to the perspective projection in equation (5.6) by a translation by the vector $(0, 0, -z_0)$. For the understanding of the properties of perspective projections it is therefore sufficient to examine only the specific projection in equation (5.6). All other perspective projections can be interpreted as this specific projection together with an affine mapping which is applied to the virtual world before the projection. The matrix in equation (5.6) can be decomposed into a product of two matrices.

$$
\begin{pmatrix} 1 & 0 & 0 & 0 \\ 0 & 1 & 0 & 0 \\ 0 & 0 & 0 & 0 \\ 0 & 0 & \frac{1}{z_0} & 1 \end{pmatrix} = \begin{pmatrix} 1 & 0 & 0 & 0 \\ 0 & 1 & 0 & 0 \\ 0 & 0 & 0 & 0 \\ 0 & 0 & 0 & 1 \end{pmatrix} \cdot \begin{pmatrix} 1 & 0 & 0 & 0 \\ 0 & 1 & 0 & 0 \\ 0 & 0 & 1 & 0 \\ 0 & 0 & \frac{1}{z_0} & 1 \end{pmatrix}. \tag{5.7}
$$

The left matrix on the right-hand side of this equation corresponds exactly to the matrix in equation (5.2) with $z_0 = 0$, encoding a parallel projection to the x/y-plane. It was shown before that any perspective projection A_{persp} can be reduced to the perspective projection A_{persp,z_0} in equation (5.6) by applying a suitable transformation in advance.

$$
A_{\mathrm{persp}} = A_{\mathrm{persp},z_0} \cdot T.
$$

Based on the decomposition of the perspective projection A_{persp,z_0} in equation (5.7) one obtains

$$
A_{\mathrm{persp}} = \begin{pmatrix} 1 & 0 & 0 & 0 \\ 0 & 1 & 0 & 0 \\ 0 & 0 & 0 & 0 \\ 0 & 0 & 0 & 1 \end{pmatrix} \cdot \widetilde{T}
$$

where

$$
\widetilde{T} = \begin{pmatrix} 1 & 0 & 0 & 0 \\ 0 & 1 & 0 & 0 \\ 0 & 0 & 1 & 0 \\ 0 & 0 & \frac{1}{z_0} & 1 \end{pmatrix} \cdot T.
$$

This means that even any perspective projection can be considered as a suitable transformation $\widetilde{T}$ followed by a parallel projection to the x/y-plane. As explained before, also all parallel projections can be reduced to this special parallel projection. Therefore, projection can always be viewed as applying some transformation to the virtual world and then applying a parallel projection to the x/y-plane. For this reason it is sufficient to consider only the parallel projection to the x/y-plane whenever projections are mentioned.

The parallel projection to the x/y-plane simply assigns the value zero to the z-coordinate. In order to understand the effects of perspective projections a little better, the right matrix

$$\begin{pmatrix} 1 & 0 & 0 & 0 \\ 0 & 1 & 0 & 0 \\ 0 & 0 & 1 & 0 \\ 0 & 0 & \frac{1}{z_0} & 1 \end{pmatrix} \tag{5.8}$$

in the decomposition in equation (5.7) is examined in more detail. The x/y-plane, i.e., all points with $z = 0$, remains unchanged, since it is the projection plane. Considering a point of the form $\left(0, 0, \frac{1}{w}\right)$ with $w \in \mathbb{R}$, $w \neq 0$, it can be written in homogeneous coordinates as $(0, 0, 1, w)$. The matrix (5.8) maps this point to the point $\left(0, 0, 1, \frac{1}{z_0} + w\right)$ in homogeneous coordinates. In Cartesian coordinates this means

$$\left(0, 0, \frac{1}{w}\right) \mapsto \left(0, 0, \frac{z_0}{1 + z_0 \cdot w}\right).$$

Letting the parameter w go to zero slowly, the point $\left(0, 0, \frac{1}{w}\right)$ slides along the z-axis to infinity whereas its image $\left(0, 0, \frac{z_0}{1+z_0 \cdot w}\right)$ converges to the finite point $(0, 0, z_0)$. This means that the hypothetical point at infinity on the z-axis is mapped to a concrete noninfinite point. Considering all lines through the point $\left(0, 0, \frac{1}{w}\right)$, the images of these lines obtained by the matrix (5.8) meet in the point $\left(0, 0, \frac{z_0}{1+z_0 \cdot w}\right)$. Letting w go to zero, the lines through the point $\left(0, 0, \frac{1}{w}\right)$ become lines parallel to the z-axis. The matrix maps these parallel lines meeting in the hypothetical point at infinity on the z-axis to lines through the point $(0, 0, z_0)$. This point is called *vanishing point*.

These theoretical considerations prove the well-known effect that parallel lines leading away from the viewer do not look parallel any more in a perspective projection. They meet in the vanishing point. Figure 5.11 shows the typical example of a railway that seems to get narrower with increasing distance until it vanishes in a single point.

Horizontal and vertical lines remain parallel when this perspective projection is applied. The vanishing point is only of interest for lines that lead away from the viewer. If another projection plane is chosen for the perspective projection, then there might be two or even three vanishing points. The number of vanishing points is equal to the number of coordinate axes that the projection plane intersects. Figure 5.12 illustrates the effects for the projection of

Figure 5.11 Vanishing point for perspective projection

a cube when there are one, two or three vanishing points. The corresponding projections are called *one-*, *two-* and *three-point perspective projections.*

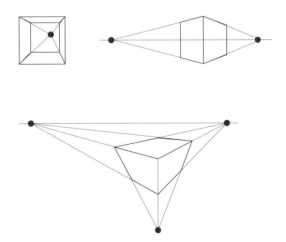

Figure 5.12 One-, two- and three-point perspective projections

In this section, it has been demonstrated that an arbitrary projection of a scene can be viewed as a suitable geometric transformation of the scene followed by a parallel projection to the x/y-plane. Changing the viewer's position or his direction of view corresponds to another transformation that is applied to the scene. Instead of transforming the viewer, the reverse transformation is simply applied to the scene. For modelling a moving viewer it is therefore sufficient to include the whole scene in its own transformation group in order to apply the reverse transformations of the viewer within this transformation group. For instance, when the viewer turns to the right, the whole scene is rotated to the left instead.

5.8.1 Projections in Java 3D

By default, perspective projection is applied in Java 3D for showing scenes. If a parallel projection is preferred, this can be achieved by the following method to be called in the constructor of the corresponding Java 3D class.

```
simpUniv.getViewer().getView().setProjectionPolicy(
                            View.PARALLEL_PROJECTION);
```

The class `ViewParallelProjection.java` uses parallel instead of perspective projection to show the static scene with the helicopter that was introduced in sections 5.3 and 5.2.2.

The method

```
simpUniv.getViewingPlatform().setNominalViewingTransform();
```

within the class `SimpleUniverse` positions the viewer such that he can see the range from -1 to 1 on the x- and the y-axis in the x/y-plane. One can also define another initial position of the viewer by defining a suitable transformation `vt` as an instance of the class `Transform3D` and applying the method

```
simpUniv.getViewingPlatform().getViewPlatformTransform().
                                            setTransform(vt);
```

If the viewer should carry out a fixed movement, this can either be implemented in Java 3D by applying the reverse movement or transformation to the whole scene or directly in the `BranchGroup` of the `ViewPlatform`. Interactive movements of the viewer, i.e., interactive navigation through the scene, controlled by the mouse can be realised with the `OrbitBehavior` that was introduced in section 5.5. As an alternative, the keyboard can also be used to navigate interactively through the scene. This technique will be introduced in section 9.7.

5.9 Exercises

Exercise 5.1

Draw a scenegraph for the chair in figure 5.2. Construct the chair with the following basic geometric objects: `box(x,y,z)` which generates a box of width $2x$, height $2y$ and depth $2z$ centred around the origin of the coordinate system, and `cylinder(r,h)` which creates a cylinder with radius r and height h also centred around the origin. Specify in each leaf of the tree the geometric object to be constructed or the corresponding transformation to be applied. The chair stands on the x/z-plane centred over the origin of the coordinate system with its rest in the back. The chair has the following measurements.

– Legs of height 1.0 with a squared profile with width 0.1

– A squared seat with width 0.8 and thickness 0.2

– A cylindrical backrest with radius 0.4 and thickness 0.2

Exercise 5.2

Extend the program `SimpleAnimation3d.java` by adding a rotating rear blade to the helicopter.

Exercise 5.3

Write a program that shows the single parts of the chair in figure 5.2 separately next to each other and then combines them to the chair in an animated scene.

Exercise 5.4

The perspective projection to the plane with normal vector $(\frac{\sqrt{3}}{3}, \frac{\sqrt{3}}{3}, \frac{\sqrt{3}}{3})^\top$ through the point $(1, 2, 3)$ and the origin of the coordinate system as centre of the projection shall be reduced to a parallel projection onto the x/y-plane. Specify a suitable transformation as a composition of elementary geometric transformations and the transformation in equation (5.7).

6

Modelling three-dimensional objects

In the previous chapter, objects of the virtual world were constructed with elementary geometric shapes like boxes, spheres, cylinders and cones. These simple shapes are not sufficient to model surfaces of more complex objects. This chapter introduces a variety of techniques for modelling three-dimensional objects and their surfaces.

6.1 Three-dimensional objects and their surfaces

Before discussing methods for modelling three-dimensional objects, it should be clarified what kind of objects are considered in computer graphics. In principle, any subset of the space $\mathbb{R}^3$ could be seen as a three-dimensional object. However, this would mean that even single points, edges or planes are considered to be three-dimensional. One could view a piece of paper as a two-dimensional plane. But even the thinnest paper has a nonzero thickness and is therefore an extremely flat box. Figure 6.1 shows some examples of how three-dimensional objects should not look like. Isolated or dangling edges and faces as seen in the figure should be avoided.

For the purpose of showing a three-dimensional object, its surface is of importance, not the set of points in the three-dimensional space that are occupied by the object. Transparent objects can be considered as an exception. Therefore, the intention of computer graphics techniques for modelling objects usually focusses on surfaces and not on sets of points in $\mathbb{R}^3$. In certain

extra edge

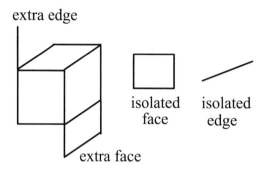

isolated
face

isolated
edge

extra face

Figure 6.1 Isolated and dangling edges and faces

applications, for instance when objects are measured with 3D scanners or in the case of tomography data, no explicit definition of the surface of the object is available. In such cases it is very common that the object is first described as a three-dimensional set of points and then the object's surface is derived from this set.

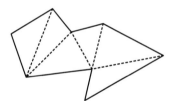

Figure 6.2 Triangulation of a polygon

There are various sophisticated techniques for modelling complex surfaces with round and bent shapes. However, these models are usually not taken directly for the generation of an image of a scene. Instead, surfaces are approximated by a larger number of polygons, triangles in most cases, in order to simplify computations for illumination and projection. For arbitrary surfaces it might even be impossible to find an analytical expression for the representation of the projection. Efficient and fast calculations of projections would become impossible. The situation is much easier for polygons. The intersection point of a plane polygon with a line representing a projector is simple and fast. The approximation of a curved surface by polygons is called *tesselation*. Using only triangles for the polygons is no real restriction since any polygon can be partitioned into triangles. Figure 6.2 shows a triangulation of a polygon. The dashed lines split the polygon into triangles. Triangles have the advantage that very

efficient computer graphics algorithms are available for them, which can also
be directly implemented on a graphics card. Another disadvantage of polygons
with more than three edges is that it must be assured that all vertices lie in
the same plane.

The single triangles or polygons for modelling a surface are usually oriented
in order to determine which side of the polygon is on the outside of the surface.
The orientation is given by the order of the polygon's vertices. The vertices are
listed in anticlockwise order when looking onto the surface from the outside of
the object.

In figure 6.3 this means that the triangle with the vertices 0,1,2 is oriented
in the direction of the viewer. The viewer can see the front of this part of the
surface. The same triangle, but with orientation 0,2,1 of the vertices would
remain invisible for the viewer since he can only see this part of the surface
from the back. The surface would be invisible since it is impossible to see the
surface of a solid three-dimensional object from the inside. When polygons have
an orientation, rendering can be accelerated significantly since surfaces that do
not point to the viewer can be ignored for the whole rendering process.

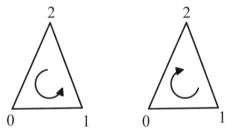

Figure 6.3   Orientation of polygons

Isolated and dangling faces should be avoided since they can lead to unrealistic effects. They can be seen from one side, but become invisible from the
other.

Figure 6.4 shows a tetrahedron with vertices $\mathbf{P}_0, \mathbf{P}_1, \mathbf{P}_2, \mathbf{P}_3$. The four faces
in the form of triangles of the tetrahedron can be defined by the following
groups of vertices.

- $\mathbf{P}_0, \mathbf{P}_3, \mathbf{P}_1$

- $\mathbf{P}_0, \mathbf{P}_2, \mathbf{P}_3$

- $\mathbf{P}_0, \mathbf{P}_1, \mathbf{P}_2$

- $\mathbf{P}_1, \mathbf{P}_3, \mathbf{P}_2$

For the specification of the triangles, the vertices of each triangle are listed in an anticlockwise manner when looking at the corresponding triangle from the outside of the tetrahedron.

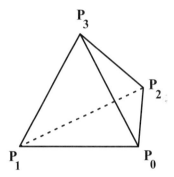

Figure 6.4 A tetrahedron

6.2 Topological notions

This section introduces elementary concepts from topology to better understand the problems of modelling three-dimensional objects and their surfaces. The definitions are given for the general case $\mathbb{R}^p$. Here they are only needed for the cases $p = 3$ and $p = 2$. The latter case is used for illustration purposes. Areas are the two-dimensional counterparts of three-dimensional objects.

In the left-hand side, figure 6.5 shows a set M of points in the plane with isolated and dangling edges. Based on the topological notions which are introduced in the following, this set of points can be *regularised*, resulting in the area on the right-hand side of the figure without isolated or dangling edges.

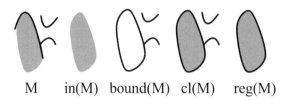

M   in(M) bound(M) cl(M)   reg(M)

Figure 6.5 A set $M \subset \mathbb{R}^2$ of points, its interior, boundary, closure and regularisation

In order to explain the topological notions, a set $M \subset \mathbb{R}^p$ is considered in the following. A subset $U \subset \mathbb{R}^p$ is called a *neighbourhood* of the point $x_0 \in \mathbb{R}^p$ if there exists $\varepsilon > 0$ such that

$$\{x \in \mathbb{R}^P \mid \parallel x - x_0 \parallel < \varepsilon\} \subseteq U.$$

In the two- and the three-dimensional case, this means that a neighbourhood of a point must contain at least a small circle or sphere, respectively, around the point. A point $x \in M$ is called an *inner point* of M if there is a neighbourhood U of x such that $U \subseteq M$ holds. In the two- and the three-dimensional case, this means that there must be at least a small circle or sphere around a point x, completely contained in M, to be an inner point of M.

The set

$$\mathrm{in}(M) \;=\; \{x \in M \mid x \text{ is an inner point of } M\}$$

of all inner points of M is called the *interior* or *kernel* of M. The interior of M is shown directly next to the set M in figure 6.5.

A point x is called a *boundary point* of M if every neighbourhood of x has nonempty intersections with M as well as with the complement of M. The set

$$\mathrm{bound}(M) \;=\; \{x \in M \mid x \text{ is a boundary point of } M\}$$

of all boundary points of M is called the *boundary* of M, which is illustrated in the middle of figure 6.5. The interior of a set can also be defined as the set without its boundary.

$$\mathrm{in}(M) \;=\; M\backslash\mathrm{bound}(M).$$

M is called an *open set* if M coincides with its interior, i.e., if $\mathrm{in}(M) = M$ holds.

The union of a set M with its boundary

$$\mathrm{cl}(M) \;=\; M \cup \mathrm{bound}(M)$$

is the *closure* of M, which is shown as the second set from the right in figure 6.5.

M is called *closed* if the closure of M is M itself, i.e., if $\mathrm{cl}(M) = M$ holds. The *regularisation* of M is the closure of the interior of M.

$$\mathrm{reg}(M) \;=\; \mathrm{cl}(\mathrm{in}(M)).$$

The regularisation of a set will cut off isolated as well as dangling edges and faces as can be seen on the right-hand side of figure 6.5.

The set M is called *regular* if $\mathrm{reg}(M) = M$ holds, i.e., if the set coincides with its regularisation.

In addition to the regularisation of three-dimensional objects, it might also be necessary to remove inner surfaces. The inner surfaces of a hollow object will never be needed for rendering so that it is better to remove them completely for efficiency reasons.

6.3 Modelling techniques

Voxels are a very simple technique for modelling three-dimensional objects. The three-dimensional space is partitioned into a grid of small, equisized cubes, called voxels. Voxels are the three-dimensional counterpart of a pixel grid. A three-dimensional object is defined by those voxels that lie within the interior of the object. Voxels are suitable for modelling objects based on tomography data, which provide information about the tissue density inside the measured body or object. For instance, if the bones of a body should be represented, those voxels would be considered where a density corresponding to bones has been measured.

Figure 6.6 illustrates the representation of a three-dimensional object based on voxels.

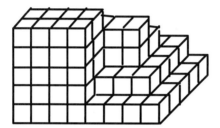

Figure 6.6   Modelling a three-dimensional object with voxels

The computational costs in terms of memory and time for handling voxel models can be enormous. Seeing the voxel grid as the three-dimensional counterpart of a two-dimensional pixel grid and using similar resolution, this would mean that instead of 1000×1000 pixels, $1000 \times 1000 \times 1000 = 10^9$ voxels are needed. It is out of discussion that such models can be used for immediate image generation.

Octrees are an efficient alternative to voxel models. They are based on voxels with varying size. Only in those parts where a fine resolution is needed, small voxels are used. For instance, when a sphere-like object should be modelled by voxels, there is no need to fill the sphere with a large number of small voxels. It is sufficient to fit one big voxel into the sphere and use smaller voxels only for the representation of the surface. For an octree, the object to be modelled is first fit into a sufficiently large cube or a box. Then this cube is split into eight smaller cubes. Smaller cubes that lie completely inside or completely outside the object are marked with *in* and *off*, respectively. For these cubes, there is no need for further refinement. The other cubes are marked with *on*, indicating that the cube intersects the surface of the object. All cubes marked with *on* are further subdivided into smaller cubes and the smaller cubes are marked and processed in the same way until the maximum desired resolution, i.e., the minimum allowed cube size, is reached.

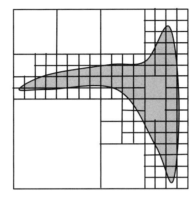

Figure 6.7 Recursive partition of an area into squares

For illustration purposes, the two-dimensional counterpart of octrees is considered here. They are based on the same principle, partitioning an area into squares or rectangles of varying size. Since larger squares are divided into four smaller squares, they are called *quadtrees*. Figure 6.7 shows an area surrounded by a square which is recursively partitioned into smaller squares. Smaller squares are only divided further if they intersect the boundary of the area. The process is stopped when the squares have reached a predefined minimum size. The corresponding quadtree is shown in figure 6.8. Octrees are similar to quadtrees, but their inner nodes have eight instead of four child nodes since cubes are divided into eight subcubes.

Voxel models and octrees are tailored for representing objects based on data obtained using specific 3D measurement techniques. For efficiency purposes, a raw voxel model can be turned into an octree easily. Nevertheless, both models are not suitable for realistic representations of object surfaces. For proper illumination and light reflection effects, it is very important to take the slope of the surface into account. The cubes in voxel models and octrees have no tilted surfaces. Their surfaces always point in the direction of the coordinate axis. Therefore, for objects that are modelled by voxels or octrees, the surfaces should be approximated by parametric freeform surfaces, which will be introduced in section 6.6.

When real objects are measured and the data should be used directly for generating 3D models, then voxels and octrees might be a good approach. But

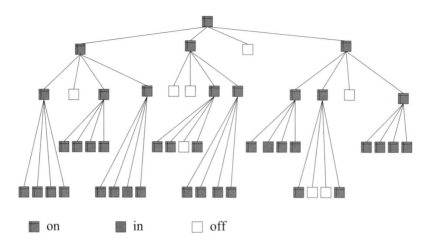

■ on   ■ in   □ off

Figure 6.8 The quadtree for figure 6.7

there are better suited techniques for modelling virtual objects that are usually integrated into specific object modelling and CAD tools. It would be too tedious to describe virtual curved objects by specifying an enormous amount of tiny voxels. One technique better suited for direct modelling is the *CSG scheme* where CSG stands for constructive solid geometry. The CSG scheme is based on a collection of elementary geometric objects. Transformations and regularised set-theoretic operations can be applied to these objects to construct more complex objects. Set-theoretic operations like union, intersection and difference were introduced in section 2.3 in the context of two-dimensional objects. The same principles apply to three-dimensional objects. Regularisation is carried out in addition to avoid isolated and dangling edges and faces. Figure 6.9 shows an object on the left which was constructed from the elementary objects box and cylinder. The right part of the figure specifies how the corresponding elementary objects were combined with set-theoretic operations to obtain the object on the left. The necessary transformations are not included in the figure. For instance, the centre part of the shown object is generated from a box from which a cylinder was subtracted, resulting in the half-circle-shaped bulge.

Another useful solid modelling technique is the *sweep representation*. A three-dimensional object is generated from a two-dimensional shape that is moved along a trajectory. For instance, the horseshoe-shaped object on the left in figure 6.10 is created from a rectangle which is moved along an arc. The tent shape on the right-hand side of the figure originates from a triangle sliding along a line.

The probably most important modelling technique, which will be introduced in section 6.6, is based on freeform surfaces that are defined by parametric

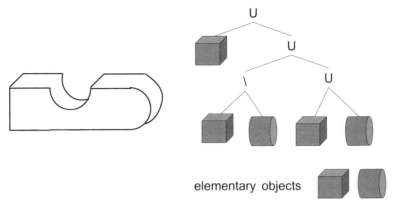

Figure 6.9 An object that was constructed using elementary geometric objects and set-theoretic operations shown on the right

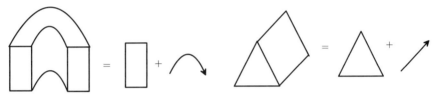

Figure 6.10 Two objects and their sweep representations

curves. As mentioned before, curved surfaces will be approximated by plane polygons for the generation of images. The description of the surface of an object by polygons requires a list of points—the vertices of the polygons—and a list of polygons composed of these points. Apart from this geometrical structure, information about the colour or texture of the surface as well as normal vectors assigned to the polygons or vertices is needed for calculating the correct illumination and shading caused by light reflections. So when a curved surface is approximated by polygons, not only the vertices and faces of the polygons are stored, but also normal vectors of the original surface in the vertices of the polygons.

Also the surfaces of the elementary geometric objects in the simple scene with the helicopter in figure 5.3 on page 121 are approximated by triangles. Figure 6.11 shows the underlying tesselation.

The larger the number of triangles, the better the curved surface can be approximated. Figure 6.12 shows a sphere for which the tesselation was refined from left to right. The left sphere is approximated by only eight triangles. The computational effort increases with the number of triangles. The approximation of a surface by triangles can be carried out off-line before the rendering

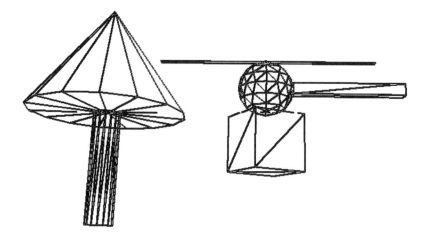

Figure 6.11 Tesselation of the helicopter scene in figure 5.3

process. But also the calculations for light reflections on the surface, the determination of which objects or polygons are hidden from view by others as well as collision detection, i.e., whether moving objects collide, become more complex with an increasing number of triangles. Usually, a higher resolution will lead to a quadratic increase of the computational costs because, for example, doubling the resolution in each dimension for a two-dimensional surface approximation requires four times as many triangles.

Figure 6.12 Representation of a sphere with different tesselations

For this reason, the same object might be stored in different resolutions in a virtual world. For instance, there is no need to have a detailed model of each tree when a forest is viewed from the distance. A very rough approximation with few triangles is sufficient for each tree. For an extremely refined resolution, each triangle might not even cover a single pixel in the projection when the tree is viewed from the distance. So the computational effort can be reduced drastically when simplified tesselations of the trees are used in this case. However, once the viewer approaches the forest, more refined tesselations are required for a realistic image. The viewer might even stand in front of a tree and look at the structure of single leaves. This requires a very high resolution with triangles. This technique of storing an object with different tesselations and deciding which resolution should be used depending on the distance of the viewer to the object is called *level of detail* (*LOD*).

6.4 Surface modelling with polygons in Java 3D

The representation of a scene in Java 3D is also based on tesselations of the objects. The elementary geometric objects in Java 3D that were introduced in section 5.4 are approximated by triangles. Figure 6.11 shows the tesselations for the elementary geometric objects in the program `StaticSceneExample.java`. A representation in the form of a *wire frame model* as shown in figure 6.11 can be achieved in Java 3D by setting the `PolygonAttributes` of the corresponding `Appearance myApp`.

```
PolygonAttributes polygAttr = new PolygonAttributes();
polygAttr.setPolygonMode(PolygonAttributes.POLYGON_LINE);
myApp.setPolygonAttributes(polygAttr);
```

Figure 6.11 was generated with the program `TesselationBWExample.java`. No colours were used, all objects are drawn with the same black `Appearance` for which the `PolygonAttributes` were set as described above. In the program `TesselationExample.java` the original colours of the scene are kept and `PolygonAttributes` were only set for the green `Appearance` so that only the cockpit of the helicopter, its tail and the treetop are shown as wire frames.

The resolution for the tesselation of the elementary geometric objects can also be controlled in Java 3D. The only exception is the box. It has six rectangular faces and each of them can be exactly modelled by two triangles so that there is no need for a higher resolution.

The constructor

```
Sphere s =
        new Sphere(r,Sphere.GENERATE_NORMALS,res,sphereApp);
```

generates a sphere with radius r and the **Appearance sphereApp** whose surface is approximated by **res** triangles at the circumference. This constructor was used in the program **TesselationResolution.java** with different values for the resolution **res** to create figure 6.12.

The constructors

```
Cylinder c =
    new Cylinder(r,h,Cylinder.GENERATE_NORMALS,xres,yres,app);
```

and

```
Cone c = new Cone(r,h,Cone.GENERATE_NORMALS,xres,yres,app);
```

generate a cylinder and a cone, respectively, with radius r, height h and **Appearance app**. For the approximation of the surfaces, **xres** triangles are used around the circumference and **yres** triangles along the height. For a nice approximation, the value **xres** should be chosen larger whereas for **yres** even the value 2 might be sufficient.

Java 3D offers a variety of ways to model surfaces of geometric objects by approximations with polygons. Here, as one representative of these methods, only approximations with triangles are considered. Usually, the approximation of complex surfaces by triangles will not be specified directly. Instead, suitable software tools are used for this purpose. For measurements of existing objects there are programs that can convert the data into surfaces. CAD programs and other design tools offer a selection of methods like freeform surfaces, CSG and sweep representation together with elementary geometric objects. How to import objects or files created with such tools into Java 3D will be explained in section 6.5.

For modelling surfaces of objects directly with triangles, the class **GeometryArray** is available. In the first step, the vertices of the triangles must be stored in an array.

```
Point3f[] vertexCoordinates =
            {
                new Point3f(x0,y0,z0),
                ...
            };
```

The coordinates of the points are given as **float**-values. For the tetrahedron in figure 6.4 on page 152, this array would contain four instances of the class **Point3f**. This array specifies only the points for vertices, but not which points should form a triangle. An integer array is responsible for this. For each triangle, the indices of the corresponding points in the `Point3f` array are entered subsequently into this array. For the tetrahedron in figure 6.4 the array would have the following entries.

```
int triangles[] = {
                    0,3,1,
                    0,2,3,
                    0,1,2,
                    1,3,2
                };
```

The number of vertices and the number of triangles coincide just by chance for a tetrahedron. For other geometrical shapes this will not be the case. A cube, for example, would require eight vertices and twelve triangles, two for each side of the cube. It is important to specify the points for each triangle in the correct order. The points should be given in anticlockwise order when looking at the surface from the outside.

The following lines of code generate an instance `ga` of the class `GeometryArray` from the specified vertices and triangles.

```
GeometryInfo gi =
              new GeometryInfo(GeometryInfo.TRIANGLE_ARRAY);
gi.setCoordinates(vertexCoordinates);
gi.setCoordinateIndices(triangles);
NormalGenerator ng = new NormalGenerator();
ng.generateNormals(gi);
GeometryArray ga = gi.getGeometryArray();
```

Then this `GeometryArray` `ga` can be used to create an instance of the class `Shape3D` with a predefined `Appearance` `app`.

```
Shape3D myShape = new Shape3D(ga,app);
```

This `Shape3D` object can be integrated into a scene in the same way as the elementary geometric objects cube, sphere, cylinder and cone.

A tetrahedron is constructed in this way in the class `GeomArrayExample.java`. It is interesting to see what happens if the vertices of one of the triangles are specified in the wrong order. One could, for instance, change the order of the points in the first triangle from 0,1,3 to 0,3,1. The front face of the tetrahedron will obtain the reverse orientation and becomes invisible from the front.

6.5 Importing geometric objects into Java 3D

Although it is in principle possible to model surfaces of complex geometric objects with triangles, it is an impossible task to specify all triangles explicitly. Various file formats for 3D computer graphics objects can be imported into Java 3D programs. In this way, modelling and design tools can be used to create complex geometric objects which can then be integrated into animated scenes in Java 3D. As an example, importing files in the *Wavefront Object* format will be explained here in detail. In the appendix and on the web site of this book, there are links to web sites where three-dimensional objects in this format can be downloaded as well as links to programs for creating objects in Wavefront Object format.

Files in Wavefront Object format are normal ASCII files containing the following information. Comment lines start with the symbol #. The vertices needed for modelling the three-dimensional object start with the letter v followed by three values determining the x-, y- and z-coordinate of the corresponding vertex. In the same way, normal vectors are specified starting with vn (vertex normals) instead of v. In addition, points for attaching textures can be defined. They are marked by vt (texture vertices). The description of polygons starts with the letter f (face). A polygon is defined by the indices of its vertices. Indices of corresponding normal vectors also belong to polygons. The letter g (group) is used for groupings. In this way, polygons can be combined to a group and can be addressed as subobjects. For example, a helicopter might have groups for the cockpit, the rotor blade and the tail. A name can be assigned to each group. Then Java 3D can directly access such groups and, for instance, assign individual colours to them.

With the following lines of code the file `filename.obj` in Wavefront Object format can be loaded to a Java 3D scene.

```
ObjectFile f = new ObjectFile(ObjectFile.RESIZE);
Scene s = null;
try
{
  s = f.load("filename.obj");
}
catch (Exception e)
{
  System.out.println("File loading failed:" + e);
}
```

Then this loaded object can be assigned to a transformation group tg, as usual, with the method addChild using the method getSceneGroup.

```
tg.addChild(s.getSceneGroup());
```

The method `getNamedObjects` provides a `Hashtable` with the names of all groups that are defined in the loaded file so that subobjects can be accessed. The following lines of code print the names of these subobjects.

```
Hashtable namedObjects = s.getNamedObjects();
Enumeration enum = namedObjects.keys();
String name;
while (enum.hasMoreElements())
{
  name = (String) enum.nextElement();
  System.out.println("Name: "+name);
}
```

If there is, for example, a subobject with the name `partName` and this subobject should obtain a new colour given by the `Appearance` app, then this can be achieved by

```
Shape3D part = (Shape3D) namedObjects.get("partName");
part.setAppearance(app);
```

In this way, it is also possible to use only parts of an object in Wavefront Object format in a scene. After loading the Wavefront Object file, the whole object is not assigned to the transformation group `tg` as above, but only the subobject with the group name `partName` is chosen and endowed with the `Appearance` app by the following lines of code.

```
Shape3D part = (Shape3D) namedObjects.get("partName");
Shape3D extractedPart = (Shape3D) part.cloneTree();
extractedPart.setAppearance(app);
tg.addChild(extractedPart);
```

The program `Load3DExample.java` demonstrates how to include an object in Wavefront Object format into a Java 3D program, how to print out all its group names, and how to assign a colour to a specific subobject. The program `Extract3DExample.java` shows how to extract a single subobject and how to include only this subobject with a desired colour in a scene.

6.6 Parametric curves and freeform surfaces

For the representation of a scene as an image, the surfaces of geometric objects are approximated by triangles. But an explicit description of surfaces with triangles is not suitable for modelling. *Freeform surfaces* are much better suited for this purpose. They are the three-dimensional counterpart of curves in the plane as described in section 2.3. Like these curves, a freeform surface is defined by a finite set of points which it approximates. Saving geometric objects based on freeform surfaces does not cause any problems when the object is scaled. Tesselations are not well suited for scaling an objects. They will lead to similar problems as scalings of raster graphics. For a given freeform surface, the number of triangles for the tesselation can be chosen depending on the desired precision and resolution. The freeform surfaces provide also exact information about the normal vectors to the surface which are very important for illumination and shading.

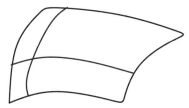

Figure 6.13 Two curves obtained from a surface that is scanned along the coordinate axes

Modelling curved surfaces is based on parametric curves. When a surface is scanned parallel to one of the coordinate axes, one obtains a curve in the three-dimensional space. Figure 6.13 shows two curves that are obtained from scanning a surface. Understanding parametric curves in the three-dimensional space is essential for the understanding of curved surfaces. Therefore, a brief introduction to parametric curves is given, before freeform surfaces are discussed.

6.6.1 Parametric curves

When a curve in the three-dimensional space or in the plane should be defined by a finite set of points—the so-called *control points*—the following properties will make modelling and adjusting such curves easier.

Controllability: The influence of the parameters on the shape of the curve can be understood in an intuitive way. When the shape of a curve has to be changed, it should be clear for the user which parameters he should modify in which way in order to achieve the desired change.

Locality principle: It must be possible to carry out local changes on the curve.

Modifying one control point should only change the curve in the neighbourhood of this control point and not alter the curve completely.

Smoothness: The curve should satisfy certain smoothness properties. It should not only be continuous without jumps, it should have no sharp bends. The latter property requires the curve to be differentiable. In some cases it is even necessary that higher derivatives exist. It also desirable that the curve is of bounded variation. This means it should stay somehow close to its control points.

Interpolation refers to curves that pass through all control points whereas *approximation* only requires that the curve gets close to the control point, but it does not have to pass through them. Given $(n+1)$ control points, there is always an interpolation polynomial of degree n or less that passes exactly through the control points. Nevertheless, interpolation with polynomials is not suited for the modelling purposes of computer graphics. Apart from the problem that the evaluation of polynomials of higher degree leads to high computational costs, interpolation polynomials do not satisfy the locality principle. The modification of a single control point usually affects all coefficients of the polynomial and changes the whole curve. Clipping for such polynomials is also not easy, since a polynomial interpolating a given set of control points can deviate arbitrarily from the region around the control points. Therefore, it is not sufficient to consider only the control points for clipping of such interpolation polynomials. The curve must be computed directly to check whether it passes through the clipping area. Another problem of polynomials of higher degree is that they tend to oscillate between the control points.

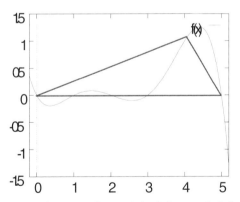

Figure 6.14 An interpolation polynomial of degree 5 defined by the control points (0,0), (1,0), (2,0), (3,0), (4,1), (5,0)

Figure 6.14 shows an interpolation polynomial of degree 5, defined by six control points through which it passes. With the exception of one control point, all others are located on the x-axis. The polynomial oscillates around the control points and has a clear overshoot above the highest control point. It does not stay within the convex hull of the control points.

The undesired properties of interpolation polynomials can be amended by dropping the strict requirement that the polynomial must pass through all control points. Instead, it is sufficient to approximate some of the control points only. *Bernstein polynomials* of degree n are a class of polynomials with better properties than interpolation polynomials. The i-th Bernstein polynomial of degree n ($i \in \{0, \dots, n\}$) is given by the equation

$$B_i^{(n)}(t) \;=\; \binom{n}{i} \cdot (1-t)^{n-i} \cdot t^i \qquad (t \in [0,1]).$$

Bernstein polynomials satisfy two important properties.

$$B_i^{(n)}(t) \in [0,1] \qquad \text{for all } t \in [0,1].$$

This means that the evaluation of a Bernstein polynomial within the unit interval will only yield values between zero and one. This property and the following one will be needed later on for constructing curves that stay within the convex hull of their control points.

$$\sum_{i=0}^{n} B_i^{(n)}(t) \;=\; 1 \qquad \text{for all } t \in [0,1].$$

In every position of the unit interval the Bernstein polynomials add up to one.

Bézier curves use Bernstein polynomials of degree n to approximate $(n+1)$ control points $\mathbf{b}_0, \dots, \mathbf{b}_n \in \mathbb{R}^p$. For the purposes of computer graphics only the cases of the plane with $p = 2$ and the three-dimensional space with $p = 3$ are of interest. The control points are also called *Bézier points*. The curve

$$\mathbf{x}(t) \;=\; \sum_{i=0}^{n} \mathbf{b}_i \cdot B_i^{(n)}(t) \qquad (t \in [0,1]) \tag{6.1}$$

defined by these points is called a *Bézier curve* of degree n.

The Bézier curve interpolates the first and the last point, this means $\mathbf{x}(0) = \mathbf{b}_0$ and $\mathbf{x}(1) = \mathbf{b}_n$ hold. In general, the curve does not pass through the other control points. The tangent vector to the Bézier curve in the first and the last point can be calculated in the following way.

$$\begin{aligned}
\dot{\mathbf{x}}(0) &= n \cdot (\mathbf{b}_1 - \mathbf{b}_0), \\
\dot{\mathbf{x}}(1) &= n \cdot (\mathbf{b}_n - \mathbf{b}_{n-1}).
\end{aligned}$$

This means that the tangent vector in the first point $\mathbf{b}_0$ points in the direction of the point $\mathbf{b}_1$ and the tangent vector in the last point $\mathbf{b}_n$ points in the direction of the point $\mathbf{b}_{n-1}$. This principle is already known from the definition of cubic curves in figure 2.7 on page 15.

Fixing the value t in equation (6.1), one obtains a convex combination of the control points $\mathbf{b}_0, \ldots, \mathbf{b}_n$, since the values $\mathbf{x}(t)$ of the Bernstein polynomials add up to one in every point t. Therefore, the Bézier curve stays within the convex hull of the control points.

When an affine transformation is applied to the control points, the resulting Bézier curve with respect to the new control points coincides with the transformed Bézier curve. Therefore, Bézier curves are invariant under affine transformations like rotation, translation or scaling. Bézier curves are also symmetric with respect to their control points. The control points $\mathbf{b}_0, \ldots, \mathbf{b}_n$ and $\mathbf{b}_n, \ldots, \mathbf{b}_0$ lead to the same curve. The curve is only passed through in the reverse direction.

When a convex combination of two sets of control points is used to define a new set of control points, then the resulting Bézier curve is the convex combination of the corresponding Bézier curves.

– If the control points $\tilde{\mathbf{b}}_0, \ldots, \tilde{\mathbf{b}}_n$ define the Bézier curve $\tilde{\mathbf{x}}(t)$ and

– the control points $\hat{\mathbf{b}}_0, \ldots, \hat{\mathbf{b}}_n$ define the Bézier curve $\hat{\mathbf{x}}(t)$,

– then the control points $\alpha\tilde{\mathbf{b}}_0 + \beta\hat{\mathbf{b}}_0, \ldots, \alpha\tilde{\mathbf{b}}_n + \beta\hat{\mathbf{b}}_n$ define the Bézier curve $\mathbf{x}(t) = \alpha\tilde{\mathbf{x}}(t) + \beta\hat{\mathbf{x}}(t)$ if $\alpha + \beta = 1$, $\alpha, \beta \geq 0$ holds.

When all control points lie on a line or a parabola, then the resulting Bézier curve will be the corresponding line or parabola. Bézier curves also preserve certain geometrical shape properties like monotonicity or convexity of the control points.

Despite the nice properties of Bézier curves, they are not suited for larger sets of control points since this would lead to polynomials of high degree. $(n+1)$ control points usually define a Bézier curve which is a polynomial of degree n. Therefore, instead of Bézier curves, *B-splines* are preferred to define approximating curves for a given set of control points. B-splines are composed of a number of Bézier curves of lower polynomial degree—usually degree three or four. For this purpose, for a sequence of n control points (for instance $n = 4$) a Bézier curve is computed and the last control point of the sequence is used as the starting point of the next sequence for the next Bézier curve. In this way, B-splines interpolate those control points where the single Bézier curves are glued together. These junctions are also called *knots*. The other control points are called *inner Bézier points*. Figure 6.15 shows a B-spline which is composed of two Bézier curves of degree 3.

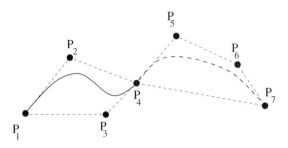

Figure 6.15 B-spline with knots P_1, P_4, P_7 and inner Bézier points P_2, P_3, P_5, P_6

In order to avoid sharp bends at junctions between the Bézier curves, each knot and its two neighbouring inner Bézier points should be collinear. In this way, the B-spline will be differentiable also in the knots. This method for avoiding sharp bends was illustrated in figure 2.8 on page 16. By choosing the inner Bézier points properly, a B-spline of degree n can be differentiated $(n-1)$ times. Cubic B-splines are based on polynomials of degree three and can therefore be twice differential when the inner Bézier points are chosen correctly. In addition to the collinearity condition, another restriction must be imposed on the neighbouring inner Bézier points. The B-spline in figure 6.16 is composed of two Bézier curves of degree 3. It is defined by the knots P_1, P_4, P_7 and the inner Bézier points P_2, P_3, P_5, P_6. In order to guarantee that the B-spline is twice differentiable, the segments of the tangents must have the same proportions as indicated in figure 6.16.

B-splines preserve the nice properties of Bézier curves. They stay within the convex hull of the control points, they are invariant under affine transformations, symmetric in the control points, they interpolate the first and the last control point and they satisfy the locality principle.

A B-spline is piecewise composed of Bézier curves. They can be described in homogeneous coordinates in the form

$$\begin{pmatrix} P_x(t) \\ P_y(t) \\ P_z(t) \\ 1 \end{pmatrix}.$$

$P_x(t), P_y(t), P_z(t)$ are polynomials in t. When a perspective projection in the form of a matrix as in equation (5.6) is applied to this representation of a Bézier

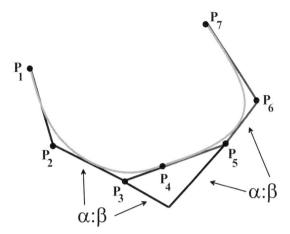

Figure 6.16 Condition for the inner Bézier points for a twice differentiable, cubic B-spline

curve, one obtains

$$
\begin{pmatrix}
1 & 0 & 0 & 0 \\
0 & 1 & 0 & 0 \\
0 & 0 & 0 & 0 \\
0 & 0 & \frac{1}{z_0} & 1
\end{pmatrix}
\cdot
\begin{pmatrix}
P_x(t) \\
P_y(t) \\
P_z(t) \\
1
\end{pmatrix}
=
\begin{pmatrix}
P_x(t) \\
P_y(t) \\
0 \\
\frac{P_z(t)}{z_0} + 1
\end{pmatrix}.
$$

Therefore, the projection of a Bézier curve as a parametric curve is no longer a polynomial in Cartesian coordinates, but a rational function.

$$
\begin{pmatrix}
\dfrac{P_x(t)}{\frac{P_z(t)}{z_0} + 1} \\[3mm]
\dfrac{P_y(t)}{\frac{P_z(t)}{z_0} + 1} \\[3mm]
0
\end{pmatrix}.
$$

Since a perspective projection of a B-spline or a Bézier curve will lead to a rational function anyway, one can already use rational functions for modelling curves in the three-dimensional space. The perspective projection of a rational function is again a rational function. Therefore, it is very common to use *NURBS* (nonuniform rational B-splines) instead of B-spline. NURBS are generalisations of B-splines based on extensions of Bézier curves to rational functions in the following form.

$$
\mathbf{x}(t) = \frac{\sum_{i=0}^{n} w_i \cdot \mathbf{b}_i \cdot B_i^{(n)}(t)}{\sum_{i=0}^{n} w_i \cdot B_i^{(n)}(t)}.
$$

The adjustable weights w_i are called *form parameters*. A larger weight w_i increases the influence of the control point $\mathbf{b}_i$ on the curve. For support of this interpretation and to avoid singularities, it is usually required that all weights w_i are positive.

6.6.2 Efficient computation of polynomials

In order to draw a parametric curve, polynomials have to be evaluated. The same applies to freeform surfaces. In most cases, polynomials of degree 3 are used. This section presents an efficient scheme for evaluating polynomials, which is based on similar principles of incremental computations as introduced in the context of the midpoint algorithm in section 3.2. Although floating point arithmetic cannot be avoided for polynomials in this way, it is at least possible to reduce the repeated calculations to additions only.

For drawing a cubic curve, the parametric curve is evaluated at equidistant values of the parameter t. The corresponding points are computed and connected by line segments. The same applies to freeform surfaces, which are also modelled by parametric curves or surfaces in the form of polynomials. For evaluating a polynomial $f(t)$ at the points t_0, $t_1 = t_0 + \delta$, $t_2 = t_0 + 2\delta, \ldots$ with a step width of $\delta > 0$, a scheme of forward differences is applied. The polynomial has to be evaluated once for the initial value $f_0 = f(t_0)$ at the point t_0 and then the changes

$$\Delta f(t) = f(t + \delta) - f(t)$$

are added in an incremental fashion as

$$f(t + \delta) = f(t) + \Delta f(t)$$

or

$$f_{n+1} = f_n + \Delta f_n.$$

For a polynomial $f(t) = at^3 + bt^2 + ct + d$ of degree 3, this leads to

$$\Delta f(t) = 3at^2\delta + t(3a\delta^2 + 2b\delta) + a\delta^3 + b\delta^2 + c\delta.$$

In this way, the evaluation of polynomials of degree 3 can be reduced to an addition of Δ-values. The computation of these Δ-values requires evaluations of polynomials of degree 2. These polynomials are also not explicitly evaluated. The same scheme of forward differences is also applied to them.

$$\Delta^2 f(t) = \Delta(\Delta f(t)) = \Delta f(t + \delta) - \Delta f(t)$$

$$= 6a\delta^2 t + 6a\delta^3 + 2b\delta^2.$$

The Δ-values of the original polynomial of degree 3 are calculated from the equation

$$\Delta f_n \;=\; \Delta f_{n-1} + \Delta^2 f_{n-1}.$$

A multiplication is still necessary for the computation of the Δ^2-values. Applying the scheme of forward differences once again, one obtains

$$\Delta^3 f(t) \;=\; \Delta^2 f(t+\delta) - \Delta^2 f(t) \;=\; 6a\delta^3.$$

With this final step, multiplications are only required for the computation of the initial value at $t_0 = 0$.

$$
\begin{aligned}
f_0 &= d, \\
\Delta f_0 &= a\delta^3 + b\delta^2 + c\delta, \\
\Delta^2 f_0 &= 6a\delta^3 + 2b\delta^2, \\
\Delta^3 f_0 &= 6a\delta^3.
\end{aligned}
$$

For the calculation of all further values, only additions are needed. Table 6.1 illustrates this principle of difference schemes. Table 6.2 shows the calculations of the forward differences for an example, the polynomial $f(t) = t^3 + 2t + 3$, i.e., $a = 1$, $b = 0$, $c = 2$, $d = 3$, with a step width of $\delta = 1$.

$t_0 = 0$		$t_0 + \delta$		$t_0 + 2\delta$		$t_0 + 3\delta$	$\cdots$
f_0	$\rightarrow$	$+$	$\rightarrow$	$+$	$\rightarrow$	$+$	$\cdots$
Δf_0	$\nearrow$	$+$	$\nearrow$	$+$	$\nearrow$	$+$	$\cdots$
$\Delta^2 f_0$	$\nearrow$	$+$	$\nearrow$	$+$	$\nearrow$	$+$	$\cdots$
$\Delta^3 f_0$	$\nearrow$	$\Delta^3 f_0$	$\nearrow$	$\Delta^3 f_0$	$\nearrow$	$\Delta^3 f_0$	$\cdots$

Table 6.1 Forward difference for a general polynomial of degree 3

6.6.3 Freeform surfaces

As mentioned in section 6.6, freeform surfaces are closely related to parametric curves. Freeform surfaces have two parameters to describe the two-dimensional surface, whereas only one parameter t is needed for curves. When one parameter of a freeform surface is considered as fixed, then the variation of the other parameter yields a curve on the surface as can be seen in figure 6.17.

$t = 0$		$t = 1$		$t = 2$		$t = 3$		$t = 4$	
3	$\rightarrow$	6	$\rightarrow$	15	$\rightarrow$	36	$\rightarrow$	75	...
3	$\nearrow\rightarrow$	9	$\nearrow\rightarrow$	21	$\nearrow\rightarrow$	39	$\nearrow\rightarrow$	63	...
6	$\nearrow\rightarrow$	12	$\nearrow\rightarrow$	18	$\nearrow\rightarrow$	24	$\nearrow\rightarrow$	30	...
6	$\nearrow\rightarrow$	6	$\nearrow\rightarrow$	6	$\nearrow\rightarrow$	6	$\nearrow\rightarrow$	6	...

Table 6.2 Forward differences for the polynomial $f(t) = t^3 + 2t + 3$ with step width $\delta = 1$

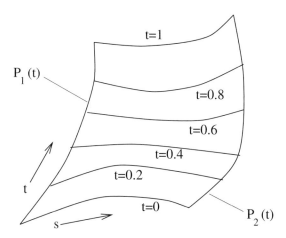

Figure 6.17 A parametric freeform surface

Bézier surfaces are composed of Bézier curves with parameters s and t.

$$\mathbf{x}(s, t) = \sum_{i=0}^{n}\sum_{j=0}^{m} \mathbf{b}_{ij} \cdot B_i^{(n)}(s) \cdot B_j^{(m)}(t) \qquad (s, t \in [0, 1]).$$

Most common are Bézier curves of degree 3. This means $m = n = 3$. For the definition of a Bézier surface $(m + 1) \cdot (n + 1)$ Bézier points $\mathbf{b}_{ij}$, i.e., 16 in the case of cubic Bézier surfaces, have to be specified. Figure 6.18 illustrates how a net of Bézier points determines the Bézier surface.

Bézier surfaces have similar nice properties as Bézier curves. The four points at the corners $\mathbf{b}_{00}, \mathbf{b}_{0m}, \mathbf{b}_{n0}, \mathbf{b}_{nm}$ lie on the surface. This does not apply to the other control points in general. The surface stays within the convex hull of the control point. Curves with a constant value $s = s_0$ are Bézier curves with respect to the points

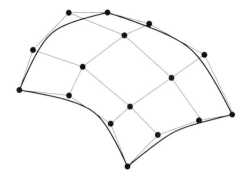

Figure 6.18 A net of Bézier points for the definition of a Bézier surface

$$\mathbf{b}_j = \sum_{i=0}^{n} \mathbf{b}_{ij} \cdot B_j^{(n)}(s_0)$$

and analogously for curves with constant parameter $t = t_0$.

Since tesselations, as they are required in computer graphics, approximate surfaces with triangles and not with rectangles, Bézier surfaces of degree n, usually $n = 3$, are sometimes defined over a grid of triangles in the following way.

$$\mathbf{x}(t_1, t_2, t_3) = \sum_{i,j,k \geq 0:\; i+j+k=n} \mathbf{b}_{ijk} \cdot B_{ijk}^{(n)}(t_1, t_2, t_3).$$

The corresponding Bernstein polynomials are given by

$$B_{ijk}^{(n)}(t_1, t_2, t_3) = \frac{n!}{i!j!k!} \cdot t_1^i \cdot t_2^j \cdot t_3^k$$

where $t_1 + t_2 + t_3 = 1$, $t_1, t_2, t_3 \geq 0$ and $i + j + k = n$ (for $i, j, k \in \mathbb{N}$). The triangular grid is shown in figure 6.19.

6.7 Normal vectors for surfaces

Aspects of illumination and shading in connection with light reflections are crucial for generating realistic 3D images. Light reflections depend on the angle of the light with respect to the surface. Surface normal vectors are needed for the calculation of these angles. Illumination and shading techniques will be described in detail in section 8. In this section, normal vectors are introduced that will be needed later on for illumination and shading purposes.

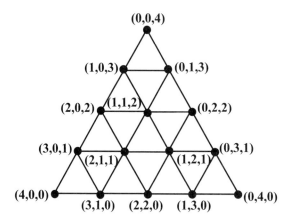

Figure 6.19 A triangular grid for the definition of a Bézier surface

A triangle always defines a plane and all normal vectors of such a flat triangle point in the same direction. If the plane induced by a triangle is given by the equation

$$Ax + By + Cz + D = 0, \tag{6.2}$$

then the vector $(A, B, C)^\top$ is a nonnormalised[1] normal vector to the plane. This is true for the following reason. If $\mathbf{n} = (n_x, n_y, n_z)^\top$ is a not necessarily normalised normal vector to the plane and $\mathbf{v} = (v_x, v_y, v_z)^\top$ is a point in the plane, then the point $(x, y, z)^\top$ lies also in the plane if and only if the vector connecting $\mathbf{v}$ and $(x, y, z)^\top$ lies in the plane. This means the connecting vector must be orthogonal to the normal vector.

$$0 = \mathbf{n}^\top \cdot \left((x, y, z)^\top - \mathbf{v} \right) = n_x \cdot x + n_y \cdot y + n_z \cdot z - \mathbf{n}^\top \cdot \mathbf{v}.$$

Choosing $A = n_x$, $B = n_y$, $C = n_z$ and $D = \mathbf{n}^\top \cdot \mathbf{v}$, equation (6.2) for the plane is obtained.

When a triangle is given by the three noncollinear points $\mathbf{P}_1, \mathbf{P}_2, \mathbf{P}_3$, the normal vector can be calculated by the cross product by

$$\mathbf{n} = (\mathbf{P}_2 - \mathbf{P}_1) \times (\mathbf{P}_3 - \mathbf{P}_1).$$

The cross product of two vectors $(x_1, y_1, z_1)^\top$ and $(x_2, y_2, z_2)^\top$ is defined as the vector

$$\begin{pmatrix} x_1 \\ y_1 \\ z_1 \end{pmatrix} \times \begin{pmatrix} x_2 \\ y_2 \\ z_2 \end{pmatrix} = \begin{pmatrix} y_1 \cdot z_2 - y_2 \cdot z_1 \\ z_1 \cdot x_2 - z_2 \cdot x_1 \\ x_1 \cdot y_2 - x_2 \cdot y_1 \end{pmatrix}.$$

---

[1] For a normalised vector $\mathbf{v}$, $\| v \| = 1$ must hold.

The cross product is zero when the two vectors are collinear.

Equation (6.2) provides a nonnormalised normal vector to the plane. The value D is obtained by inserting one of the points of the triangle, i.e., one point in the plane, into this equation.

$$D = \mathbf{n}^\top \cdot \mathbf{P}_1.$$

The normal vector at a point $\mathbf{x}(s_0, t_0)$ of a freeform surface is the normal vector to the tangent plane in the corresponding point. The tangent plane is determined by the tangent vectors at $\mathbf{x}(s_0, t_0)$ to the two parametric curves $\mathbf{p}(s) = \mathbf{x}(s, t_0)$ and $\mathbf{q}(t) = \mathbf{x}(s_0, t)$.

$$
\begin{aligned}
\left(\frac{\partial}{\partial s} \mathbf{x}(s, t_0) \right)_{s=s_0} &= \left(\frac{\partial}{\partial s} \sum_{i=0}^{n} \sum_{j=0}^{m} \mathbf{b}_{ij} \cdot B_i^{(n)}(s) \cdot B_j^{(m)}(t_0) \right)_{s=s_0} \\
&= \sum_{j=0}^{m} B_j^{(m)}(t_0) \cdot \sum_{i=0}^{n} \mathbf{b}_{ij} \cdot \left(\frac{\partial B_i^{(n)}(s)}{\partial s} \right)_{s=s_0},
\end{aligned}
$$

$$
\begin{aligned}
\left(\frac{\partial}{\partial t} \mathbf{x}(s_0, t) \right)_{t=t_0} &= \left(\frac{\partial}{\partial t} \sum_{i=0}^{n} \sum_{j=0}^{m} \mathbf{b}_{ij} \cdot B_i^{(n)}(s_0) \cdot B_j^{(m)}(t) \right)_{t=t_0} \\
&= \sum_{i=0}^{n} B_i^{(n)}(s_0) \cdot \sum_{j=0}^{m} \mathbf{b}_{ij} \cdot \left(\frac{\partial B_j^{(m)}(t)}{\partial t} \right)_{t=t_0}.
\end{aligned}
$$

These two tangent vectors are parallel to the surface in the point (s_0, t_0) and induce the tangent plane in this point. The cross product of these tangent vectors is then the normal vector to the surface at the point $\mathbf{x}(s_0, t_0)$.

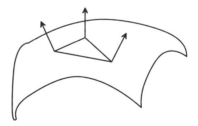

Figure 6.20 Normal vectors to the original surface in the vertices of an approximating triangle

When a freeform surface is approximated by triangles, the normal vectors for the triangles should not be derived from the triangles but from the freeform surface directly. Of course, it is impossible to store a normal vector for every single point in an approximating triangle. But at least, the normal vectors for the three vertices of the triangle should be computed and stored as the normal vectors to the surface in the corresponding points. In this way, a plane triangle can have three different normal vectors that are inherited from the original surface. None of these normal vectors might coincide with the normal vector to the plane defined by the triangle as can be seen in figure 6.20.

6.7.1 Normal vectors in Java 3D

The normal vectors for the elementary geometric objects cube, sphere, cylinder and cone are determined automatically in Java 3D. For objects loaded from a file, for instance in Wavefront Object format, the normal vectors are usually provided in the file along with object coordinates. When objects are modelled directly by triangles in Java 3D, the normal vectors can also be specified explicitly. This will seldom be needed since complex objects are usually not designed directly in Java 3D. They will be constructed with a suitable design tool and imported to Java 3D as Wavefront Object files. Nevertheless, a simple technique for controlling the generation of normal vectors in the class `GeometryArray` shall be described here.

When an object is defined by triangles in Java 3D with the class `GeometryArray`, an instance `ng` of the class `NormalGenerator` must be created as described on page 161. It is possible to modify the computation of normal vectors before the normal vectors for the `GeometryInfo` object `gi` are calculated by calling the method `ng.generateNormals(gi)`. The method

```
ng.setCreaseAngle(angle);
```

should be called directly before the method `ng.generateNormals(gi)`. The value `angle` specifies up to which angle the normal vectors of neighbouring triangles should be interpolated. The idea behind this interpolation is that neighbouring triangles with a very flat angle approximate a smooth curved surface. So the edge between the triangles is not part of the approximated surface. However, if the angle is too sharp, then the neighbouring triangles model a real edge on the approximated surface and this edge should be preserved. Figure 6.21 illustrates the principle of interpolated normal vectors on the left-hand side. The angle between the two triangles is so flat that it can be assumed that the edge is not desired and therefore, the normal vectors are interpolated. There is a very sharp angle between the two triangles on the right-hand side of figure 6.21. The resulting edge is intended and the normal vectors should not be interpolated.

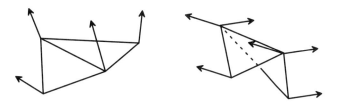

Figure 6.21 Interpolated and noninterpolated normal vectors

When the default constructor `new NormalGenerator()` is used, the angle will be set to zero. Interpolation between normal vectors will not be carried out. The method `setCreaseAngle` can change the angle and set it even to a value that will cause interpolation between triangles with a very sharp edge in between. In the program `NormalsForGeomArrays.java`, the same tetrahedron as in the program `GeomArrayExample.java` is generated. However, the angle for interpolation is set to π, i.e., $180°$, so that normal vectors between neighbouring triangles are always interpolated. The edges of the tetrahedron, which were clearly visible in the program `GeomArrayExample.java`, become almost invisible now.

6.8 Exercises

Exercise 6.1

The surface of the object on the right shall
be modelled with triangles. Define suitable coordinates for the six vertices and
specify the triangles based on the vertices.
Make sure that the orientation of each
triangle is chosen correctly. The vertices
of a triangle should occur in anticlockwise
order when looking at the surface from
outside the object. The object itself is
two units high, one unit in depth and
five units wide. Write a Java 3D program to model and display the object. Use
the technique that was explained in section 6.4.

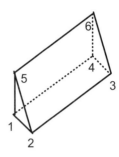

Exercise 6.2

Draw the quadtree for the triangle on the right
up to a depth of two. The root (level 0) of the
quadtree corresponds to the dashed square.

Exercise 6.3

Display the spheres from figure 6.12, which were generated with the program
TesselationResolution.java, as wire frame models. Display also the ship
which is loaded in the program Load3DExample.java as a wire frame model.

Exercise 6.4

Use Java 2D to draw a twice differentiable curve based on the technique described for figure 6.16.

7

Visible surface determination

In order to display a three-dimensional scene, the visible objects must be determined. There are two aspects of such visibility considerations. First of all, clipping will remove all objects that are not in the range that the viewer can oversee. Rendering is only necessary for the objects inside the clipping region. Problems in connection with clipping for two-dimensional graphics have been discussed in chapters 3 and 4. Clipping for three-dimensional scenes will be slightly more complicated. However, there is an additional aspect which only occurs in the three-dimensional case. An object might be in the viewer's viewing range, but it is invisible for the viewer since it is covered by other objects from sight. This chapter focusses on three-dimensional clipping and algorithms for determining visible objects.

7.1 The clipping volume

The specification of a number of parameters concerning the viewer is needed, before a scene from a three-dimensional world can be displayed. The coordinates of the point where the viewer stands are needed as well as in which direction the viewer looks. This information is still not sufficient. The projection plane must be defined as well. The projection plane corresponds to the plane for displaying, usually the computer screen. The computer screen or any other display can only show a limited sector of the infinite projection plane. This sector is usually rectangular. Instead of defining the rectangle explicitly on the

projection plane, an angle of view can be specified. This angle determines the
viewer's field of vision. The angle defines how far the field of view extends to
the left and the right from the viewer. This determines the width of the clipping
rectangle on the projection plane. It corresponds to the width of the window
on the computer screen that is used for displaying the scene. The height of
the rectangle can then be chosen proportionally to the height of the display
window. Figure 7.1 shows a view from above on the field of view.

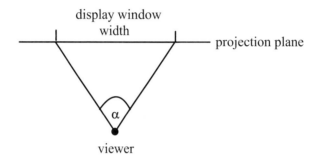

Figure 7.1 The angle α determines the range on the projection plane that
corresponds to the width of the display window

In principle, these specifications are sufficient for clipping. Then the three-
dimensional clipping region—the *clipping volume*—corresponds to a pyramid
of infinite height in case of perspective projection and to a box with infinite
extension in one direction in case of parallel projection. As a consequence, an
arbitrary large number of objects might be located in the clipping volume.
When the viewer takes a closer look at a flower on a meadow in the virtual
world, the city in the far background of the scene must still be rendered completely. The resulting computational effort can be unacceptable. The following
considerations show also that this approach is not realistic.

The distance a person can see is almost unlimited. One can even see stars
in the night sky that are light-years away. A person can also see a finger positioned closely in front of his eyes. But it is impossible to see the finger and the
night sky at the same time. The eyes adjust to a specific distance. Only objects
approximately in this distance are in focus. Objects much farther away or much
closer are out of focus. For instance, when one focusses on a very distant object
and then places a finger close in front of one eye, one can almost not notice
the finger. The same effect also occurs when one focusses on something very
close. While reading a book, one will not notice birds flying in the sky or cars
passing by in the distance. At one moment in time, the focus is adjusted to a
fixed distance and there is a range around this distance in which objects can

be seen in focus. This fact is modelled in computer graphics by clipping planes, the *front* and the *back clipping plane*. The front clipping plane specifies the shortest distance in which objects can still be seen and the back clipping plane defines the largest distance in which objects are still in focus. For a perspective projection, the clipping volume has the shape of a frustum of a pyramid, a pyramid whose tip was cut off. The clipping volume for a parallel projection reduces to a box. The projection plane lies in between the front and the back clipping plane and corresponds to the distance of optimal focus. Objects located between the front clipping plane and the projection plane should occur in front of the computer screen. However, this effect can only be achieved with techniques supporting stereoscopic viewing, which will be discussed in chapter 9. The relations between the front and back clipping plane and the projection plane are illustrated in figure 7.2.

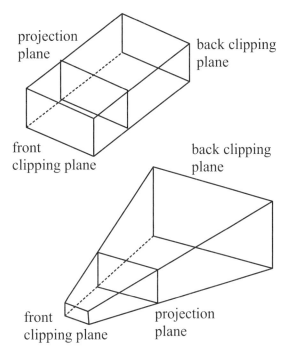

Figure 7.2 The clipping volume for parallel projection (top) and perspective projection (bottom)

It was explained in section 5.8 how any projection can be decomposed into a transformation T followed by a parallel projection onto the x/y-plane. Therefore, three-dimensional clipping can be carried out in a simple and efficient way by first applying the transformation T to all objects and then computing the parallel projection onto the x/y-plane. In this way, the clipping volume even for perspective projections will be transformed to the box-shaped clipping volume of the parallel projection. The edges of this box are parallel to the coordinate axes. The box can be defined by two vertices on its diagonal with coordinates $(x_{\min}, y_{\min}, z_{\min})$ and $(x_{\max}, y_{\max}, z_{\max})$, respectively. In order to check whether an object lies within the clipping volume, it is sufficient to find out whether at least one point (p_x, p_y, p_z) of the object is located in the box. This is satisfied if and only if

$$x_{\min} \leq p_x \leq x_{\max} \quad \text{and} \quad y_{\min} \leq p_y \leq y_{\max} \quad \text{and} \quad z_{\min} \leq p_z \leq z_{\max}$$

holds.

7.1.1 Clipping in Java 3D

Within the class `SimpleUniverse` default settings for the clipping parameters are automatically chosen. How to change the position of the viewer was explained in section 5.8.1.

In order to modify the angle for the field of view or the clipping planes, it is necessary to access the `View` of the `SimpleUniverse`, which is obtained by the following method.

```
View v = simpUniv.getViewer().getView();
```

The method

```
v.setFieldOfView(angle);
```

sets the angle for the field of view to the value `angle` (in radians). The methods

```
v.setFrontClipDistance(fcdist);
v.setBackClipDistance(bcdist);
```

allow the user to define the distances `fcdist` and `bcdist` of the viewer to the front and the back clipping plane, respectively. With

```
v.getPhysicalBody().setNominalEyeOffsetFromNominalScreen(
                                                distance);
```

the distance of the projection plane to the viewer can be modified to the value `distance`.

In the class `ClippingPlanes.java` the angle for the field of view is narrowed to $30°$ compared to the default value of $45°$. In addition, the front clipping plane is moved backwards and the back clipping plane is moved closer to the viewer. The helicopter scene in figure 5.3 on page 121, originally generated with the program `StaticSceneExample.java`, is shown again with these modified clipping parameters. Since the clipping volume is significantly narrowed, parts of the scene are no longer visible.

7.2 Principles of algorithms for visible surface determination

Clipping is responsible for determining which objects of a virtual 3D world are at least partly within the clipping volume. These objects are candidates for the visible objects in the scene. Not all of these objects will be visible since objects farther away from the viewer might be hidden from sight by other objects closer to the viewer. The problem of determining which objects are visible and which ones are not is referred to as *hidden line* and *hidden surface elimination* or *visible line* and *visible surface determination*.

Since any projection can always be decomposed into a suitable geometric transformation of the virtual world followed by a parallel projection to the x/y-plane, considerations concerning the visibility of objects will refer to this special case of a parallel projection in this chapter.

7.2.1 Image-precision and object-precision algorithms

A simple algorithm for determining the visible objects in a scene might be based on the following principle. The rectangle on the projection plane corresponding to the display window for the scene is endowed with the same pixel raster. Then a ray is cast through each pixel in the direction of projection, i.e., parallel to the z-axis. The colour of the pixel is given by the object which the ray first hits. The technique is referred to as an *image-precision algorithm* since it is based on the pixel raster of the image to be computed. An image-precision algorithm has a complexity of $n \cdot p$ for an image with p pixels and n objects. For a typical resolution of a computer screen, p would be around one million pixels. The number of objects can vary strongly with the scene. Objects are the polygons or triangles that model the surface. Therefore, thousands or even 100,000 objects might be contained in a complex scene.

Other strategies for visible surface determination than image-precision algorithms are not based on the pixel raster, but take the relative positions among the objects into account. Such techniques are called *object-precision algorithms*. After it has been determined which objects or which parts of the objects are visible, only those objects are projected onto the pixel raster. Object-precision algorithms have to compare objects pairwise to find out which objects are hidden from view. This leads to a quadratic complexity in the number of objects, i.e., a complexity of $n(n-1)/2$ for a scene with n objects in the worst case. Usually, the number of objects in a scene will be much smaller than the number of pixels so that $n^2 \ll n \cdot p$ holds and object-precision algorithms seem to be superior to image-precision algorithms. However, the single steps of object-precision algorithms are much more complex than those of image-precision algorithms. One advantage of object-precision algorithms is that they work independent of the resolution since they carry out the determination of visible objects independent of the pixel raster. Only for the final projection of the visible objects the pixel raster is needed.

7.2.2 Back-face culling

Independent of the chosen strategy for determining the visible surfaces, the number of candidate objects, i.e., the number of triangles or polygons, should be reduced to a minimum. Clipping already removes all objects outside the clipping volume. But even roughly 50% of the objects within the clipping volume can also be ignored for visibility considerations. Those polygons that do not face the viewer can neither be visible nor can they hide other objects from view. The latter point assumes that all geometric objects are solid. This means if the backside of an object hides another object from view, then this object must also be hidden from view by the frontside. Removing all triangles or polygons that point away from the viewer before starting the actual visibility determination is called *back-face culling*.

It was explained in section 6.1 that triangles and polygons for surfaces obtain an orientation by the order in which their vertices are specified. A polygon is visible only from that side where its vertices appear in anticlockwise order. Taking this into account, the normal vector of a polygon can also be oriented in such a way that it always points in the direction from where the polygon is visible. If such a normal vector points away from the viewer, he is looking at the polygon from its backside so that it cannot be visible for him. The polygon can be ignored for visibility considerations. For a parallel projection to the x/y-plane, the direction of projection is parallel to the z-axis. The z-axis points to the viewer. A polygon can only be visible from the front in the case of an acute angle between the polygon's normal vector and the direction of projection, i.e., the z-axis.

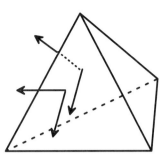

Figure 7.3 A front face whose normal vector forms an acute angle with the direction of projection and a back face whose normal vector forms an obtuse angle with the direction of projection

The tetrahedron in figure 7.3 illustrates this principle. The two parallel vectors indicate the direction of projection. They point in the same direction as the z-axis. The other two vectors are the normal vectors to two faces of the tetrahedron. The normal vector of the front face forms an acute angle with the direction of projection. Therefore, this face will be visible unless there is some other object between it and the observer. The normal vector of the back face forms an obtuse angle with the direction of projection. Back-face culling will remove the corresponding triangle. It will be ignored for visibility considerations.

A face can be removed by back-face calling if and only if its normal vector forms an obtuse angle with the direction of projection, i.e., when the angle is larger than $90°$. The dot product of the normal vector $\mathbf{n} = (n_x, n_y, n_z)^\top$ and the unit vector in the direction of projection $\mathbf{e}_z = (0,0,1)^\top$ yields

$$\mathbf{e}_z^\top \cdot \mathbf{n} \; = \; \cos(\varphi) \cdot \| \, \mathbf{e}_z \, \| \cdot \| \, \mathbf{n} \, \| \tag{7.1}$$

where φ is the angle between the two vectors and $\| \, \mathbf{v} \, \|$ is the length of the vector $\mathbf{v}$. The length of a vector can never be negative and both vectors are not the zero-vector. This means that the right-hand side of equation (7.1) is negative if and only if $\cos(\varphi) < 0$, i.e., if $\varphi > 90°$ holds. The sign of the dot product (7.1) indicates whether the face with the normal vector $\mathbf{n}$ has to be taken into account for the visibility considerations. All faces where the dot product yields a negative value can be neglected for the visibility considerations. Since one of the vectors in the dot product is the unit vector for the z-axis, the dot product simplifies to

$$\mathbf{e}_z^\top \cdot \mathbf{n} \; = \; (0,0,1) \cdot \begin{pmatrix} n_x \\ n_y \\ n_z \end{pmatrix} \; = \; n_z.$$

Therefore, no multiplications or additions are needed to determine the sign of this dot product. It is sufficient to check the sign of the z-component of the normal vector **n**.

For a parallel projection to the x/y-plane, back-face culling means that all polygons whose normal vectors have a negative z-component can be removed before further visibility considerations are carried out.

7.2.3 Spatial partitioning

Back-face culling reduces the computational effort for visibility considerations. *Spatial partitioning* also tries to remove the computational effort further. The clipping volume is subdivided into disjoint regions, for instance into eight boxes of equal size. The objects are assigned to the corresponding box or boxes with which they have a nonempty intersection. An object that crosses the boundary of a box will be assigned to more than one box.

In case of an object-precision algorithm, only the objects within the same box have to be checked for visibility considerations for visible surface determination. If one box is behind another, all its objects will be projected before the objects from the box in front. In this way, objects from the front box will automatically overwrite objects from the box behind it that are hidden from view. For a partition of the clipping volume into k boxes, the n objects in the scene will be equally distributed over the boxes in the ideal case. This means that the computational complexity is reduced from n^2 to $k \cdot \left(\frac{n}{k}\right)^2 = \frac{n^2}{k}$. This is, however, only true if no object crosses the border of a box and the objects are equally distributed over the boxes, i.e., each box contains $\frac{n}{k}$ objects. This assumption will definitely not be valid anymore when the partition contains a larger number of boxes and the boxes become too small.

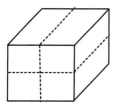 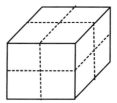

Figure 7.4 Partitioning of the clipping volume for image-precision (left) and object-precision algorithms (right)

For image-precision algorithms it is better to partition the clipping volume into boxes as is shown on the left of figure 7.4. The clipping rectangle on the projection plane is partitioned into smaller rectangles and each smaller rectangle induces a box in the clipping volume. For each pixel only those objects have to be considered that lie within the box that is associated with the smaller rectangle in which the pixel lies.

Recursive subdivision algorithms divide the clipping region farther and further until a region is small enough to decide which object is visible in it. An upper bound for the maximum depth of such recursive partitioning is given by the resolution of the image. *Area subdivision algorithms* partition the clipping rectangle on the projection plane recursively so that they are image-precision methods. *Octree algorithms* partition the clipping volume and are therefore object-precision methods.

7.3 Image-precision techniques

Three image-precision techniques will be introduced in this section. The most popular and important one is the z-buffer or depth-buffer algorithm.

7.3.1 The z-buffer algorithm

The *z-buffer* or *depth-buffer algorithm* is the most often applied technique for determining visible surfaces. The z-buffer algorithm is an image-precision technique which is based on the following principle. It uses a frame buffer for the colours of the pixels in the image and a z- or depth-buffer in which a z-value is entered for each pixel. The z-buffer is initialised with the distance or z-coordinate of the back clipping plane. The frame buffer is initialised with the background image or background colour. The objects are projected in an arbitrary order and the projections are stored in the frame buffer. If all objects were entered in this way into the frame buffer, then objects projected later would overwrite earlier projected objects when their projections overlap. Since the order of projection is not fixed, this could lead to the wrong result that objects farther away from the viewer hide objects from view that are closer to the viewer. Therefore, before a pixel of a projected object is entered into the frame buffer, its z-value, i.e., its distance to the projection plane, is compared to the value entered for the corresponding pixel so far in the z-buffer. If the value in the z-buffer is larger than the z-value of the point of the object that led to the projected pixel, then the new pixel colour is entered into the frame buffer and the z-value is also updated. If, on the other hand, the z-value corresponding to the projected pixel is larger than the value in the z-buffer, then neither the frame buffer nor the z-buffer is changed.

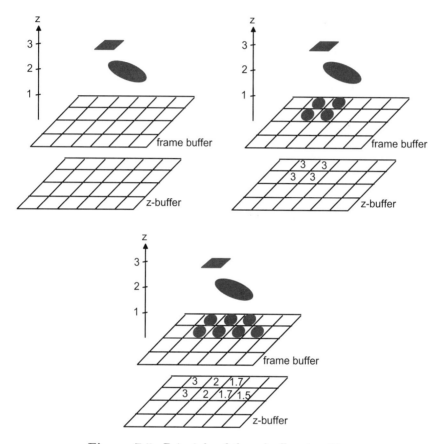

Figure 7.5 Principle of the z-buffer algorithm

The principle of the z-buffer algorithm is illustrated in figure 7.5. There are two objects to be projected, a rectangle and an ellipse. The viewer looks at the scene from below the projection plane or the frame buffer. The frame buffer is initialised with the background colour—in this case white—and the z-buffer is initialised with the z-value of the back clipping plane. The values are not shown here. They could be $-\infty$ here, i.e., the back clipping plane could be moved to infinity. The rectangle is projected first. Since the rectangle lies within the clipping volume and its z-values are smaller than the z-values of the back clipping plane, the rectangle is projected to the frame buffer and its z-

coordinates are entered in the z-buffer. When the ellipse is projected afterwards, it turns out that its z-values are even smaller where the ellipse and the rectangle overlap. Therefore, the ellipse overwrites the projection of the rectangle partly in the frame buffer and its z-values are also entered in the z-buffer.

Had the ellipse been projected before the rectangle, then the following would happen. When the rectangle is projected, there are already values in the z-buffer that are smaller than the z-values of the rectangle. Therefore, the rectangle will not be projected into the frame buffer where already smaller z-values coming from the ellipse are entered in the z-buffer. So even in this order of projection, the final result would be the same as in figure 7.5.

It should be noted that the z-values of an object are usually not constant. It must be decided individually for each pixel whether it should be entered into the frame and the z-buffer or not.

The z-buffer algorithm can be applied in a very efficient manner for animated scenes with moving objects when the viewer does not change his position. All objects that do not move form the background of the image. They need to be entered into the frame and the z-buffer just once. So each time a new image for the animated scene is generated, the frame and z-buffer are initialised with the static part of the scene. Only the moving objects have to be re-entered into the buffers. If a moving object is hidden from another static object in the scene, then this will be noticed since the z-value has been initialised with a corresponding lower value. The moving object will not be entered into the buffers in this case.

In order to enter polygons into the frame and the z-buffer, a scan line technique is applied to each pixel row in the projection plane. Let the plane induced by the polygon be given by the equation

$$A \cdot x + B \cdot y + C \cdot z + D \ = \ 0. \tag{7.2}$$

The z-value along a scan line can be computed in the following form.

$$z_{\mathrm{new}} \ = \ z_{\mathrm{old}} + \Delta z$$

since the z-values of a plane change in a linear fashion when they are sampled along a line. Let z_{old} be the z-coordinate of the projected polygon at pixel (x, y). The new z-coordinate z_{new} for the following pixel $(x + 1, y)$ must satisfy equation (7.2) for the plane as well as the previous point (x, y, z_{old}) since both points lie in the plane.

$$
\begin{aligned}
0 &= A \cdot (x+1) + B \cdot y + C \cdot z_{\text{new}} + D \\
&= A \cdot (x+1) + B \cdot y + C \cdot (z_{\text{old}} + \Delta z) + D \\
&= \underbrace{A \cdot x + B \cdot y + C \cdot z_{\text{old}} + D}_{=\,0} + A + C \cdot \Delta z \\
&= A + C \cdot \Delta z.
\end{aligned}
$$

Therefore, the change of the z-coordinate along the scan line is

$$
\Delta z = -\frac{A}{C}.
$$

7.3.2 Scan line technique for edges

For the z-buffer algorithm, the projection of single polygons can be carried out on the basis of a scan line technique. As an alternative it is also possible to project the edges of all polygons and to apply a scan line technique to determine which polygons should be drawn.

The coordinate axes of the rectangular clipping area on the projection plane are denoted by u and v. This scan line technique is based on three tables. The edge table contains all nonhorizontal edges and has the following structure.

$v_{\min}$	$u(v_{\min})$	$v_{\max}$	Δu	Polygon numbers

$v_{\min}$ is the smallest v-value of the projected edge, $u(v_{\min})$ the u-value corresponding to $v_{\min}$. $v_{\max}$ denotes the largest v-value of the edge. Δu is the slope of the projected edge. The column polygon numbers contains the list of all polygons to which the edge belongs. The edges are sorted in increasing order with respect to their $v_{\min}$-values. For identical $v_{\min}$-values, edges with a smaller $u(v_{\min})$-value come first.

The second table of this scan line technique is the polygon table, containing information about the polygons in the following form.

Polygon No.	A	B	C	D	Colour	In-flag

The polygon number serves as a key or identifier for the polygon. The coefficients A, B, C, D define the plane corresponding to the polygon in terms of the equation

$$
Ax + By + Cz + D = 0.
$$

The column colour contains the colour or information about the shading of the polygon. If only a single value can be entered there, the possibilities for realistic shading are very restricted. In-flag indicates whether the actual position on the scan line lies within or outside the polygon.

The last table contains the list of all active edges. Active edges are those edges which intersect the actual scan line. These edges are sorted by the u-components of the intersection points in increasing order. The number of rows of the table of active edges can be different for each scan line. The number of rows and the entries of the other two tables remain constant except for the entries in the column with the In-flag.

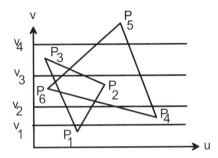

Figure 7.6   Determining the active edges for the scan lines v_1, v_2, v_3, v_4

For the configuration shown in figure 7.6, the following edges are active for the scan lines v_1, v_2, v_3, v_4, respectively.

$$v_1 : P_3P_1, \; P_1P_2$$
$$v_2 : P_3P_1, \; P_1P_2, \; P_6P_4, \; P_5P_4$$
$$v_3 : P_3P_1, \; P_6P_5, \; P_3P_2, \; P_5P_4$$
$$v_4 : P_6P_5, \; P_5P_4.$$

When a single scan line is considered, the active edges are determined first and all In-flags are set to zero. When the line is scanned, each time an edge is crossed, the In-flags of the associated polygons have to be inverted from 0 to 1 or from 1 back to 0 since crossing an edge means that one enters or leaves the polygon. At each pixel, the visible polygon among those with In-flag=1 has to be determined. For this purpose, the z-value of each polygon with In-flag=1 is computed based on the equation for the plane. The polygon with the smallest z-value is the one that is visible at the considered pixel. The corresponding z-value of the polygon can be determined in an incremental fashion in the same way as in the z-buffer algorithm.

7.3.3 Ray casting

Ray casting is another image-precision technique for visible surface determination. For each pixel in the clipping rectangles of the projection plane a ray parallel to the direction of projection is cast. The ray should start at the front clipping plane and end at the back clipping plane. The first object that the ray meets determines the colour of the pixel. Ray casting is suitable for parallel projection as well as perspective projection without an additional transformation that turns the perspective projection into a parallel projection. The rays are parallel to the direction of projection for a parallel projection and for a perspective projection the rays are cast along the connections between the centre of projection and the pixels. Figure 7.7 illustrates the ray casting technique. Pixels correspond to the centres of the centres of the squares of the projection plane in the figure.

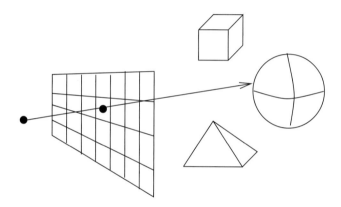

Figure 7.7   Ray casting

For a perspective projection with its centre of projection in the point (x_0, y_0, z_0), the ray to the pixel with the coordinates (x_1, y_1, z_1) can be parameterised by

$$x = x_0 + t \cdot \Delta x, \qquad y = y_0 + t \cdot \Delta y, \qquad z = z_0 + t \cdot \Delta z \qquad (7.3)$$

where

$$\Delta x = x_1 - x_0, \qquad \Delta y = y_1 - y_0, \qquad \Delta z = z_1 - z_0.$$

For values $t < 0$ the ray is behind the centre of projection, for $t \in [0, 1]$ between the centre of projection and the projection plane, and for $t > 1$ it is behind the projection plane.

In order to determine whether the ray intersects a polygon and, if yes, where it meets the polygon, the intersection point of the ray with the plane $Ax + By + Cz + D = 0$ induced by the polygon is calculated. Afterwards a test is carried out, yielding whether the intersection point lies within the polygon.

Inserting the ray (7.3) into the equation for the plane, one obtains for t the solution

$$t = -\frac{Ax_0 + By_0 + Cz_0 + D}{A\Delta x + B\Delta y + C\Delta z}.$$

Given that the equation $Ax + By + Cz + D = 0$ describes a plane, i.e., at least one of the coefficients A, B, C is nonzero, the denominator can become zero if and only if the ray is parallel to the plane. In this case, the plane is not important for the projection to the considered pixel.

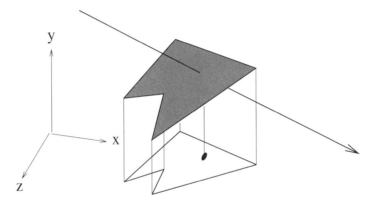

Figure 7.8 Projection of a polygon to decide whether a point lies within the polygon

In order to determine whether the intersection point lies within the polygon, the polygon is projected together with the intersection point to one of the planes defined by the axes of the coordinate system. This means that one of the coordinates is set to zero. To avoid problems with roundoff errors, the plane that should be chosen for projection should be the one that is most parallel to the plane of the polygon. This means that the normal vector to the polygon plane and the normal vector to the projection plane should be as parallel as possible. The angle between these two normal vectors should be close to $0°$ or $180°$. In other words, their dot product should either be close to one or -1 given that the normal vectors are normalised. The dot product of the normal vector (A, B, C) with a normal vector to a plane defined by two coordinate axes is simply the component of (A, B, C) that will be set to zero for the projection. Therefore, the projection plane is chosen orthogonal to the component which has the greatest absolute value in (A, B, C). After the projection, the odd parity rule is applied to decide whether the intersection point lies within the projected polygon as is illustrated in figure 7.8.

Coherence should be taken into account for ray casting in order to reduce the computational complexity. Coherence refers to exploiting considerations like the following ones.

– Neighbouring pixels usually obtain their colour from the same polygon.

– Once a ray intersects a polygon, it is not necessary to calculate intersections with polygons which are farther away.

Without exploiting coherence, $1000 \cdot 1000 \cdot 100$, i.e., 100 million intersection tests would have to be carried out for a resolution of 1000×1000 pixels and 100 objects in the scene. Coherence can, for instance, reduce the computation time in the following way. When the polygon has been computed which determines the colour of a pixel, the intersection test for the neighbouring pixels should be applied first to this polygon. When the new ray intersects this polygon as well—and the chance is quite high—no intersection tests with polygons farther away are required anymore.

Ray casting can lead to aliasing effects when the back clipping plane is very far away. The background is composed of more or less randomly intersected objects in the far distance so that neighbouring pixels representing the background might not have the same or a similar colour. To avoid this effect, *supersampling* can be applied. For one pixel more than one ray is cast as shown in figure 7.9. The colour of the pixel is calculated as the mean or weighted mean of the corresponding colours obtained from the objects that the rays meet.

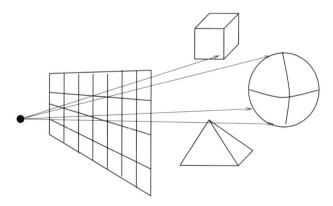

Figure 7.9 Supersampling

The computational effort will increase only slightly in this case since most of the additional rays can be used for more than one pixel. In figure 7.9 where four rays are cast for each pixel in an $m \times n$ pixel matrix, only $(m+1) \cdot (n+1)$ different rays instead of $m \cdot n$ without supersampling have to be computed. The additional effort is

$$(m+1) \cdot (n+1) - m \cdot n \; = \; m + n + 1.$$

For a resolution of 1000×1000 pixels the computational costs increase by approximately 0.2%.

7.4 Priority algorithms

The order in which objects are projected is not important at all for the z-buffer algorithm. By taking the information in the z-buffer into account, it can be guaranteed that objects which are farther away from the viewer will not overwrite closer objects, even if a distant object is projected later. The aim of *priority algorithms* is to find a suitable order in which objects can be projected so that no conflicts occur during the projection. This means that the distant objects have to be projected first and the closer objects later on. This would also guarantee that the projection of a distant object cannot overwrite a closer object. If a suitable order of projection can be found for the objects, there is no need for a z-buffer. The order of projection is also independent of the resolution so that priority algorithms belong to the class of object-precision techniques.

In the following, two objects, i.e., two polygons P and Q, are considered. The aim is to find out whether the order in which the polygons are projected is important. In other words, does one polygon hide at least parts of the other from view? It should be made sure that in such case the polygon closer to the viewer is projected after the other one. If there is no overlap of the z-coordinates of the two polygons, then the one with larger z-coordinates, the more distant one, is projected first. If the z-coordinates overlap, further tests have to be carried out.

In order to check whether the polygons overlap in the z-coordinate, it is sufficient to compare the z-components of their vertices. If the z-components of all vertices of one polygon are smaller than the z-components of all vertices of the other polygon, then there is no overlap in the z-coordinates.

If the x- or the y-coordinates of the polygons P and Q do not overlap, then the order of projection is not important for these polygons since their projections will be next to each other, as can be seen in figure 7.10 and neither of the two can hide the other from view. The test whether the x- or the y-coordinates do not overlap, can be carried out in the same way as for the z-coordinate.

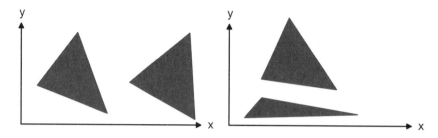

Figure 7.10 No overlap in the x-coordinate (left) or the y-coordinate (right)

If there are overlaps in all coordinates, the next test to be carried out is whether one polygon lies completely in front of or behind the plane that is induced by the other polygon. These two possibilities are illustrated in figure 7.11. In the left-hand side of the figure, the polygon should be projected first which lies behind the plane induced by the other. In the right-hand side of the figure, the polygon that lies completely in front of the plane induced by the other should be projected later.

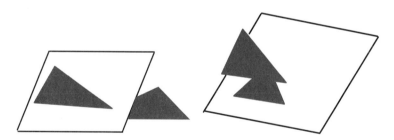

Figure 7.11 Does one polygon lie completely in front or behind the plane induced by the other?

These two cases can be checked based on correctly oriented normal vectors. As an example, only the case in the right-hand side of figure 7.11 will be explained in detail. The normal vector to the plane induced by the polygon is the same normal vector as for the polygon itself. The normal vector must point to the viewer and not away from him. Otherwise, the polygon had been removed before by back-face culling. An arbitrary point in the plane is chosen and the vectors connecting the point in the plane with the vertices of the other polygon are considered. If the one polygon lies completely in front of the other polygon, then all these vectors must have an angle of less than 90° with the normal vector to the plane. This is the case if and only if the dot product of each of these vectors with the normal vector to the plane is positive. Figure 7.12 illustrates this fact. The angles between the normal vector to the plane and the vectors to the vertices of the other polygon are all smaller than 90°.

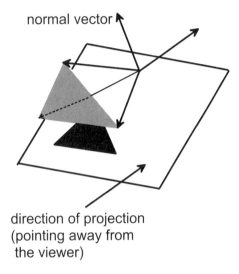

Figure 7.12 Determining whether a polygon lies completely in front of the plane induced by the other polygon

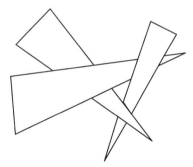

Figure 7.13 A case where no correct order exists in which the polygons should be projected

Unfortunately, these criteria are not always sufficient to determine a suitable order of projection for the objects. There are cases as in figure 7.13 where it is impossible to achieve a correct image by any order of projection. If none of the above criteria is applicable, it is necessary for the priority algorithm to further subdivide the polygons participating in the conflict in order to find a correct order of projection. Even if such cases will not happen very often, it is not easy to determine a suitable subdivision of the corresponding polygons.

7.5 Exercises

Exercise 7.1

Change the clipping volume in the program `TesselationResolution.java` in such a way that only the two spheres in the middle are visible and that their front parts are also cut off.

Exercise 7.2

If one assumes in figure 7.8 that the polygons are triangles, it is necessary to project the polygons and apply the odd parity rule afterwards in order to determine whether the intersection point lies within the triangle. Describe an algorithm for triangles without using projections.

Exercise 7.3

Describe an algorithm for testing whether the case in the left-hand side of figure 7.11 applies. The solution can be based on similar considerations as in figure 7.12.

Illumination and shading

Projections, required for displaying a three-dimensional scene on a two-dimensional plane or screen, were discussed in section 5.8. A projection is a special type of mapping from the three-dimensional space to a plane. In this sense, a projection describes only where a point or an object has to be drawn on the projection plane. The determination of visible surfaces in chapter 7 also focussed only on the question which objects should be drawn or projected and which ones are hidden from view by others. The information where an object should be drawn on the projection plane, i.e., which pixels are covered by the object, is not at all sufficient for a realistic representation of a three-dimensional scene. Figure 8.1 shows the projections of a grey sphere and a grey cube, both in two variants. The first variant simply assigns the colour of the sphere and the cube directly to the pixels that are occupied by the corresponding object. This leads to geometric shapes with a homogeneous colour losing almost the

Figure 8.1 Objects with and without illumination and shading effects

complete information about the three-dimensional structure. The projection of the sphere is a grey circle, the cube becomes a grey hexagon.

Taking illumination and light reflections into account leads to different light effects on the surfaces of the three-dimensional objects and to a non-homogeneous shading of their projections. In this way, even the flat images appear vivid and provide a three-dimensional impression as can be seen in figure 8.1 where the effects of illumination were taken into account for the second sphere and the second cube. *Shading* refers to rendering an object's surface with illumination and light reflection effects. This chapter introduces the necessary background and techniques for illumination and shading in computer graphics.

From a theoretical point of view, the computations for shading described in the following sections would have to be carried out for each wavelength of the light individually. Since this is impossible, the computations will always be restricted to the three primary colours red, green and blue in order to determine the RGB-values for the representation.

8.1 Light sources

In addition to information about the objects and the viewer, the description of a three-dimensional scene must also include information about illumination of the scene. A single light source or a number of light sources can contribute to the illumination of a scene. In most cases, light sources will provide white or "grey" light, i.e., white light which does not have the full intensity. But also coloured light coming from a traffic light or the more red or orange light from the sun at dawn can occur in a scene. The colour and intensity of a light source are defined by suitable RGB-values.

The simplest form of light is *ambient light*. Ambient light does not come from a specific light source and has no direction. It represents the light that is more or less everywhere in the scene, originating from multiple reflections of light at various surfaces. In a room with a lamp on a table, it will not be completely dark under the table although the lamp cannot shed its light directly under the table. The light is reflected by the surface of the table, the walls, the ceiling and the floor. Of course, the light under the table will have a lower intensity, but it will still be there with approximately the same intensity everywhere, not coming from a specific direction. Ambient light is a simplification of the computations for illumination. From the theoretical point of view, there is nothing like ambient light. The correct way to take ambient light into account would be to trace the multiple reflections of the light completely. This would increase the computational effort enormously, so that this approach is not (yet) well suited for real-time computer graphics. An approach to compute the ambient light correctly is introduced in section 8.10.

For ambient light it is sufficient to specify its colour. A *directional light source* has in addition to a colour also a direction. The light rays from a directional light source are parallel. Directional light is used to model light coming from a source in almost infinite distance, for instance sunlight.

A lamp is modelled as a *point light source*. A point light source has a position and the light rays spread in all directions from this position. The intensity of the light decreases with increasing distance. This effect is called *attenuation*. The following argument shows that the intensity of the light decreases quadratically with the distance to the light source. If a point light source is in the centre of a sphere with radius r, then the full energy of the light will be distributed equally on the inner part of the surface of the sphere. If the sphere is replaced by a bigger sphere with radius R, then the full energy of the light will not change. But it is now distributed to a larger surface. The ratio of the surfaces of the two spheres is

$$\frac{4\pi r^2}{4\pi R^2} = \left(\frac{r}{R}\right)^2.$$

For a ratio of $r/R = 1/2$ each point on the inner part of the surface of the larger sphere receives therefore only one quarter of the energy of a point on the inner part of the surface of the smaller sphere.

The theoretical model for attenuation would then be to multiply the intensity of the light from a point light source by the factor $1/d^2$ when it hits the surface of an object at distance d to the light source. The intensity of the light source will decrease very quickly with the distance so that the intensity differences for larger distances will be almost unnoticeable. However, for objects very close to the light source, drastic differences will occur. The intensity could be arbitrarily large and would tend to infinity when a surface is directly in front of the light source. In order to avoid these effects, the decrease of the intensity caused by attenuation is modelled by a general quadratic polynomial in the denominator in the form

$$f_{\text{att}} = \min\left\{\frac{1}{c_1 + c_2 d + c_3 d^2}, 1\right\} \tag{8.1}$$

where the constants c_1, c_2, c_3 can be chosen individually for each point light source. d is the distance of an object to the light source. This formula guarantees that the intensity can never exceed the value 1. The constants can also be adjusted so that a more moderate attenuation effect occurs than with the simple form $1/d^2$. The coefficient c_2 for the linear term can also be used to model *atmospheric attenuation*. The quadratic decrease of the light intensity comes from the distribution of the energy of the light onto a larger surface for an increasing distance. In addition, part of the light is absorbed by dust particles in the air causing atmospheric opacity. This leads obviously to a linear decrease of the intensity with increasing distance. The number of dust particles a light ray can hit grows proportionally with distance it covers.

Another common light source are *spotlights*. In contrast to a point light source, a spotlight has a direction in which it spreads its light in the form of a cone. A spotlight is characterised by the colour of its light, its location, the direction in which it shines and an angular limit that describes the extension of the cone of light. Attenuation is computed for a spotlight on the basis of equation (8.1) in the same way as for point light sources. The quadratic decrease of the intensity with increasing distance can also be deduced from figure 8.2 where it can be seen that the full energy of the light from the spotlight is distributed over a circle whose radius growth is linear with the distance. Therefore, the surface grows quadratically with the distance.

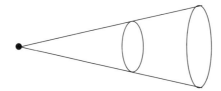

Figure 8.2 Cone of light from a spotlight

For a more realistic model of a spotlight, it should be taken into account that the intensity of the light is smaller close to the boundary of the cone of light than at the centre. In the *Warn model* [49], a parameter p is used to control how fast the intensity of the light decreases from the centre of the cone to its boundary. Consider a point on a surface that is illuminated by a spotlight. Let $\mathbf{l}$ be a vector that points from the point where the spotlight is located to a point on the surface of the illuminated object, and let $\mathbf{l}_S$ be the axis of the cone pointing in the direction of the light. Then the intensity of light at the point on the surface coming from the spotlight is computed in the Warn model by

$$I = I_S \cdot f_{\mathrm{att}} \cdot (\cos\gamma)^p = I_S \cdot f_{\mathrm{att}} \cdot \left(-\mathbf{l}_S^\top \cdot \mathbf{l}\right)^p. \qquad (8.2)$$

I_S is the intensity of the spotlight, f_{att} is the distance-dependent factor for attenuation as in equation (8.1) and γ is the angle between $\mathbf{l}$ and $\mathbf{l}_S$. The value p controls how much the spotlight is focussed. For $p = 0$ the spotlight behaves in the same way as a point light source. The larger p is chosen, the more the light concentrated around the axis of the cone and the smaller is the intensity at the boundary of the cone. The cosine in equation (8.2) can be computed as the dot product of the vectors l and l_S if they are normalised, i.e., if both of them have the length one. Figure 8.3 illustrates the situation in the Warn model.

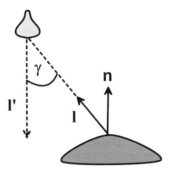

Figure 8.3 The Warn model for a spotlight

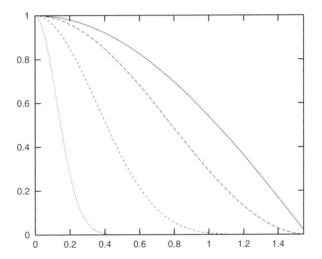

Figure 8.4 The functions $(\cos \gamma)^{64}$, $(\cos \gamma)^8$, $(\cos \gamma)^2$, $\cos \gamma$

Figure 8.4 shows the effect of the parameter p. The function $(\cos \gamma)^p$ is drawn for the values $p = 1, 2, 8, 64$. For $p = 1$, the rightmost curve, the intensity drops slowly to zero with increasing angle γ. For higher values of p, even small deviations from the axis of the cone, i.e., small angles γ, lead already to very small intensities, since $(\cos \gamma)^p$ is almost zero.

It should be noted that the intensity I_S in equation (8.2) of the Warn model can have different values for each colour, or at least for each of the primary colours red, green and blue.

8.2 Light sources in Java 3D

Java 3D provides classes for all light sources which have been introduced in the previous section. As mentioned in section 5.5, most of the programs here will have a separate branch in the scenegraph for the lights. In the same way as for objects in the scene, an instance bgLight of the class BranchGroup has to be created first. All lights will be entered into this branch group with the method addChild. The branch group bgLight itself will be included in the scene by adding it to the SimpleUniverse with the method addBranchGraph.

For each light source, a colour must be defined by three float-values between zero and one for the RGB-intensities.

```
Color3f lightColour = new Color3f(r,g,b);
```

Each light source can have a different colour. In the same way as for interpolators in section 5.7, a bounding region must be assigned to each light source. For this purpose, one can generate an instance bs of the class BoundingSphere as was described on page 137.

Ambient light is then created with the class AmbientLight in the following way.

```
AmbientLight ambLight = new AmbientLight(lightColour);
ambLight.setInfluencingBounds(bs);
bgLight.addChild(ambLight);
```

The colour of ambient light will usually be a grey one, i.e., the intensities for red, green and blue will be chosen equally, but definitely lower than one. The methods setInfluencingBounds and addChild have to be applied in the same way for all other light sources to specify the bounding region of the light source and to add it to BranchGroup bgLight.

A directional light source is generated with the class DirectionalLight. In addition to the colour, the direction of the parallel light rays must be specified in the form of a vector $(x, y, z)^\top$ consisting of three float-values. An instance of the class Vector3f is used for this purpose.

```
Vector3f lightDir  = new Vector3f(x,y,z);
DirectionalLight dirLight =
                new DirectionalLight(lightColour,lightDir);
```

For a point light source, a colour must be defined and two instances `location` and `attenuation` of the class `Point3f` that are determined by three float-values in the same way as `Vector3f`.

```
PointLight pLight =
          new PointLight(lightColour,location,attenuation);
```

The instance `location` determines the position of the point light source. The three components of `attenuation` specify the coefficients in equation (8.1) for attenuation.

The class `SpotLight` models spotlights.

```
SpotLight spLight =
          new SpotLight(lightColour,location,attenuation
                        direction,angle,concentration);
```

The same parameters as for point light sources are required, i.e., colour, position and attenuation. In addition, the direction in which the spotlight shines is defined by the `Vector3f direction`. The `float`-value `angle` defines the angular limit corresponding to half of the opening angle of the cone of light. The `float`-value `concentration` between 0 and 120 determines how much the spotlight is focussed to the centre axis. For the value zero, the light will have the same intensity at the axis of the cone and at the boundary. The intensity drops abruptly to zero at the boundary of the cone. The value 120 defines a spotlight whose light is strongly focussed on the axis of the cone and very weak at the boundary.

The `BranchGroup` for the light can contain an arbitrary number of light sources of the same or of different type. If the light sources are directly assigned to the `BranchGroup`, they remain static where they were positioned. Moving light sources can be implemented in the `BranchGroup bgLight` in the same way as moving objects in the `BranchGroup theScene` as was described in section 5.7. Instead of assigning a light source directly to the `BranchGroup bgLight`, a transformation group with an interpolator can be defined to which the light source is added. Then this transformation group is assigned to the `BranchGroup bgLight`. It is also possible to include light sources in the `BranchGroup theScene` or in a transformation group within `theScene` when a light source is directly connected with an object. In this way, the object and the light source will carry out the same movement.

As an example, the class `MovingLight.java` implements a moving directional light source. Other example programs where different light sources are used will be described in section 8.4.

Light sources themselves are invisible. They only send out light which is reflected by objects in the scene. For instance, if a scene contains a point light source, the viewer cannot see it, even if he look in the direction of the light source. When there are no objects in the scene, the scene will remain completely dark. If a light source should be visible, it is necessary to include a corresponding object in the scene, for instance a light bulb or a torch. It is also necessary to assign the corresponding bright colour of the light to the object or the part of the object that is intended to emit the light. How surfaces or objects can be defined which emit light themselves will be explained in section 8.4.

8.3 Reflection

In order to achieve illumination and shading effects as in figure 8.1 on page 201, it necessary to specify for all surfaces of objects in the scene how they reflect light. The illumination model that is constructed here is not correct from the physical point of view. Ambient light as it is modelled in scenes so far does not exist in reality per se, nor is it constant everywhere. Ambient light is a simplification of real illumination for the purpose of computational simplicity and efficiency. For the same reasons, the light which is reflected by objects is not taken into account for further illumination calculations. Objects in a virtual scene only reflect light from defined light sources. They do not reflect the light which is shed on them by reflections of other objects. Ambient light replaces these complex reflections. Section 8.10 will introduce a far more complex model where the light reflections between objects are explicitly calculated.

This section explains light reflection on a surface in detail. A point on a surface of an object is considered and for this point the colour is computed which should be assigned to it taking all light sources in the scene into account as well as the reflection properties of the surface. The single effects introduced in the following usually occur in combination. For each effect, an RGB-value is determined, modelling the reflection of the surface in the corresponding point when only this effect is considered. In order to determine the final colour of the point on the surface, all these effects have to be added. It should be taken into account that the overall intensity for each of the three primary colours red, green and blue is limited by one.

Objects might emit light themselves. It should be emphasised again that the emitted light is only taken into account for this object so that it will occur brighter for the viewer. The emitted light will not illuminate other objects in this simple model. If an object emits light, then this emission contributes a corresponding intensity to each of the primary colours red, green and blue. By this light emitting effect alone, a pixel on the surface of the object i will obtain an intensity of

$$I = k_i.$$

This intensity must be specified separately for red, green and blue. The object might not emit white light and have therefore different intensities for the three primary colours. The correct specification would be

$$I^{(\text{red})} = k_i^{(\text{red})} \qquad I^{(\text{green})} = k_i^{(\text{green})} \qquad I^{(\text{blue})} = k_i^{(\text{blue})}.$$

Since the structure of the illumination equation for all effects will always be the same for the three primary colours, for each effect only one equation for the computation of the intensity will be provided. The corresponding computations have to be carried for the three primary colours and might also lead to different intensities as in the above case when the object does not emit white light, but light of a different colour.

An object emitting light is not considered as a light source in the scene. It only shines for the viewer. Objects emitting light should be combined with a corresponding light source. A light bulb would be modelled by a point light source and a geometric object emitting light. The point light source illuminates the scene, but remains invisible itself. The object does not illuminate other objects, but it shines for the viewer and makes the point light source visible. The intensity on the surface generated by emitting light is constant and does not lead to any 3D effects. When there are no light sources in the scene and only objects emitting light, this will result in the same homogeneous flat projections as in figure 8.1 on page 201 for the leftmost object and the second object from the right.

All following illumination effects result from reflections of light coming from light sources in the scene. The illumination equation is always of the form

$$I = I_{\text{light source}} \cdot f_{\text{pixel}}.$$

$I_{\text{light source}}$ is the intensity of the light coming from the light source. f_{pixel} is a factor that depends on various parameters. For instance, the colour of the surface, its shininess, the distance to the light source in case attenuation must be taken into account, and the angle at which the light hits the surface in the considered pixel.

For ambient light, the illumination equation is

$$I = k_a \cdot I_S$$

where I_S is the intensity of ambient light. k_a is the reflection coefficient of the surface for ambient light. In the same way as for objects emitting light, ambient light alone will not lead to any 3D effects. The projections of objects occur flat and have a homogeneous colour. 3D effects result only from light to which a direction can be assigned, in contrast to ambient light coming from all directions or no specific direction. Only if light has a direction, can a nonhomogeneous *shading* occur on an object's surface. On dull surfaces, a light ray is reflected into all directions equally. How much light is reflected depends on the intensity of the light, the reflection coefficient of the surface and the angle at which the light hits the surface. Figure 8.5 illustrates the influence of the angle at which the light hits the surface. The same energy of light, i.e., the full energy of the light source, reaches the circle, no matter whether it stands perpendicular to the axis of the cone of light or whether it is tilted. But the tilted area is larger than the perpendicular one. This means that the tilted area receives less light per point or pixel than the perpendicular one. The more the area is tilted, the less energy of light will be available per point.

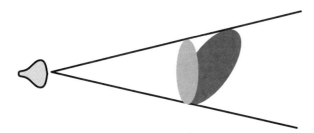

Figure 8.5 Light intensity depending on the angle of the light

This effect is also responsible for the fact that it is warmer at the equator, where the sun's rays hit the surface of the earth perpendicular, at least in spring and autumn, and colder at the north and south pole. The seasons also result from this effect since the axis of the earth is tilted differently to the sun over the year. During the time between March and September the northern hemisphere is tilted to the sun, during the other half of the year the southern hemisphere is tilted to the sun.

This effect of light reflection for purely dull surfaces can be computed according to Lambert's cosine law by the illumination equation

$$I = I_L \cdot k_d \cdot \cos\theta \qquad (8.3)$$

where I_L is the intensity of the light hitting the surface, $0 \leq k_d \leq 1$ is the reflection coefficient of the surface or the material, and θ is the angle between the normal vector **n** to the surface in the considered point and the vector **l** pointing in the direction where the light comes from. Figure 8.6 illustrates this situation. This kind of reflection on dull surfaces is called *diffuse reflection*.

The illumination equation (8.3) for diffuse reflection is only valid for angles θ between $0°$ and $90°$. Otherwise, the light ray hits the surface from the backside

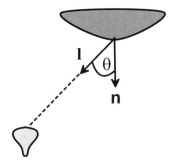

Figure 8.6 Diffuse reflection

so that no reflection occurs. In the case of directional light coming from a light source in infinite distance, the variable I_L in equation (8.3) has the same value everywhere. In the case of a point light source, I_L is the intensity of the light source multiplied by the attenuation factor in equation (8.1), which depends on the distance of the point on the surface to the light source. For a spot light in addition to attenuation, the factor in equation (8.2) modelling how much the spotlight is focussed must be taken into account.

In principle, the illumination equations have to be evaluated for each pixel. Section 8.5 will introduce approximation techniques by which the illumination equations are only evaluated explicitly for certain pixels, usually the vertices of the surface polygons, and for the remaining pixels the value resulting from their illumination equation is estimated by simpler interpolation schemes. Nevertheless, even if the illumination equations are only computed for the vertices of the surface polygons in the scene, this might still be a large number. Therefore, the computationally expensive cosine in equation (8.3) is computed based on the dot product of the normal vector $\mathbf{n}$ to the surface and the vector $\mathbf{l}$ pointing in the direction where the light comes from. Both vectors must be normalised for this purpose. The same principle has already been applied in the context of equation (8.2) on page 204. In this way, equation (8.3) becomes

$$I \;=\; I_L \cdot k_d \cdot (\mathbf{n}^{\top} \cdot \mathbf{l}).$$

In the case of a directional light source and a plane surface, the vectors $\mathbf{l}$ and $\mathbf{n}$ remain constant on the surface. Then the surface will be shaded homogeneously with the same colour. One can see this effect in figure 8.1 on page 201 for the cube on the right which was illuminated by directional light. The faces of the cube are shaded differently since the light hits them in different angles. But the shading on a single face is constant.

Diffuse reflection on dull surfaces reflects the light into all directions. *Specular reflection* occurs on shiny surfaces. Such shiny surfaces reflect at least a portion of the light in a similar way as a mirror. In contrast to diffuse reflection, ideal specular reflection takes place only in one direction. The vector pointing to the source of light is mirrored about the normal vector of the surface. The vector in the direction of the light and the vector pointing in the direction of the reflection have the same angle with the normal vector to the surface. The difference between diffuse and specular reflection is illustrated in figure 8.7.

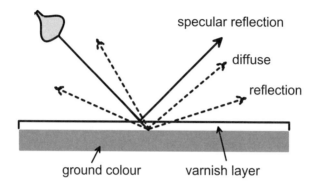

Figure 8.7 Diffuse and specular reflection

Shiny surfaces very often have a very thin transparent layer, for instance varnish. When light hits the surface, part of the light penetrates the varnish layer and is reflected on the dull surface of the object. This part of the light is subject to diffuse reflection and the colour of the reflected light depends strongly on the ground colour of the dull surface. Another part of the light is directly reflected on the transparent layer by specular reflection. Therefore, specular reflection does usually not change the colour of the light. This effect can also be seen in figure 8.1 on page 201. The second object from the left has a shiny white spot on its surface although the colour of the object itself is grey. This white spot is due to specular reflection. Shading caused by diffuse reflection depends only on the angle at which the light hits the surface and on the reflection coefficient. The position of the viewer is of no importance for calculating effects coming from diffuse reflection. Whether or where the viewer can see specular reflection depends on his position. In the case of a plane surface which is illuminated by a single light source, there will be exactly one point on the surface where the viewer can see ideal specular reflection. This is, however, only true for perfect mirrors. For surfaces that are more or less shiny, the light vector is reflected roughly in the direction around the ideal specular reflection. In this way a circular brighter area occurs on the surface instead of only a single light point in which ideal specular reflection takes place. Before models for nonideal specular reflection can be introduced, it is necessary to find a computation scheme for the direction of ideal specular reflection.

In figure 8.8, l denotes the vector pointing in the direction from which the light hits the surface in the considered point. n is the normal vector to the surface in this point. The vector v points in the direction of the viewer, i.e., in the direction of projection. r denotes the direction of ideal specular reflection. The normal vector n has the same angle with the vectors l and r.

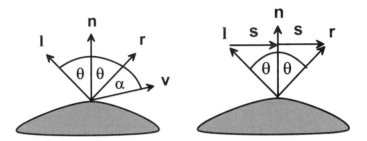

Figure 8.8 Computation of ideal specular reflection

In order to compute the direction r of ideal specular reflection for normalised vectors n and l, the auxiliary vector s is introduced, as can be seen in figure 8.8 on the right. The projection of l to n corresponds to the shortened vector n, denoted by s in the figure. Since n and l are assumed to be normalised, this projection vector is $s = n \cdot \cos\theta$. The vector r must therefore satisfy

$$r = n \cdot \cos(\theta) + s. \tag{8.4}$$

The auxiliary vector s can be determined from l and the projection of l onto n.

$$s = n \cdot \cos(\theta) - l.$$

Inserting s into equation (8.4) yields

$$r = 2 \cdot n \cdot \cos(\theta) - l.$$

As already in the case of diffuse reflection, the dot product can be used to calculate the angle between the vectors n and l: $n^\top \cdot l = \cos\theta$. Therefore, the normalised vector in the direction of ideal specular reflection is

$$r = 2 \cdot n(n^\top \cdot l) - l.$$

It is again assumed that the surface is not illuminated from the backside. This means $0° \leq \theta < 90°$ must hold. This is true if and only if the dot product $n^\top \cdot l$ is positive.

Only for an ideal mirror, specular reflection will take place exclusively in the direction of the vector $\mathbf{r}$. For most shiny surfaces, specular reflection can be seen around the ideal direction. The more the viewer deviates from the direction of ideal specular reflection, the smaller the effect of nonideal specular reflection will be. The *Phong illumination model* [34] takes this into account by reducing the intensity of specular reflection based on the angle α in figure 8.8. The intensity of specular reflection decreases while α increases.

$$I \;=\; I_L \cdot W(\theta) \cdot (\cos(\alpha))^n. \tag{8.5}$$

I_L is the intensity of the light which might have been reduced already by an attenuation factor for a point light source and by an additional factor for a spotlight, depending on the deviation from the axis of the cone of light. The value $0 \leq W(\theta) \leq 1$ is the fraction of the light which is directly reflected at the shiny surface, i.e., the fraction of the light to which specular reflection applies. In most cases, $W(\theta) = k_{\mathrm{sr}}$ will be a constant *specular reflection coefficient* of the surface independent of the angle θ. n is the *specular reflection exponent* of the surface. For a perfect mirror, $n = \infty$ would hold. A smaller n leads to a less focussed specular reflection. Figure 8.4 on page 205 shows the cosine function with different exponents n. For $n = 64$, the function tends to zero very quickly so that specular reflection can be seen only very close to the ideal direction of specular reflection. Choosing $n = 1$ would result in a much larger area of visible specular reflection. The more shiny a surface is, the higher the value of the specular reflection exponent should be chosen.

The value of the cosine function in equation (8.5) can again be computed by the dot product when the vectors $\mathbf{n}$ and $\mathbf{r}$ are normalised. $\cos \alpha = \mathbf{r}^\top \cdot \mathbf{v}$. The vector $\mathbf{r}$ will be normalised already when the vectors $\mathbf{l}$ and $\mathbf{n}$ are normalised. This follows directly from figure 8.8.

The Phong illumination model is not based on principles of physics. It is a heuristic method to enhance realistic effects of specular reflection. A modified version of the Phong illumination model replaces the deviation of the view direction from the direction of ideal specular reflection, the angle α, by another angle based on the halfway vector between the direction of the light source and the viewer direction. The viewer can see ideal specular reflection when the halfway vector between $\mathbf{l}$ and $\mathbf{v}$ coincides with the normal vector $\mathbf{n}$ to the surface. A reasonable measure for the deviation from the direction of specular reflection is therefore the angle β between the normal vector $\mathbf{n}$ and the halfway vector $\mathbf{h}$ of $\mathbf{l}$ and $\mathbf{v}$, as is shown in figure 8.9.

In the modified Phong illumination model, the term $\cos \alpha$ in equation (8.5) is replaced by the term $\cos \beta$, which can again be written as a dot product.

$$\cos \beta \;=\; \mathbf{n}^\top \cdot \mathbf{h}.$$

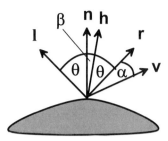

Figure 8.9 The halfway vector **h** in Phong's model

The halfway vector **h** is given by

$$\mathbf{h} = \frac{\mathbf{l} + \mathbf{v}}{\|\, \mathbf{l} + \mathbf{v} \,\|}.$$

In case of directional light and parallel projection, the halfway vector **h** does not change, in contrast to the vector **r** in the original Phong illumination model so that the calculations for illumination can be reduced in the modified Phong illumination model.

The considerations in this section always referred to one light source, a single point on a surface and three primary colours red, green and blue. When there is more than one light source and also ambient light $I_{\text{ambient\_light}}$ in the scene, the single computed intensities have to be summed up. In case the corresponding surface is also emitting light itself, this intensity $I_{\text{self\_emission}}$ must also be added. This leads to the following overall illumination equation for the point on the surface.

$$I = I_{\text{self\_emission}} + I_{\text{ambient\_light}} \cdot k_a \tag{8.6}$$

$$+ \sum_j I_j \cdot f_{\text{att}} \cdot g_{\text{cone}} \cdot \left(k_d \cdot (\mathbf{n}^\top \cdot \mathbf{l}_j) + k_{\text{sr}} \cdot (\mathbf{r}_j^\top \cdot \mathbf{v})^n \right).$$

k_a is the reflection coefficient for ambient light which is usually identical to the reflection coefficient k_d for diffuse reflection. I_j is the intensity of the j-th light source. For a directional light source, the two factors f_{att} and g_{cone} are equal to one. Only for a point light source, the first factor, modelling attenuation, depends on the distance and for a spotlight the second factor takes into account how fast the intensity of the light decreases to the boundary of the cone of light. **n**, **l**, **v** and **r** are the vectors known from figure 8.8 and 8.6, respectively. Equation (8.6) is based on the original Phong illumination model for specular reflection. The reflection coefficient k_{sr} for specular reflection is usually not identical to the coefficients k_d and k_a.

The intensity I in equation (8.6) is bounded by one. If the sum exceeds one, then the intensity is simply cut off at one.

The application of equation (8.6) for the three colours red, green and blue does not require much additional computational costs since the coefficients $I_{\text{self-emission}}$, $I_{\text{ambient-light}}$, I_j, k_a, k_d and k_{sr} might be different for each colour, but are given and do not have to be computed by an algorithm. The other coefficients need more complex calculations. They are the same for every colour, but depend on the chosen point on the surface and the properties of the light source.

Deferred Shading [45] is a recent technique to speed up the calculations when there are multiple light sources in the scene. It is based on the z-buffer algorithm. The original z-buffer might carry out all these complex computations for the projection of a surface only to find out at a later stage that all efforts were superfluous since the surface is not visible and another surface overwrites the projection. In the worst case, unnecessary computations for illumination are carried out again and again until finally the surface or object closest to the viewer is rendered. Deferred Shading first applies the z-buffer algorithm only to fill the depthbuffer with the corresponding z-values of the visible objects and ignores the frame buffer. In the second pass of the algorithm the frame buffer is also filled. But since the z-values are already entered, only those objects need to be projected to the frame buffer that are really visible.

8.4 Shading in Java 3D

In Java 3D, an `Appearance` is assigned to each object to characterise the properties of the object's surface. The class `Appearance` was already used in section 6.4 to display objects as wire frame models. A very important attribute of `Appearance` is the `Material`. The properties of the material and therefore the surface are specified in the following constructor.

```
Material ma = new Material(ambientColour,emissiveColour,
                           diffuseColour,specularColour,
                           shininessValue);
```

The first four parameters are colours that are defined by instances of the class `Color3f` which was introduced in section 5.4. The colour `ambientColour` defines how much ambient light is reflected by the material. If ambient light is added to the scene by an instance of the class `AmbientLight` as was described in section 8.2, then the contribution of ambient light reflection for a surface of the corresponding material is computed in the following way.

Given the RGB-values (r_a, g_a, b_a) of ambientColour for the material and the RGB-values (r_l, g_l, b_l) for ambient light in the scene, the intensities for the reflection of ambient light are determined by $(r_a \cdot r_l, g_a \cdot g_l, b_a \cdot b_l)$. To these intensities the values for self-emitting light specified in emissiveColour and the calculated values for diffuse and specular reflection have to be added. How much light is reflected for diffuse and specular reflection is defined by diffuseColour and specularColour. These colours correspond to the intensities k_d and k_{sr}, respectively, in equation (8.6). They are multiplied with the corresponding values coming from light sources of the classes DirectionalLight, PointLight and SpotLight. The last parameter shininessValue is a float-value between 1 and 128 for the shininess of the material or surface. The larger the value, the more shiny the surface will be. The value shininessValue is the specular reflection exponent in the Phong illumination model.

Once a Material ma has been generated in this way, an Appearance having the reflection properties ma can be created with the method setMaterial.

```
Appearance app = new Appearance();
app.setMaterial(ma);
```

This Appearance app can be used for objects to let the object's surface appear with the corresponding colour and reflection properties of the Material ma.

Although it is possible to use four different colours in the constructor for materials, it is not recommended to do so. Most objects do not emit light themselves so that emissiveColour will be black in most cases. The colours for diffuse reflection and for the reflection of ambient light should be identical or ambientColour could be chosen slightly less intense than diffuseColour. The colour for specular reflection is very often white, a light grey or the same colour as for diffuse reflection, but with higher intensity.

The program LightingExample.java displays two objects, a shiny sphere and a dull cube, that are illuminated by four light sources: ambient light, a directional light source, a point light source and a spotlight. For a better understanding of illumination and shading effects, it is recommended to the reader to modify the parameters of the instances of the class Material and to observe the changes. It is also possible to switch off light sources, simply by declaring the line where the corresponding light source is added to the BranchGroup bgLight with the method addChild as a comment line.

The program LightingExample2.java demonstrates undesired effects that can occur when the four colours in the constructor of Material are chosen completely different. The program uses a moving light source. The program MovingSpotLight.java illustrates how a spotlight with abruptly dropping intensity at the boundary of its cone of light can also lead to unrealistic effects. If the last parameter in the constructor SpotLight is changed from 0 to 1 in the program, the undesired effect vanishes.

8.5 Shading

For the computation of light reflections on a surface in section 8.3, it was
assumed that the normal vector to the surface is known in each point. In
order to compute the correct colour of a pixel on the projection plane, it is
not only necessary to determine which object surface is visible at the pixel,
but also in which point the projector through the pixel meets the surface. For
cubic freeform surfaces this would mean that a system of equations had to be
solved whose variables occur in the power of three, leading to unacceptable
computational effort per pixel. Therefore, light reflections are not calculated
directly for the freeform surfaces, but for their approximations with polygons.
What does this mean for the normal vectors to the surface? A very simple
approach would ignore the original normal vectors to the freeform surfaces and
use the normal vectors to the plane polygons instead.

Figure 8.10 A sphere in different tesselations rendered with flat shading

Constant or *flat shading* simplifies this idea even further. For a polygon,
the colour is determined only for a single pixel based on one normal vector.
All other pixels resulting from the projection of the polygon obtain the same
colour, leading to a homogeneous colour for the projection of the polygon. This
approach is correct under the following assumptions.

– The light source is in infinite distance so that $\mathbf{n}^\top \cdot \mathbf{l}$ is constant. This applies
  only to directional light sources.

– The viewer is in infinite distance so that $\mathbf{n}^\top \cdot \mathbf{v}$ is constant. This is true for
  parallel projections.

– The polygon represents the real surface of the object and is not just an
  approximation of a curved surface.

– No specular reflection occurs.

With these assumptions, shading can be computed in a fast and simple way, but will not lead to realistic images. Figure 8.10 shows the same sphere as in figure 6.12 on page 158, also in different tesselations. However, flat shading was applied in figure 8.10. Even the rightmost refined approximation by triangles still shows clear faces on the surface of the sphere whereas they are almost invisible already for a medium resolution in the figure on page 158.

An extremely refined resolution is needed for flat shading to avoid the effects of visible faces. One reason for this problem is also the preprocessing carried out automatically in the human vision system which intensifies contrast, i.e., edges, so that even small edges are already noticed.

Therefore, instead of flat shading *interpolated shading* is preferred. Interpolated shading requires the definition of normal vectors in the vertices of a polygon or triangle. Here only the case of triangles will be considered. The normal vectors in the three vertices of a triangle can be different for interpolated shading when the triangle is supposed to approximate a part of a curved surface. If the triangles are not derived from a freeform surface, but where specified manually, different normal vectors in the vertices of the triangle can still be computed. In each vertex, the standard normal vectors to the triangles that share the vertex are interpolated. This technique has been described in section 6.7.1.

When a curved surface is approximated by triangles and suitable normal vectors are specified in the vertices of the triangles, *Gouraud shading* [21] computes the colour in each of the three vertices based on the corresponding normal vectors. The shading of the other points in the triangle is based on colour interpolation derived from the three vertices. This leads to a linear colour gradient over the triangle. Figure 8.11 illustrates the colour intensity as a function over the triangle.

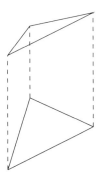

Figure 8.11 The colour intensity as a function over a triangle for Gouraud shading

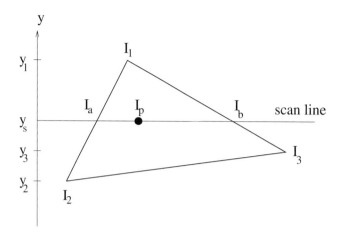

Figure 8.12 Scan line technique for the computation of Gouraud shading

An efficient scheme for the computation of the intensities in the triangle uses a scan line technique. For a scan line y_s the intensities I_a and I_b on the edges of the triangles are calculated where the scan line intersects the triangle. These values are obtained by weighted interpolation between the vertices of the corresponding edges of the triangle. The intensity changes in a linear way along the scan line with initial value I_a and final value I_b. Figure 8.12 illustrates this principle. The intensities are computed based on the following equations.

$$I_a = I_1 - (I_1 - I_2)\frac{y_1 - y_s}{y_1 - y_2},$$

$$I_b = I_1 - (I_1 - I_3)\frac{y_1 - y_s}{y_1 - y_3},$$

$$I_p = I_b - (I_b - I_a)\frac{x_b - x_p}{x_b - x_a}.$$

The colour intensities to be calculated are integer values between 0 and 255. Usually, the intensities on a single triangle will not differ strongly so that the absolute slope of the linear intensity curve along the scan line will be small. In this case, the midpoint algorithm could be applied to determine the discrete intensity values.

The undesired effect of visible faces and edges is already amended by Gouraud shading. Nevertheless, because of the linear interpolation scheme for Gouraud shading, the minimum and maximum intensity on a triangle will always be in one of the vertices. This might still lead to the effect of visible protruding edges or vertices. *Phong shading* [34] is also based on interpolation as Gouraud shading. However, instead of interpolating the computed colour intensities in the vertices for shading the triangle, the normal vectors in the vertices are interpolated for the calculation of the colour intensities of the other points. In this way, it is also possible that the minimum and maximum colour intensity can occur inside the triangle depending on the configuration of the normal vectors in the vertices and on the direction from which the light comes. Figure 8.13 shows a curved surface and a triangle which approximates a part of the surface. The normal vectors in the vertices of the triangle are the normal vectors to the surface in these points. Inside the triangle, the normal vectors are convex combinations of these normal vectors.

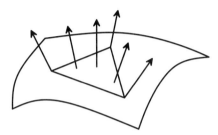

Figure 8.13 Interpolated normal vectors for Phong shading

From the computational point of view, Phong shading requires much more time than Gouraud shading. For the latter technique, the complex computations for illumination involving light sources and reflections need to be carried out only for the three vertices of a triangle. The remaining triangle is shaded by a simple scan line technique with simple calculations. For Phong shading, after interpolating the normal vectors, the full computations for illumination have to be carried out still for each pixel.

Gouraud and Phong shading provide good approximations for shading of the curved surface. From the theoretical point of view, it would even be better to derive the normal vector for a point in the triangle directly from the corresponding point on the curved surface in order to determine the colour of the corresponding pixel. This would mean that it is not sufficient to store only predefined normal vectors of selected points—the vertices—but that the information about the original curved surface is still necessary for shading. This would be unacceptable from the computational point of view.

8.5.1 Constant and Gouraud shading in Java 3D

Gouraud shading is the default shading technique in Java 3D. One can also switch to constant shading for an object by changing its `Appearance`. First an instance of the class `ColoringAttributes` has to be generated and then the shading mode can be set with the method `setShadeModel`.

```
ColoringAttributes ca = new ColoringAttributes();
ca.setShadeModel(ColoringAttributes.SHADE_FLAT);
app.setColoringAttributes(ca);
```

`app` is an instance of the class `Appearance`. The method

```
ca.setShadeModel(ColoringAttributes.SHADE_GOURAUD);
```

switches back to the default shading in Java 3D. Figure 8.10 on page 218 was generated by the program `ShadingExample.java` using constant shading.

8.6 Shadows

An important aspect, which has been neglected for shading so far, is *shadows*. "Casting a shadow" is not an active matter, but simply the lack of light from a light source that does not reach the object's surface with the shadow on it. The illumination equation including shadows becomes

$$I = I_{\text{self\_emission}} + I_{\text{ambient\_light}} \cdot k_a \qquad (8.7)$$

$$+ \sum_j S_j \cdot I_j \cdot f_{\text{att}} \cdot g_{\text{cone}} \cdot \left(k_d \cdot (\mathbf{n}^\top \cdot \mathbf{l}_j) + k_{\text{sr}} \cdot (\mathbf{r}_j^\top \cdot \mathbf{v})^n \right).$$

This is the same illumination equation as (8.6) except for the additional factors

$$S_j = \begin{cases} 1 & \text{if the light from light source } j \text{ reaches the surface} \\ 0 & \text{otherwise (shadow).} \end{cases}$$

When does the light of a light source reach a surface and when is it blocked by another object leading to a shadow? Chapter 7 has introduced methods for visibility determination, i.e., to decide whether an object in the scene is visible for the viewer or blocked from view by other objects. The problem of determining shadow is the same, only the light source instead of the viewer has to be considered. When a surface is visible for a light source, then $S_j = 1$ and there is no shadow for this light source on the surface. When the surface is not visible from the light source, then $S_j = 0$ and a shadow is cast on the object. Figure 8.14 shows a shadow on a cube caused by a tetrahedron which blocks the light from a light source from above. Shadow does not mean that the surface will be black. Ambient light will still be reflected. And if there is more than one light source in the scene, a surface might be blocked from one light source, but not from the others.

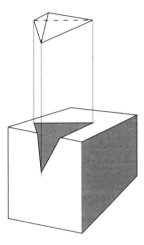

Figure 8.14 Shadow on an object

The connection between shadows and visibility determination is exploited by the *two-pass z-* or *two-pass depth buffer algorithm*. In the first pass of this algorithm, the standard z-buffer algorithm is carried out with the following modifications. The viewer is replaced by a light source. For a directional light source, a parallel projection in the opposite direction of the direction of the light is applied. For a point light source and a spotlight, a perspective projection is applied with its centre of projection at the position of the light source. In all cases the projection is reduced to a parallel projection to the x/y-plane by a suitable transformation T_L. In this first pass of the two-pass z-buffer algorithm only the values for the z-buffer Z_L are entered. The frame buffer and its calculations are not needed. The second pass of the algorithm is identical to the standard z-buffer algorithm for the viewer with the following modification.

A transformation T_V turning the perspective projection with the viewer as the centre of projection into a parallel projection to the x/y-plane is needed as usual. The viewer z-buffer Z_V is also treated as usual in the second pass of the algorithm. But before a projection is entered into the frame buffer F_V for the viewer, an illumination test is carried out to check whether the surface is illuminated by the considered light source. If the coordinates of a point on the surface to be projected are (x_V, y_V, z_V), the transformation

$$\begin{pmatrix} x_L \\ y_L \\ z_L \end{pmatrix} = T_L \cdot T_V^{-1} \cdot \begin{pmatrix} x_V \\ y_V \\ z_V \end{pmatrix}$$

yields the coordinates of the same point from the viewpoint of the light source. T_V^{-1} is the inverse transformation, i.e., the inverse matrix to T_V. The value z_L is compared to the entry in the z-buffer Z_L for the light source at the position (x_L, y_L). If a smaller value than z_L is entered in the z-buffer Z_L at this position, then there must be an object between the light source and the considered surface so that this surface does not receive any light from this light source. The surface is in the shadow of this light source, and the corresponding factor S_j in equation (8.7) must be set to zero. When there is more than one light source in the scene, the first pass of the algorithm is carried out for each light source. In the second pass it is determined for each light source whether a surface receives light from the corresponding light source and the factors S_j are chosen correspondingly.

8.7 Transparency

Transparent surfaces reflect a part of the light, but objects behind them can also be seen. A typical transparent object is a coloured glass pane. Transparency means that only a fraction of the light of the objects behind the transparent surface can pass through the transparent surface, but no distortion as with frosted glass happens. Such objects like milk glass are called *translucent*. Translucent surfaces will not be considered here. Refraction will also not be taken into account.

In order to explain how transparency is modelled, a surface F_2 is considered that is positioned behind a transparent surface F_1. For *interpolated* or *filtered transparency* a transmission coefficient $k_{\text{transp}} \in [0, 1]$ is needed. k_{transp} specifies the fraction of light that can pass through the transparent surface F_1. The surface is completely transparent, i.e., invisible, for $k_{\text{transp}} = 1$. For $k_{\text{transp}} = 0$, the surface is not transparent at all and can be handled in the same way as surfaces have been treated so far. The colour intensity I_P of a point P on the transparent surface F_1 is determined by

$$I_P = (1 - k_{\text{transp}}) \cdot I_1 + k_{\text{transp}} \cdot I_2 \qquad (8.8)$$

where I_1 is the intensity of the point that would result if the surface F_1 would be treated like a normal nontransparent surface. I_2 is the intensity of the corresponding point on the surface F_2 when the surface F_1 would be completely invisible or completely removed from the scene. The values I_1 for red, green and blue result from the colour assigned to the transparent surface. In this way it is also possible to model coloured glass panes, although this model is not correct from the theoretical point of view. A colour filter would be the correct model.

Transparent surfaces complicate the visible surface determination. Especially when the z-buffer algorithm is used, the following problems can occur.

− Which z-value should be stored in the z-buffer when a transparent surface is projected? If the z-value of an object O behind the transparent surface is kept, an object between O and the transparent surface could overwrite the frame buffer later on completely, although it is located behind the transparent surface. If instead the z-value of the transparent surface is used, then the object O would not be entered into the frame buffer although it should be visible behind the transparent surface.

− Which value should be entered in the frame buffer? If interpolated transparency is computed according to equation (8.8), the information about the value I_1 is lost for other objects that might be located directly behind the transparent surface. Even the value I_1 would not be sufficient. It is possible to apply *alpha-blending*. Since the coding of RGB-values requires three bytes and blocks of four bytes are handled more efficiently in the computer, it is common to use the fourth byte for an alpha-value. This alpha-value corresponds to the transmission coefficient k_{transp} for transparency. But even with this alpha-value it is not clear to which object behind the transparent surface alpha-blending should be applied, i.e., how to apply equation (8.8), since the choice of the object for alpha-blending depends on the z-value.

Opaque objects should be entered first for the z-buffer algorithm and afterwards the transparent surfaces. When the transparent surfaces are entered, alpha-blending should be applied for the frame buffer. There will still be problems when transparent surfaces cover other transparent surfaces from sight. In this case, the order in which they are entered must be correct, i.e., from back to front. For this purpose, it is common to sort the transparent surfaces with respect to their z-coordinates.

Figure 8.15 50% (left) and 25% (right) screen-door transparency

Screen-door transparency is an alternative solution based on a similar principle as halftone techniques from section 4.5. The mixing or interpolation of the colours of a transparent surface with an object behind it as defined in equation (8.8) is not carried out per pixel but per pixel group. A transmission coefficient of $k_{\text{transp}} = 0.25$ would mean that every fourth pixel obtained its colour from the object behind the transparent surface and the other pixels obtain the colour from the transparent surface. Figure 8.15 illustrates this principle for magnified pixels. The darker colour comes from the transparent surface, the lighter colour from an object behind it. For the left-hand side of the figure $k_{\text{transp}} = 0.5$ was used, for the right-hand side $k_{\text{transp}} = 0.25$.

Screen-door transparency is well suited for the z-buffer algorithm. The z-values are chosen according to the surface they come from. Either the transparent one or a surface behind it. For $k_{\text{transp}} = 0.25$, 75% of the pixels would have the z-value of the surface and the other 25% the z-value of the object behind it. An object that is projected later on in the z-buffer algorithm will be treated correctly. If it is in front of the transparent surface, it will overwrite everything. If it is behind another object to which screen-door transparency has been applied already, it will not be entered at all. If the object is behind the transparent surface and closer than all other objects that were entered there before, the corresponding fraction of the pixels will automatically get the colour from this object.

Although screen-door transparency works well together with the z-buffer algorithm, the same problems as for halftone techniques occur. The results are only acceptable when the resolution is high enough. For a transmission coefficient of about 50% the results for screen-door and interpolated transparency are almost indistinguishable. But for transmission coefficients close to one or zero, screen-door transparency tends to show dot patterns instead of a realistic transparency effect.

8.7.1 Transparency in Java 3D

Java 3D provides the class `TransparencyAttributes` to model transparency. The method `setTransparencyMode` defines the chosen type of transparency, i.e., interpolated or screen-door transparency. The transmission coefficient is specified with the method `setTransparency` as a `float`-value between zero and one. The instance of the class `TransparencyAttributes` must then be assigned to an `Appearance` app by the method `setTransparencyAttributes`.

```
TransparencyAttributes ta = new TransparencyAttributes();
ta.setTransparencyMode(TransparencyAttributes.BLENDED);
ta.setTransparency(transpCoeff);
```

```
app.setTransparencyAttributes(ta);
```

The second line chooses interpolated transparency by specifying BLENDED. For screen-door transparency, BLENDED has to be replaced by SCREEN_DOOR. The program TransparencyExample.java demonstrates the use of these two types of transparency.

8.8 Textures

Textures are images on surfaces of objects. A simple texture might use a colour gradient or a pattern instead of the same colour on the surface everywhere. Modelling a wallpaper with a pattern on it, needs a texture to be assigned to the walls. In this case, multiple copies of the same texture are attached to the surface. A picture hanging on a wall could also be modelled by a texture which would be applied only once.

Textures are also used to model fine structures like ingrain wallpaper, wood grain, roughcast or even brick patterns. In contrast to a normal smooth wallpaper, an ingrain wallpaper has a fine three-dimensional structure that can be felt and seen. The same applies to a bark of a tree, a wall of bricks or pleats on clothes. The correct way to model such small three-dimensional structures would be an approximation by extremely small polygons. However, the effort for modelling as well as the computational effort for rendering are unacceptable.

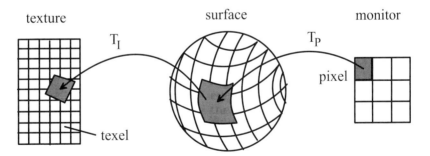

Figure 8.16 Using a texture

A texture is an image that is mapped to a surface as is sketched in figure 8.16. A *texture map* T_I is defined that maps the surface or its vertices to the pixel raster of the image for the texture. When a pixel of the screen or projection plane is interpreted as a small square, then this square corresponds to a small area on the surface. This small area is mapped by the texture map to the image for the texture. In this way, the corresponding *texels*—the pixels of the texture image—can be determined to calculate the colour for the pixel. This colour value has to be combined with the information from illumination taking into account whether the surface with the texture is shiny or not.

Textures are useful for a variety of problems in computer graphics. A background texture like a clouded sky can be defined. This texture is not assigned to any surface but simply used as a constant background. More complex illumination techniques like the radiosity model introduced in section 8.10 lead to more realistic images but are too slow for interactive real-time graphics. Under certain conditions, textures can be used to calculate diffuse reflection with these techniques in advance and apply the results as textures to the surfaces in the form of so-called *light maps* so that only specular reflection is needed for the real-time graphics.

Environment or *reflection mapping* is a technique to model mirrors or reflecting surfaces like the surface of calm water. For this purpose, the viewer is first reflected at the corresponding surface. Then the image is computed which the reflected viewer would see. This image is then used as a texture for the reflecting surface when the image for the original position of the viewer is computed. Figure 8.17 illustrates this idea.

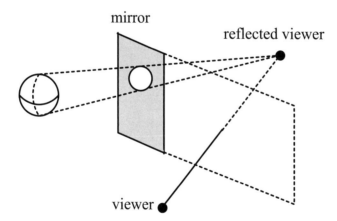

Figure 8.17 Modelling a mirror by a reflection mapping

When textures are used to model small three-dimensional patterns like reliefs, viewing them from a shorter distance might give the impression of a flat image, especially when there is a strong light source. No information about the three-dimensional structure is contained in the image for the texture itself. In order to provide a more realistic view without representing the three-dimensional structure with extremely small polygons, *bump mappings* [3] are introduced. The surface to which the texture is applied still remains flat. But in addition to the colour information coming from the image of the texture, a bump map is used to modify the normal vectors of the surface. A bump map assigns to each texture point a perturbation value $B(i,j)$ specifying how much the point on the surfaces should be moved along the normal vector for the relief. If the surface is given in parametric form and the point to be modified is $P = P(x(s,t),\, y(s,t),\, z(s,t))$, then the nonnormalised modified normal vector at P is obtained from the cross product of the partial derivatives with respect to s and t.

$$\mathbf{n} \;=\; \frac{\partial P}{\partial s} \times \frac{\partial P}{\partial t}.$$

If $B(T(P)) = B(i,j)$ is the corresponding bump value, one obtains

$$P' \;=\; P + B(T(P)) \cdot \frac{\mathbf{n}}{\|\,\mathbf{n}\,\|}$$

as the lifted or perturbed point on the surface with the relief structure. A good approximation for the new normal vector in this point is then given by

$$\mathbf{n}' \;=\; \frac{\mathbf{n}+\mathbf{d}}{\|\,\mathbf{n}+\mathbf{d}\,\|} \quad \text{where} \quad \mathbf{d} \;=\; \frac{\frac{\partial B}{\partial u} \cdot \left(\mathbf{n} \times \frac{\partial P}{\partial t}\right) - \frac{\partial B}{\partial v} \cdot \left(\mathbf{n} \times \frac{\partial P}{\partial s}\right)}{\|\,\mathbf{n}\,\|}.$$

In this way, bump mapping can induce varying normal vectors on a flat plane. Figure 8.18 shows how normal vectors modelling a small dent can be applied to a flat surface.

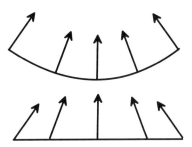

Figure 8.18 Bump mapping

8.9 Textures in Java 3D

Java 3D provides a variety of methods to apply textures to surfaces. It is possible to specify in detail how the texture should be attached to the vertices

of a surface that is modelled by polygons. The details of these methods will not
be included in this introductory book. It should be sufficient here to explain
how a texture can be applied to a surface without worrying about how to
position it exactly.

First of all, an image is needed for the texture. The image can be loaded from
a file and is then transformed into an instance of the class `ImageComponent2D`
with the method `getScaledImage`. A scaling to a specified width w and height
h is carried out. The values of w and h must be powers of two, i.e., they must
be chosen from the set $\{1, 2, 4, 8, 16, 32, 64, \ldots\}$.

```
TextureLoader textureLoad =
                    new TextureLoader("image.jpg",null);
ImageComponent2D textureIm =
                    textureLoad.getScaledImage(w,h);
```

Then an instance of the class `Texture2D` is generated which is then assigned
to an instance of the class `Appearance`.

```
Texture2D myTexture =
          new Texture2D(Texture2D.BASE_LEVEL,Texture2D.RGB,
                        textureIm.getWidth(),
                        textureIm.getHeight());
myTexture.setImage(0,textureIm);
Appearance textureApp = new Appearance();
```

The following lines of code assign the texture to the `Appearance textureApp`.

```
textureApp.setTexture(myTexture);
TextureAttributes textureAttr = new TextureAttributes();
textureAttr.setTextureMode(TextureAttributes.REPLACE);
textureApp.setTextureAttributes(textureAttr);
Material mat = new Material();
mat.setShininess(shininess);
textureApp.setMaterial(mat);
TexCoordGeneration tcg =
    new TexCoordGeneration(TexCoordGeneration.OBJECT_LINEAR,
                    TexCoordGeneration.TEXTURE_COORDINATE_2);
textureApp.setTexCoordGeneration(tcg);
```

The `Appearance textureApp` can then be assigned to an elementary geometric object or a `Shape` as usual. Depending on the size of the surface, the texture is applied more than once to cover the surface completely. The program
`TextureExample.java` loads a texture from an image file and applies it to a
sphere.

In Java 3D textures can also be used as background images easily. The colour of the background has already been changed in some of the example programs for better illustration purposes, for example in the program `StaticSceneExample.java`. Changing the colour of the background requires an instance of the class `Background`. The desired colour is assigned to the `Background` as an argument in the constructor. When a `Background` has been created in this way it also needs a bounding region where it should be valid. The bounding region is specified with the method `setApplicationBounds`, as usual in the form of a `BoundingSphere bounds` or a bounding box. Then the background can be added to the scene with the method `addChild`.

```
Background bg = new Background(new Color3f(r,g,b));
bg.setApplicationBounds(bounds);
theScene.addChild(bg);
```

If an image from a file `image.jpg` should be used as a background instead of a fixed colour, the image must be loaded first using a `TextureLoader`. Then the constructor of `Background` is called with the image instead of the colour in the above example. The image is obtained from the `TextureLoader` with the method `getImage`.

```
TextureLoader textureLoad =
                      new TextureLoader("image.jpg",null);
Background bgImage = new Background(textureLoad.getImage());
```

The definition of a bounding region and the assignment of the background to the scene is required in the same way as for a fixed colour as background. In the program `BackgroundExample.java`, an image is loaded from a file and the image is then used as the background of a scene.

8.10 The radiosity model

It was already mentioned for the illumination model introduced in section 8.3 that an object emitting light is not considered as a light source in the scene and does not contribute to the illumination of other objects, except a light source is added to the scene where the object is located. But, in principle, all objects in the scene emit light, namely, the light they reflect. Ambient light is introduced to model this effect in a very simplified way. Unrealistic sharp edges and contrasts are the consequence of this simplification. For example, if a dark and bright wall meet in a corner of a room, the bright wall will reflect some light to the darker wall. This effect is especially visible where the bright wall meets the dark wall, i.e., at the edge between the two walls. The illumination model from section 8.1 and the reflection and shading models in section 8.3 ignore the interaction of the light between the objects. This results in a representation of the two walls as can be seen in figure 8.19 on the left-hand side. A very sharp edge is visible between the two walls. In the right part of the figure the effect was taken into account that the bright wall will reflect light to the dark wall. Therefore, the dark wall becomes slightly less dark close to the corner and the edge is less sharp.

Figure 8.19 Illumination among objects

Environment mappings from section 8.8 are a simple approach to take this effect into account. Environment mappings are not used as textures but for modelling the light that is cast by other objects onto a surface. For this purpose, shading is first computed as described in section 8.3, neglecting the interaction of light between objects. Then an environment map is determined for each object considering the other objects as light sources. The shading resulting from the environment maps is then added to the intensities that were computed before for the object's surface. Of course, in the ideal case, this process should be repeated again and again until more or less no changes occur in the intensities anymore. But this is not acceptable from the computational point of view.

The *radiosity model* [20, 32] avoids these recursive computations. The radiosity B_i is the rate of energy emitted by a surface O_i in the form of light. This rate of emitted energy is a superposition of the following components when only diffuse reflection is considered.

- E_i is the rate at which light is emitted from surface O_i as an active light source. E_i will be zero for all objects in the scene except for the light sources.

- The light coming from light sources and other objects that is reflected by surface O_i. If the surface O_i is the part of the dark wall in figure 8.19 close to the corner and O_j is the corresponding part of the bright wall, the light reflected by O_j that comes from O_i is computed as follows.

$$\varrho_i \cdot B_j \cdot F_{ji}.$$

ϱ_i is the reflection coefficient of the surface O_i, B_j is the rate of energy coming from O_j. B_j has still to be determined. F_{ji} is a dimensionless form or configuration factor specifying how much of the energy coming from O_j reaches O_i. In F_{ji}, the shape, the size and the relative orientation of the surfaces O_i and O_j are taken into account. For example, when the surfaces are perpendicular, less light will be exchanged among them compared to the case that they face each other directly. The calculation of the *form factors* will be explained later on.

– For transparent surfaces, the light coming from behind the surface must also be taken into account. Since this will make the matter more complicated, transparent surfaces will not be considered here for the radiosity model.

The total rate of energy coming from the surface O_i is the sum over these single rates. For n surfaces including the light sources, this leads to the equations

$$B_i \;=\; E_i + \varrho_i \cdot \sum_{j=1}^{n} B_j \cdot F_{ji}. \tag{8.9}$$

Taking these equations for the surfaces together leads to a system of linear equations with unknown variables B_i.

$$
\begin{pmatrix}
1 - \varrho_1 F_{1,1} & -\varrho_1 F_{1,2} & \cdots & -\varrho_1 F_{1,n} \\
-\varrho_2 F_{2,1} & 1 - \varrho_2 F_{2,2} & \cdots & -\varrho_2 F_{2,n} \\
\vdots & \vdots & \vdots & \vdots \\
-\varrho_n F_{n,1} & -\varrho_n F_{n,2} & \cdots & 1 - \varrho_n F_{n,n}
\end{pmatrix}
\cdot
\begin{pmatrix}
B_1 \\ B_2 \\ \vdots \\ B_n
\end{pmatrix}
=
\begin{pmatrix}
E_1 \\ E_2 \\ \vdots \\ E_n
\end{pmatrix}.
$$
$$\tag{8.10}$$

This system of linear equations must be solved for the primary colours red, green and blue. The number of equations is equal to the number of surfaces or surface patches—usually triangles—plus the number of light sources. The latter will be very small compared to the number of triangles. The system can have hundreds or thousands of equations and variables. In most cases it will be a sparse system of equations, in which most of the entries are zero since most of the surfaces do not exchange any light so that most of the form factors will be zero.

For the computation of the form factor from the surface A_i to the surface A_j, both surfaces are partitioned into small area patches dA_i and dA_j. The influence between the patches is computed and added. Since the patches should be arbitrarily small, the sum will become an integral. If the patch dA_j is visible from dA_i, then the differential form factor with the notation from figure 8.20

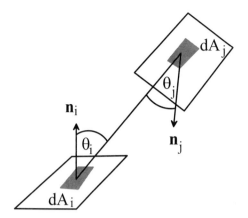

Figure 8.20 Determination of the form factors

is

$$dF_{d_i,d_j} = \frac{\cos(\theta_i) \cdot \cos(\theta_j)}{\pi \cdot r^2} \cdot dA_j.$$

dF_{d_i,d_j} decreases quadratically with increasing distance according to attenuation. The angle at which the patches face each other is also important. If the patches face each other directly, the form factor has the largest value. In this case, the normal vectors to the patches are parallel and point in opposite directions. The form factor decreases with increasing angle and becomes zero at $90°$. For angles larger than $90°$ when the patches face in opposite directions, the cosine would lead to negative values. For this reason, the factor

$$H_{ij} = \begin{cases} 1 & \text{if } dA_j \text{ is visible from } dA_i \\ 0 & \text{otherwise} \end{cases}$$

is introduced so that the differential form factor becomes

$$dF_{d_i,d_j} = \frac{\cos(\theta_i) \cdot \cos(\theta_j)}{\pi \cdot r^2} \cdot H_{ij} \cdot dA_j.$$

By integration the differential form factor for the patch dA_i to the surface A_j is obtained.

$$dF_{d_i,j} = \int_{A_j} \frac{\cos(\theta_i) \cdot \cos(\theta_j)}{\pi \cdot r^2} \cdot H_{ij} \, dA_j.$$

Another integration finally yields the form factor from the surface A_i to the surface A_j.

$$F_{i,j} = \frac{1}{A_i} \int_{A_i} \int_{A_j} \frac{\cos(\theta_i) \cdot \cos(\theta_j)}{\pi \cdot r^2} \cdot H_{ij} \, dA_j \, dA_i.$$

For small surfaces, i.e., for small polygons, an approximate value for the form factor is calculated in the following way. A hemisphere is constructed over the surface A_i with the centre of gravity of A_i as the midpoint of the hemisphere. The surface A_j is projected onto the hemisphere and then this projection is projected to the circle which the hemisphere defines. The proportion of the circle that is covered by this projection determines the form factor. This principle is illustrated in figure 8.21. The quotient of the dark grey area and the circle is the form factor. A simpler, but less accurate approximation for the form factor was proposed by Cohen and Greenberg [13]. In this approach, the hemisphere is replaced by a half-cube.

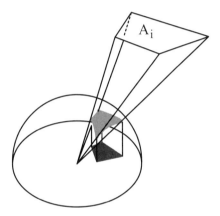

Figure 8.21 Determination of the form factors according to Nusselt

There are also algorithms to find approximate solutions of the system of linear equations (8.10) to estimate the radiosity value B_i. The *progressive refinement approach* [12] determines the values B_i in equation (8.9) by stepwise improved approximate solutions of the system of linear equations (8.10). In the first step, only the light sources are taken into account and $B_i = E_i$ is defined for all object i. In the first step, all objects remain completely dark. Only the light sources emit light. In addition to estimations for the values B_i, the algorithm also uses values ΔB_i that are updated in each step. ΔB_i specifies the change of the radiosity of object i since it has last been considered as a light source to illuminate the other objects. In the beginning $\Delta B_i = E_i$ is defined. Then the light source or object O_{i_0} with the greatest change, i.e., with the greatest value for ΔB_{i_0}, is chosen. In the first step, this would be the light source with the highest intensity. Then all B_i-values are updated by

$$B_i^{(\text{new})} \; = \; B_i^{(\text{old})} + \varrho_i \cdot F_{i_0 i} \cdot \Delta B_{i_0}. \qquad (8.11)$$

The changes ΔB_i are updated by

$$\Delta B_i^{(\text{new})} = \begin{cases} \Delta B_i^{(\text{old})} + \varrho_i \cdot F_{i_0 i} \cdot \Delta B_{i_0} & \text{if } i \neq i_0, \\ 0 & \text{if } i = i_0. \end{cases} \tag{8.12}$$

The light emitted from the object O_{i_0} so far is distributed over the objects in this way. Then the next object with the largest value ΔB_{i_0} is chosen and the update schemes (8.11) and (8.12) are applied again. This procedure is repeated until convergence is reached, i.e., until all ΔB_i are almost zero. But the procedure can be stopped earlier as well yielding a reasonable approximation. If the computation time is strictly limited as in the case of interactive graphics, a good approximation of the radiosity values is obtained in this way, under the restrictions for the computation time.

Radiosity models produce more realistic images than the simplified illumination models neglecting the reflections of light between objects. But the required computations are too complex to be used for real-time interactive graphics. A radiosity model can nevertheless be applied in static scenes and animations where the computations can be carried out in advance like in the case of an animated movie. The fast and ever-improving graphics cards might allow the application of approximation techniques like progressive refinement in the near future even for interactive real-time graphics. Radiosity models can be used to calculate diffuse reflection in advance when the light sources are fixed and there are not too many moving objects in a scene. The results from the radiosity model are stored as light maps and are applied as textures to the objects in the real-time graphics. The real-time computations only have to take care of specular reflection.

8.11 Ray tracing

The ray casting technique presented in section 7.3.3 in the context of visibility considerations is a simple ray tracing model whose principle can also be used for shading. Rays are cast from the viewer or for parallel projection parallel through the pixels on the projection plane. Each ray is traced until it hits the first object. There the usual calculations for shading are carried out. In figure 8.22, the ray hits the pyramid first. In this point the light from the light sources is taken into account for diffuse reflection. The ray is then further traced as in the case of specular reflection, only in the opposite direction, not starting from a light source but from the viewer. When the ray hits another object, this backwards specular reflection is traced again until a maximum depth for the recursion is reached, until no object is hit or until the ray meets a light source.

At the end of this procedure, the shading of the first object has to be corrected by the possible contribution of light from specular reflection at other objects along the reflected ray.

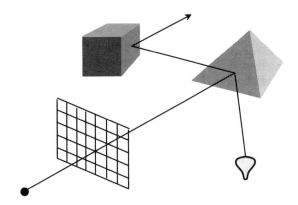

Figure 8.22   Recursive ray tracing

This technique is called *ray tracing* or *recursive ray tracing*. The computational demands are quite high for this technique.

8.12 Exercises

Exercise 8.1

Define spotlights in Java 3D in the colours red, green and blue. Point the spotlights to the front face of a white cube such that the centre of the face will be shaded white and the border areas with the different colours of the spotlight.

Exercise 8.2

A viewer is in the point $(2, 1, 4)$ and looks at the (y, z)-plane which is illuminated by a directional light source. The light source lies in infinite distance in the direction of the vector $(1, 2, 3)$. At which point on the plane can the viewer see specular reflection?

Exercise 8.3

Define a `Shape` in Java 3D that looks like a lamp and assign a light source to the same transformation group in the `BranchGroup theScene` to which the `Shape` belongs. Move the lamp with the attached light source through the scene.

Exercise 8.4

Use a JPEG image of your choice as a texture for cylinders in various sizes and for the ship in the program `Load3DExample.java`.

Exercise 8.5

A background image remains unchanged, even when the viewer moves around in the scene. Apply a background image as a texture to a large box in the far distance so that the viewer can see changes in the background image when he moves.

Exercise 8.6

Should back-face culling be applied in the context of radiosity models, before equation (8.10) is established?

Special effects and virtual reality

This last chapter presents a selection of special topics as well as basic techniques that are required for *virtual reality* applications. Virtual reality comprises more than just displaying a scene or a sequence of scenes on a computer screen. Stereoscopic viewing which is necessary for real 3D effects belongs to virtual reality. In addition to seeing a virtual world, virtual reality can also involve sound. Even tactile information might be incorporated with wire gloves. An important feature of virtual reality applications is also that the user can move around in the virtual world and interact with the virtual world. Moving through the virtual world means here that the person is moving, not just controlling the navigation through the scene by mouse commands. For this purpose, sensors to locate the position of the viewer are required. Interaction means that objects in the scene can be manipulated, for example shifted to other positions in the scene. Even if the necessary technical equipment for virtual reality applications is not available for most computer users, the principles of virtual reality can also be understood when a normal computer screen is used. From the computer graphics point of view, moving around in a virtual world is nothing else than a viewer who navigates through the scene, i.e., by changing the position of the viewer which is nothing else than translating the centre of projection. This topic was treated in detail in section 5.8 and all example programs allow a navigation through the scene. Of course, the mouse must be used for navigation in these programs. But the computations for the projections are identical as long as reliable data are available about the position of a viewer in a virtual world. The same applies to interaction. A wire glove might be the better choice in a virtual reality environment. But the computational and programming part

remain the same when the stimuli for interaction come from the mouse instead
of a wire glove. Acoustic effects do not cause any problems. They can even be
created with a normal PC.

9.1 Fog and particle systems

Fog has a similar, but not the same effect as atmospheric attenuation. In the
case of atmospheric attenuation, light is absorbed by dust particles in the air.
Fog does not consist of dust particles but of extremely small drops of water that
do not absorb the light, but disperse it in all directions. Because of this disper-
sion or diffuse reflection of the light, fog tends to have an almost white colour.
As in the case of atmospheric attenuation, the visibility of objects decreases
with increasing distance in the presence of fog. In contrast to atmospheric attenuation, fog also causes a white or grey background colour. The colour of an
object is blended with the colour of the fog. Attenuation corresponds to black
fog.

Fog is based on an increasing blending function $b : \mathbb{R}_0^+ \to [0,1]$ where
$b(0) = 0$ and $\lim_{d \to \infty} b(d) = 1$. Given the distance d of an object to the viewer, the
colour intensity I_{object} of the object and the colour intensity I_{fog} of the fog, the
intensity of the object in the fog is computed in a similar way as in the case of
interpolated transparency.

$$b(d) \cdot I_{\text{fog}} + (1 - b(d)) \cdot I_{\text{object}}.$$

Since $b(d)$ approaches the value one with increasing distance d, the colour of
the fog dominates the colour of the object in larger distances.

The blending function has usually either a linear or an exponential slope.
Linear fog does not reduce the sight up to the distance $d = d_0$, i.e., no blending
with the fog takes place. For distances larger than $d = d_1$, the fog dominates
completely so that objects farther away than distance d_1 become invisible. The
effect of the fog increases in a linear fashion between d_0 and d_1. The blending
function for linear fog is given by

$$b(d) = \begin{cases} 0 & \text{if } d \leq d_0, \\ \frac{d - d_0}{d_1 - d_0} & \text{if } d_0 < d < d_1, \\ 1 & \text{if } d_1 \leq d. \end{cases} \tag{9.1}$$

The more realistic *exponential fog* is based on an exponential increase of the
effect of fog controlled by the factor $\alpha > 0$. The blending function is given by

$$b(d) = 1 - e^{-\alpha \cdot d}. \tag{9.2}$$

The larger the value α, the more dense is the fog.

Figure 9.1 shows an example of linear fog on the left and an example of exponential fog on the right. It is recommended to adjust the background colour to the colour of the fog.

 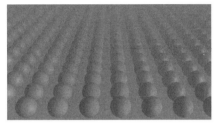

Figure 9.1 Linear and exponential fog

Linear and exponential fog model fog of continuous density. Single wafts of fog hovering in the air are not included in these models. Wafts of fog and related effects like smoke are modelled by *particle systems* [37, 38]. A particle system is composed of many small particles that are not controlled individually, but by a few parameters and random mechanisms. All particles have the same underlying basic behaviour pattern. Individual variations in the behaviour pattern are caused by the random mechanism. A particle usually has a random life span, it moves in a certain direction which can also be changed by a random mechanism and sometimes it can also split and generate new particles. For example, a fire could be modelled by a particle system. The particles would be generated on the ground where the fire is burning. All particles carry out an upwards movement with a constant speed. The direction and the speed are modified by random values. The life span of the particles is also determined on a random basis. The mean life span should be chosen in such a way that the particles reach half the height of the fire on average. The particles can also split with a certain probability while they fly upwards.

An explosion would be modelled in a similar way with the differences that the speed of the particles would be much higher and that the particles start off in a random direction from the centre of the explosion, not mainly upwards as in for the fire.

Swarm behaviour [40] for modelling, e.g., flocks of birds or shoals, is related to particle systems. A swarm can be considered as a particle system plus a control for the coordination of the particles. The particles or individuals in a swarm move approximately with the same speed and in the same direction, but not exactly. An important aspect for swarm behaviour in contrast to simple particle systems is avoidance of collisions. Rule-based methods from artificial intelligence are very often used for modelling swarm behaviour.

For clouds a quite realistic animation model has been proposed in [15]. The sky is partitioned into voxels and the voxels function as cells of a cellular automaton. Depending on the definition of the state transitions for the automaton, different kinds of clouds can be modelled. Each cell of the automaton determines a sphere as well as a colour for its associated voxel and a cloud pattern is created in this way.

9.2 Fog in Java 3D

Java 3D provides classes for linear and exponential fog. An instance of the corresponding class must be generated and a bounding region must be specified. Then the object has to be assigned to the scene with the method addChild. The class LinearFog is for creating linear fog.

```
LinearFog fog = new LinearFog(colour,d_0,d_1);
fog.setInfluencingBounds(bounds);
theScene.addChild(fog);
```

colour is an instance of the class Color3f and determines the colour of the fog. d_0 and d_1 are the parameters d_0 and d_1, respectively, of the blending function (9.1). The bounding region of the fog is defined by an instance bounds of the class BoundingSphere or BoundingBox. Exponential fog is created analogously with the class ExponentialFog.

```
ExponentialFog fog = new ExponentialFog(colour,alpha);
```

The parameter alpha is the exponent α in the exponential blending function (9.2).

The two images in figure 9.1 were generated with the programs LinFogExample.java and ExpFogExample.java, respectively. The programs show identical spheres which were positioned on a grid. The class Link was used in the programs to use the same sphere multiple times in the scenegraph. A sphere is a very simple object. Especially for more complex objects it is very convenient when the object can be defined only once and then copies of it can be used directly in different places in the scenegraph. For example, the doors in a house or the wheels of a car would be modelled only once, but occur in the scenegraph in more than one node. This also makes changes easier. When the object is modified, there is only one place where the changes have to be made and not in every copy of the object. When an object is used more than once in a scenegraph, it should be assigned to a transformation group tgMult which should then be assigned to an instance of the class SharedGroup. In each node of the scenegraph where `tgMult` should occur, the instance of the class `SharedGroup` should be assigned as a `Link` to the transformation group of the node.

```
SharedGroup sgMult = new SharedGroup();
sgMult.addChild(tgMult);
```

After the `SharedGroup sgMult` has been defined, it can be used in the scenegraph as a `Link` in the transformation groups `tg1`, `tg2`,....

```
tg1.addChild(new Link(sgMult));
tg2.addChild(new Link(sgMult));
...
```

The classes `Link` and `SharedGroup` were used in the programs `LinFogExample.java` and `ExpFogExample.java` to have multiple copies of the same sphere in the scene.

9.3 Dynamic surfaces

Movements of objects are modelled by applying suitable transformations to the objects, usually based on an interpolator. The transformations describe the movement of the whole object and are not responsible for any kind of deformation of the object. This model is sufficient for rigid objects like a car or a crane. But when persons or animals move, the skin and the muscles should also move in a suitable way, otherwise the movements will give a robot-like impression. For surfaces which should follow a movement in a flexible way, other models are applied. It would be too inefficient and complex to model the movement of the surface by individual descriptions for the movements of its surface polygons. For instance, the movement of a human arm is mainly restricted by the bones and the joints. The bone in the upper arm can be turned more or less arbitrarily in the shoulder joint. The bones in the lower arm can only be bent but not turned in the elbow joint. These few facts are almost sufficient to characterise arm movements. When only the movements of the bones are considered, a simplified model with only one bone for the upper and one for the lower arm is sufficient. When the hand of the arm carries out a movement, the bones simply follow the hand's movement under the restrictions that are imposed by the joints. A swaying movement must automatically be carried out in the shoulder joint of the upper arm since the elbow joint cannot conduct such a rotational movement. The bones themselves are not visible so that their movements have to be carried over to the surface, i.e., to the skin.

The position of the bones of the arm is determined by three skeleton points: the shoulder, the elbow and the wrist.

When the surface of the arm has been modelled by freeform surfaces or triangles, the control points or vertices are assigned to these skeleton points in a weighted manner. The weights indicate how much a point on the surface is influenced by the skeleton points. The closer a point on the surface is to a skeleton point, the larger will be the weight of the skeleton point. Points that are approximately in the middle between two skeleton points will be assigned a weight of 50% to each of the neighbouring skeleton points. Figure 9.2 shows such a *skeleton* as it might be used to model the arm.

Figure 9.2 Skeleton and skinning

The skeleton is drawn with dashed lines. The three squares indicate the skeleton points. The grey-scale of the vertices of the rough tesselation of the skin indicates the assignment of the vertices to the skeleton points. The vertex in the lower right is assigned to the right skeleton point with a weight of one. The vertices next to it have already positive weights for the right and the middle skeleton point.

When different transformations T_1, T_2, T_3 are applied to the three skeleton points s_1, s_2 and s_3, respectively, a vertex point p on the surface with the weights $w_1^{(p)}$, $w_2^{(p)}$, $w_3^{(p)}$ to the skeleton points would be transformed according to the transformation

$$T_p = w_1^{(p)} \cdot T_1 + w_2^{(p)} \cdot T_2 + w_3^{(p)} \cdot T_3.$$

It is assumed that the weights form a convex combination, i.e., $w_1^{(p)}, w_2^{(p)}, w_3^{(p)} \in [0,1]$ and $w_1^{(p)} + w_2^{(p)} + w_3^{(p)} = 1$.

This approach assumes that the surface follows the skeleton like a flexible hull. When noticeable movements of the muscles should be modelled, the tensing and relaxing of muscles will initiate an additional movement of the surface. In this case it is better to describe the surface of the arm in different elementary positions—for example straight and bent—and then apply convex combinations of elementary positions for the movement of the skin.

Instead of such heuristic techniques, mathematical models for the surface movements can also be specified. An example of cloth modelling for virtual try-on based on finite element methods can be found in [17].

9.4 Interaction

The simplest form of interaction of a user with a three-dimensional world modelled in the computer is the navigation through the virtual world. A suitable projection must be computed based on the position of the viewer. The position of the viewer might be modified by mouse movements, keyboard commands or—in the case of virtual reality—by tracking the position of the viewer. This topic has been treated in detail in section 5.8.

When the viewer should be able to interact with objects in the scene, suitable techniques are required to choose and pick objects for the interaction. It should be indicated in the scenegraph which objects can be picked at which level and what should happen when an object is picked. In the simplest case, the three-dimensional model serves only as a training tool in which the user can click on parts of a complex technical object like the cockpit of an aeroplane and information like the object's name and function is provided when it is picked. When the viewer should initiate dynamic changes in the scene by picking objects, for instance by pressing a button in the scene, the desired changes or movements have to be implemented and must be started when the user initiates them by picking the corresponding object.

When object picking is carried out with the mouse, the problem of finding out which object has been picked must be solved. The mouse can only indicate a point on the projection plane so that the object in the scene must be found to which the projected point belongs. A ray casting technique as was described in section 7.3.3 is suitable for this problem.

9.5 Interaction in Java 3D

The class `Behavior` and its subclasses offer a variety of possibilities for interaction with a scene in Java 3D. The subclass `OrbitBehavior` has already been used in all example programs to allow navigation through the scene with mouth movements.

The class `PickMouseBehavior` is designed to enable picking objects by clicking on them with the mouse. The following modifications have to be included in the scene for this purpose. The pickable objects should either be elementary geometrical objects of the class `Primitive`, i.e., `Box`, `Sphere`, `Cylinder` or `Cone`, or of the class `Shape3D`. It is also possible to define a region which can be picked by using a completely transparent pickable elementary geometric object.

The method `setUserData` assigns additional information to an object which can be used to identify the object when it is picked. Any Java object can function as a parameter of the method. In the example program only instances of the class `String` will be used to be able to identify objects by their names. If a green sphere `greenSphere` of the class `Sphere` has been included in the scene, one could assign the string "green sphere" to it by

```
greenSphere.setUserData("green sphere");
```

When there are objects in the scene which should not be pickable, for example a red sphere `redSphere`, this can be achieved by

```
redSphere.setPickable(false);
```

In order to define which actions should be initiated when a certain object has been picked, a class `MyPickingBehaviour` must be written that extends the class `PickMouseBehavior`. This class must be instantiated in the scene and the created instance must be assigned to the scene with the method `addChild`.

```
MyPickingBehaviour mpb =
        new MyPickingBehaviour(myCanvas3D,theScene,bs,...);
theScene.addChild(mpb);
```

When the class is instantiated, i.e., when the constructor of `MyPickingBehaviour` is called, at least the following parameters should be used: `Canvas3D`, the canvas on which the scene is drawn, the scene object `theScene` and a bounding region `bs`, e.g., in the form of a `BoundingSphere`. Further parameters can serve to control certain events in the scene. An example with further arguments in the constructor will be given at the end of this section.

The definition of the class `MyPickingBehaviour` with its constructor has the following structure.

```
public class MyPickingBehaviour extends PickMouseBehavior
{

    ...
    public MyPickingBehaviour(Canvas3D myCanvas,
                              BranchGroup theScene,
                              Bounds bs,...)
```

```
  {
    super(myCanvas,theScene,bs);
    setSchedulingBounds(bs);
    ...
  }
  ...
}
```

Depending on what should happen after an object has been picked, more attributes can be defined and initialised with values within the constructor. Further parameters in the constructor method can be used to hand over values for
the initialisation.

The method `updateScene` must be overwritten in the class
`MyPickingBehaviour`. Within this method it is defined what should happen
when an object is picked. The first step is usually to identify the picked object.
One way to identify an object is to check its user data. If an instance of the
class `String` with a suitable name for the object has been assigned to it with
the method `setUserData`, then the identification could look as follows.

```
public void updateScene(int xpos, int ypos)
{
  Primitive pickedShape = null;
  pickCanvas.setShapeLocation(xpos,ypos);
  PickResult pResult = pickCanvas.pickClosest();
  if (pResult != null)
  {
    pickedShape =
        (Primitive) pResult.getNode(PickResult.PRIMITIVE);
  }

  if (pickedShape != null)
  {
    System.out.println("The object "
                      +pickedShape.getUserData()
                      +" has been picked.");
  }
  else
  {
    System.out.println("No object has been picked.");
  }
}
```

The method `pickClosest`, which is applied to the attribute `pickCanvas` of the superclass `PickMouseBehavior`, yields the object which has been picked in terms of ray casting. The closest object, i.e., the first object that the ray starting from the mouse position hits, is the picked object. Other methods for this purpose are `pickAll` and `pickAllSorted` which return an array of all objects which are hit by the ray starting at the mouse position. The method `pickAny` returns the object which was found first on the ray, not necessarily the one closest to the viewer.

The program `InteractionTest.java` demonstrates this simple application of picking objects with the mouse. It uses a modified version of the class `MyPickingBehaviour` described above in the form of the program `PickingTest.java`.

When picking an object should not only lead to print out the object's name, but to some reaction within the scene, for example a movement, this can be implemented in the following way. For each pickable object the desired movement is defined in the scene. In the scene itself the waiting time until the movement should begin is set to the latest possible time. This is achieved by applying the method `setStartTime` to the `Alpha` object `delayedAlpha` associated with the movement and using the value `Long.MAX_VALUE` as argument.

```
delayedAlpha.setStartTime(Long.MAX_VALUE);
```

All instances of the class `Alpha` that control a movement which is initiated by picking are collected in an array and are handed over to the constructor of the class `MyPickingBehaviour`. Therefore, this class should also have an array `alphas` of `Alpha` objects as an attribute which is initialised with the array coming from the scene. In the method `updateScene` the line where the command `System.out.println` stands must be replaced by the following line when the object is picked whose `Alpha` is at the i-th position in the array.

```
alphas[i].setStartTime(
        System.currentTimeMillis()-alphas[i].getTriggerTime());
```

This method changes the starting time of the movement for the corresponding `Alpha` object. `alphas[i]` is the `Alpha` object associated with the object whose movement should be initiated. The starting time was initially set to `Long.MAX_VALUE`. The starting time is the waiting time after the animation has started. Since the movement should start now, the starting time should be set to the length of time the animation has been running. This is exactly the value computed in `setStartTime`. `triggerTime` is the time when the animation has been started.

The program `InteractionExample.java` demonstrates this principle with a simple example. The scene contains a cube and a sphere. When the cube is picked, i.e., clicked with the mouse, then it rotates. The sphere shrinks and extends alternatingly when it is clicked. Since the sphere must carry out two different movements, two `Alpha` objects are needed for the sphere so that the array `alphas` contains three elements including the `Alpha` object for the cube rotation. A Boolean variable is also used for switching between shrinking and extending for the sphere. The class `MyPickingBehaviour` is implemented here in the form of the program `PickingExample.java`.

9.6 Collision detection

Collision detection refers to the problem of determining whether moving objects collide, in other words, whether the corresponding shapes intersect. Without collision detection objects can penetrate each other. A car in a virtual would pass through a virtual wall without problems or accident. Collision detection for objects with a complicated geometric shape is a computationally complex task when it is carried out on the level of the polygons that model the surfaces of the objects. Even if there are only two objects in a scene, each one composed of 100 triangles, then, without further information about the configuration of the triangles, $100 \cdot 100 = 10,000$ intersection tests need to be carried out for collision detection.

For this reason, *bounding volumes* are introduced that are used to enclose objects with complex geometries. Bounding volumes are simple geometric shapes like spheres or boxes for which collision detection is much easier.

When an object is defined by a finite set of control points and assuming that the object lies within the convex hull of the control points, an enclosing cube can be defined by determining the smallest and largest values for the x-, y- and z-coordinate of all control points. In this way, two points $(x_{min}, y_{min}, z_{min})$ and $(x_{max}, y_{max}, z_{max})$ are obtained. These two points define a box that can be used as a bounding volume. The computation of the bounding volume is quite simple in this case. But the decision whether two boxes overlap for the purpose of collision detection is not as simple, especially when the objects have been moved and the bounding boxes are no longer axes-parallel.

A small bounding sphere enclosing a geometric object is more difficult to find, but the test for collision is simple for spheres. Figure 9.3 shows an object composed of a cylinder and a cone. An enclosing box is easy to find, whereas determining the smallest enclosing sphere needs some computation. Collision detection for two spheres is extremely simple. Two spheres collide or overlap if and only if the distance between their midpoints is smaller than the sum of their radii.

Figure 9.3 Bounding volume in the form of a cube and a sphere

It is very often sufficient to compute collision detection only on the basis of bounding volumes and not exactly on the level of polygons. This strategy cannot be applied in the context of dynamic surfaces as they were described in section 9.3. It can happen that the dynamic surface pervades itself when no collision detection is carried out for the polygons. In [17] a method for simulating cloth is proposed where complex computations are carried out to avoid that the fabric pervades itself.

9.7 Collision detection in Java 3D

The use of collision detection in Java 3D will be explained by an example that is implemented in the program `CollisionExample.java`. The program creates a scene in which a cube can be moved around in the scene by clicking on it with the right mouse button and moving the mouse. The scene also contains a sphere and a cylinder. When the cube collides with the sphere, the sphere will change its colour from green to red. A collision of the cube with the cylinder causes the cylinder to move to the left and right alternatingly.

First of all, the class `PickTranslateBehavior` is needed for moving the cube with the mouse. So far, this has nothing to do with collision detection. The following settings are required for the transformation group `tgBox` of the cube.

```
tgBox.setCapability(TransformGroup.ALLOW_TRANSFORM_WRITE);
tgBox.setCapability(TransformGroup.ALLOW_TRANSFORM_READ);
tgBox.setCapability(TransformGroup.ENABLE_PICK_REPORTING);
```

If there are also other objects that should be movable with the mouse, these settings are also needed for the corresponding transformation groups. The implementation of this mouse control is done in the class `PickTranslateBehavior` from which an instance is needed which must also be assigned to the scene.

```
PickTranslateBehavior pickTrans =
                new PickTranslateBehavior(theScene,
                                          myCanvas3D,
                                          bounds);
theScene.addChild(pickTrans);
```

The constructor of `PickTranslateBehavior` requires the specification of the scene, the `Canvas3D` for the scene and a bounding region, for example a `BoundingSphere`.

For the objects for which collision detection should be carried out a bounding volume `colVol` in the form of a `BoundingSphere` or a `BoundingBox` must be specified with the method `setCollisionBounds`. Then the object should be marked as relevant for collision with the method `setCollidable`.

```
colObject.setCollisionBounds(colVol);
colObject.setCollidable(true);
```

`colObject` can be an elementary geometric object, a `Shape3D` or also a transformation group. Since bounding volumes can only be defined as bounding boxes or bounding spheres, complex objects can only be approximated for collision.

The actions to be carried out when a collision occurs are implemented in a separate class in a similar way as was done for interaction with the class `PickMouseBehavior` in section 9.5.

The cylinder is considered first. The cylinder shall move from left to right or from right to left each time a collision with the cube happens. Its behaviour is controlled in the class `CollisionBehaviour2.java`. As already for interaction, the desired movements are defined directly in the scene with the starting time of the `Alpha` objects set to the maximum possible value. An instance of the class `CollisionBehaviour2` needs to be generated in the scene. The parameters for the constructor are the object for which collision detection should be carried out, i.e., the cylinder, an array of `Alpha` objects with the movements initiated by collisions and a bounding region. After the instance has been created with the constructor, it is assigned to the scene.

```
CollisionBehaviour2 scb2 =
        new CollisionBehaviour2(cyli,cylAlphas,bounds);
theScene.addChild(scb2);
```

The class CollisionBehaviour2 has to extend the class Behavior. Some additional attributes are also needed. It must be specified when during a collision the movement should be initiated. The following criteria are available.

– WakeupOnCollisionEntry: At the beginning of the collision.

– WakeupOnCollisionExit: At the end, when the collision is resolved.

– WakeupOnCollisionMovement: During the collision, when the object causing the collision is moving.

– WakeupOr: When more than one of the above criteria should be combined.

For the movement of the cylinder only the first criterion is needed. For the change of the colour of the sphere the second criterion WakeupOnCollisionExit will also be used later on. One of the attributes of the class CollisionBehaviour2 is therefore a WakeupOnCollisionEntry object. An array with the Alpha objects is also needed to initiate the movements of the cylinder. And two attributes to control which of the two movements should be carried out next are also introduced. The definition of the class with the constructor is therefore

```
public class CollisionBehaviour2 extends Behavior
{
  public WakeupOnCollisionEntry hit;
  public Primitive collidingShape;
  public Alpha[] movement;
  public boolean toRight;
  int whichAlpha;

  public CollisionBehaviour2(Primitive theShape,
                             Alpha[] theAlphas,
                             Bounds theBounds)
  {
    collidingShape = theShape;
    movement = theAlphas;
    setSchedulingBounds(theBounds);
    whichAlpha = 0;
    toRight = true;
  }
  ...
}
```

Then the method initialize of the superclass Behavior must be overwritten. Within this method it is defined which criteria with which objects or

transformation groups or nodes of the scene graph lead to calling the method
processStimulus which will be defined later on.

```
public void initialize()
{
  hit = new WakeupOnCollisionEntry(collidingShape);
  wakeupOn(hit);
}
```

The action to be carried when a collision occurs is specified in the method
processStimulus. This method contains an enumeration of all relevant collisions which have happened to the considered object. This enumeration is
scanned for a WakeupOnCollisionEntry entry. When it is found in the enumeration, the starting time of the corresponding Alpha object is set to the
current time in order to initiate the associated movement.

```
public void processStimulus(Enumeration criteria)
{
  while (criteria.hasMoreElements())
  {
    WakeupCriterion theCriterion =
             (WakeupCriterion) criteria.nextElement();
    if (theCriterion instanceof WakeupOnCollisionEntry)
    {
      ...
      movement[whichAlpha].setStartTime(
               System.currentTimeMillis()
               -movement[whichAlpha].getTriggerTime());
      ...
    }
    wakeupOn(hit);
  }
}
```

In addition to the activation of the Alpha object, it must be remembered which
movement comes next, the movement to the right or to the left. These lines of
code are not shown here to keep the printed source code short.

The change of the colour of the sphere after a collision with the cube is
implemented in the class CollisionBehaviour1.java. The class has a similar
structure as CollisionBehaviour2. The change of the colour is not a movement, but a sudden change of the state which can be modelled by an instance
of the class Switch. A Switch is a node in the scenegraph which has a number
of child nodes from which only a subset is visible. In the case of the sphere, the

Switch has two child nodes, one for the green and one for the red sphere. To use a Switch in the scenegraph, the constructor of the switch must be called and the Switch must be activated. Then an arbitrary number of children, i.e., transformation groups, can be assigned to the switch.

```
Switch sw = new Switch();
sw.setCapability(Switch.ALLOW_SWITCH_WRITE);
sw.addChild(transformgroup0);
sw.addChild(transformgroup1);
...
```

Then the Switch can either be assigned directly to the scene or to another transformation group within the scene. The method

```
sw.setWhichChild(nodeNumber);
```

is used to determine which of the child nodes of the switch should be visible in the scene. The child node is identified by its number. If more than one child node should be visible, the class BitSet (in java.util) can be used to define a bitmask bm. Calling the methods bm.set(childNumber) or bm.clear(childNumber) determines whether the child node childNumber is visible or invisible, respectively. The bitmask is assigned to the Switch with the method sw.setChildMask(bm).

In the class CollisionBehaviour1 the Alpha objects from the class CollisionBehaviour2 are replaced by the Switch as attribute. It is also necessary to distinguish in this class between collision entry and collision exit. The colour should jump back to green after the collision is over. A change of the colour should happen when a collision entry or exit happens. The definition of the attributes and the constructor are as follows.

```
public class CollisionBehaviour1 extends Behavior
{
  public WakeupCriterion[] theCriteria;
  public WakeupOr oredCriteria;
  public Switch collidingShape;

  public CollisionBehaviour1(Switch theShape,
                             Bounds theBounds)
  {
    collidingShape = theShape;
    setSchedulingBounds(theBounds);
  }
  ...
}
```

In the initialisation method, the logical disjunction of the criteria should be
defined as the wake-up criterion for this class.

```
public void initialize()
{
  theCriteria = new WakeupCriterion[2];
  theCriteria[0] =
                new WakeupOnCollisionEntry(collidingShape);
  theCriteria[1] =
                new WakeupOnCollisionExit(collidingShape);
  oredCriteria = new WakeupOr(theCriteria);
  wakeupOn(oredCriteria);
}
```

The method `processStimulus` has to handle the collision entry as in the class
CollisionBehaviour1, but also the end of the collision. The actions to be carried
out were initiated by setting the start values of `Alpha` objects. Here, instead,
the `Switch` with the red and green sphere must be changed from one sphere to
the other with the method `setWhichChild`.

The program `CollisionExample.java` does not use the class
`OrbitBehavior` to allow navigation through the scene with the mouse. Since
the movement of the cube is already controlled by the mouse, the mouse movements for placing the cube in the scene would also be interpreted as navigation
through the scene so that a simultaneous navigation would take place with
every movement of the cube. Instead of the class `OrbitBehavior`, the class
`KeyNavigatorBehavior` is used to allow navigation through the scene by keyboard commands. The scene as a `BranchGroup` cannot be assigned to this
extension of the class `Behavior`. A new transformation group `tgAll` is therefore introduced. All objects in the scene are assigned to this transformation
group and not to `theScene`. This transformation group is then assigned to
the scene. For navigation with the keyboard, tracking and controlling transformations must be allowed for `tgAll`. After this, an instance of the class
`KeyNavigatorBehavior` is created and a bounding region is assigned to it.
The instance of the class `KeyNavigatorBehavior` is finally assigned to `tgAll`
with the method `addChild`.

```
TransformGroup tgAll = new TransformGroup();
tgAll.setCapability(TransformGroup.ALLOW_TRANSFORM_READ);
tgAll.setCapability(TransformGroup.ALLOW_TRANSFORM_WRITE);
...
theScene.addChild(tgAll);
KeyNavigatorBehavior knb = new KeyNavigatorBehavior(tgAll);
knb.setSchedulingBounds(bounds);
```

```
tgAll.addChild(knb);
tgAll.addChild(...);
```

In connection with collision detection it is very often necessary to stop the movements of objects when they collide. This can be achieved by the method `pause()` applied to the corresponding `Alpha` objects.

9.8 Sound effects

Sound effects do not belong to the core part of computer graphics. They are nevertheless needed for many realistic animations and are part of virtual reality applications. There are different categories of sound effects. A sound can be background music or background noise like wind or rain. Background noise does not seem to come from a source with a well-defined position. It is present everywhere in the scene or a part of the scene. Background is similar to ambient light which also does not have a specific source and location or direction. It is simply present everywhere in the scene.

Most sound effects have a concrete source located in the scene, e.g., the voice of a person or an animal, the knocking at a door or the humming of a motor. Background noise differs in that the sources of these sounds have a specific position in the scene. For stereo effects it must be taken into account whether the source of the sound is more to the left or to the right of the viewer. The volume of the sound also depends on the distance between the viewer and the source of the sound.

The ability to locate a sound is mainly based on the use of two ears for hearing. The two ears will hear the sound with a slightly different volume and also with a short time delay. The volume of a sound depends also on the distance from its source. This means that realistic sound effects must at least take into account the level of the volume depending on the distance and a separation of the channels when more than one loudspeaker is available. The volume and the distribution of the sound to the channels can only be derived from the geometric context in the scene and the position of the viewer. Dynamic changes happen when moving objects produce sound or when the viewer navigates through the scene.

For more realistic sound effects even the Doppler frequency shift would have to be taken into account. When an object producing a sound approaches the viewer, the pitch of the sound is higher than for a static object. When the same object has passed the viewer and moves away from him, the pitch is lowered. This effect can be experienced when police and ambulance cars pass by with their sirens switched on. The implementation of Doppler's effect is quite complicated and usually not integrated into virtual scenes.

The sounds are usually stored as sound files in Wave or MP3 format. They can then be triggered by events. The volume of the sound must be adapted depending on the distance to the viewer, and also the distribution of sound to the channels depends on the position of the viewer.

9.9 Sound effects in Java 3D

Sound effects can be easily integrated into scenes with Java 3D. There are three different types of sounds. The class BackgroundSound is for background noise. A BackgroundSound has the same volume everywhere in its bounding region and the sound is equally distributed to the channels. Background sounds are handled in a similar way as ambient light.

The class PointSound is the soundequivalent of a point light source. A PointSound has a specific location in the scene and its volume decreases with increasing distance. When more than one channel is available, the PointSound can also be distributed to the channels depending on the direction it comes from.

The class ConeSound is the spotlight among the sounds. Like a PointSound it has a location, but it spreads only in one direction within a cone of sound. A pure ConeSound is not realistic, since noise cannot be directed in the same way as light. A ConeSound in connection with a PointSound at the same position leads to more realistic effects.

In order to integrate sound effects in Java3D, an instance of the desired Sound class is created, for instance

```
PointSound theSound = new PointSound();
```

Then a sound file in *Wave format* (wav) or *Audio format* (au) is loaded with the class MediaContainer and assigned to the instance of theSound with the method setSoundData.

```
MediaContainer medCon;
try
{
  FileInputStream is = new FileInputStream("mysound.wav");
  medCon = new MediaContainer(is);
  theSound.setSoundData(medCon);
}
catch(Exception e){...}
```

The method `setEnable` allows the use of this sound. Otherwise it will not be played. How often the sound should be repeated can be defined with the method `setLoop`. The method `setInitialGain` is needed to set the initial volume of the sound. A bounding region is also required for a sound.

```
theSound.setEnable(true);
theSound.setLoop(Sound.INFINITE_LOOPS);
theSound.setInitialGain(0.9f);
theSound.setSchedulingBounds(bs);
```

In this example the sound is repeated without stopping by choosing `Sound.INFINITE_LOOPS`. When the sound should be played only once or a specific number of times, the desired number should be entered instead. The sound can then be assigned to a transformation group or directly to the scene. The sound can be positioned and move around in the scene when it is assigned to a suitable transformation group. When the sound is produced by a specific object in the scene, the sound should be assigned to the same transformation group as this object.

The program `SoundExample.java` demonstrates the use of sound effects in Java 3D.

9.10 Stereoscopic viewing

Stereoscopic viewing, the ability to extract 3D information from what the two eyes see, is based on a variety and combination of factors. Even seeing with one eye only, will still provide some 3D information based on monocular factors. Binocular factors exploit the richer information combining the images coming from both eyes. Monocular factors are

- *The focus (accommodation)*: When the eye views an object, the lens has to be adjusted by muscle contractions in the eye so that the object is in focus. Objects in the far background get out of focus. This provides a certain information about distances.

- *Parallax of movements*: Parallax of movements can be observed when objects move relative to each other. The position and the size of the objects are crucial for this information. Moving objects change their distance to the viewer.

- *Masking*: When one object is hidden partly from sight by another object it can be concluded that the completely visible object must be closer to the viewer than the other object.

- *Light and shadows*: From the location, the direction, the shape and the size of the shadow cast by an object, conclusions can be drawn about the location of the object itself and about the shape of the object on which the shadow is cast. Figure 8.14 on page 223 is an example where a shadow from a tetrahedron is deformed since it is cast on two faces of a cube.

- *Size*: From the size of an object in an image compared to the size of other objects and the known size of the object, the distance of the object to the viewer can be estimated. Closer objects are larger. This means if an object that is known to be large occurs small, it must be far away from the viewer.

- *Attenuation*: The effects of atmospheric attenuation increase with the distance. Objects in the far distance appear less contrasted than closer ones.

- *Head movements*: Seeing with two eyes has the advantage that two images from slightly different positions are available at the same time. From the differences in the two images, the three-dimensional information can be retrieved. But even with one eye it is possible to have images from different positions by moving the head or the whole body. The different images do not come in parallel as with two eyes. But the small difference in time can be compensated, at least with some effort.

The binocular factors combine and aggregate the information coming from both eyes for stereoscopic viewing.

- *Difference of the images*: Since the two eyes view the same scene from two slightly different positions[1], three-dimensional information can be retrieved from a comparison of the two images.

- *Convergence*: The eyes have the ability to modify the direction of view by turning the eyeballs slightly. The closer an object is to the eyes, the more the eyeballs are turned inside. Based on this slight turn of the eyeballs, the distance of an object in focus can also be roughly estimated.

- *Pulfrich effect*: This effect was discovered in 1922 by the German physicist Carl Pulfrich. A bright stimulus is noticed or processed faster by the brain than a dark one. Wearing glasses with one darkened side, this effect can be used to generate 3D impressions for special image sequences.

In order to enable *stereoscopic viewing* with both eyes in computer graphics, it is necessary to provide different images for the left and right eye. The generation of the two images does not cause any problems from the viewpoint of computer graphics. Two perspective projections of the same scene with slightly different centres of projection are needed. Of course, the computational effort

---

[1] Roughly 6.5 cm difference.

is increased, in the worst case it is doubled. But coherence considerations can simplify the rendering tasks. Clipping, back-face culling and the computation of shadows are identical or almost identical for the two images. To present the two computed images to the eyes separately is the greater problem.

Anaglyph images are a very old approach to stereoscopic viewing. The two images are drawn with different colours, in most cases one in red and the other one in green. To view the two overlaid images special glasses must be worn with different colour filters for the two eyes. A disadvantage of anaglyph images is the loss of colour information.

Polarised light is a better alternative. Light waves oscillate around the axis of the direction in which they spread. Polarised light oscillates only in one plane. The images for the two eyes are projected to a screen with different polarisations. The viewer must wear glasses with the corresponding polarisations for the two eyes.

Polarisation is well suited for projectors, but not for computer monitors. *Liquid crystal shutter glasses* are more common for computer monitors. The images for the two eyes are presented alternatingly on the computer screen. The user must wear liquid crystal shutter glasses which are synchronised with the monitor. The liquid crystals can be switched from transparent to dark by an electric voltage. The shutter glasses darken the eye whose image is not shown at that moment on the computer screen. Since the image frequency for each eye is reduced by half in this way, it is recommended to use a special monitor with a higher frequency of at least 100 Hz. The frequency is also limited by the phosphorescence effect of monitors.

A *head-mounted display* is usually a small helmet with two LCD displays with magnifying lenses, one for each eye. Head tracking is required when the viewer can move around in the scene wearing the helmet. Headphones can also be integrated into the helmet for sound effects. The disadvantage is that wearing a helmet is not as comfortable as wearing glasses.

In recent years progress has been made in constructing specific displays that do not need specific glasses for the separation of the images for the two eyes [2, 19, 44]. Some techniques use a specific mask of lenses or prisms in front of the display so that each eye can only see one half of the pixels. The images for the two eyes must then be distributed accordingly to the pixels. There are also advanced techniques based on holographic methods.

A principal problem for these stereoscopic viewing techniques is the contradiction of constant focussing for varying distances. The focus of the eyes should always be kept fixed on the computer monitor, even if objects in the virtual world are viewed that seem to be far away behind the computer monitor or that appear to be in front of the monitor. This contradiction can cause headaches for some people when they use such techniques for stereoscopic viewing. The

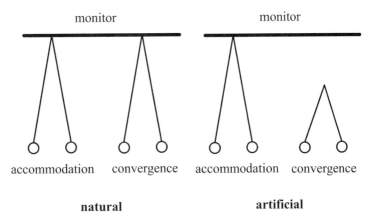

Figure 9.4 Parallax and accommodation for natural and artificial stereoscopic viewing

contradiction is illustrated in figure 9.4. Accommodation refers to the point where the lens of the eye should be focussed, convergence to the turning of the eyeballs.

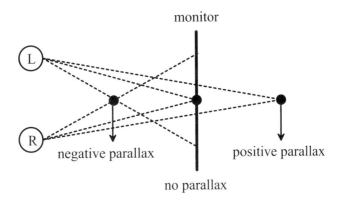

Figure 9.5 Parallax for stereoscopic viewing

Stereoscopic techniques are based on the correct choice of the parallax. Parallax refers to the difference of the images for the two eyes, when the same object is projected. Figure 9.5 illustrates the principle of parallaxes. A virtual object which is exactly in the distance of the projection plane, i.e., the computer monitor, has no parallax. Its projections are identical for the two eyes. The projection of an object behind the projection plane is shifted farther to the right for the right eye and farther to the left for the left eye. This is called a *positive parallax*. For objects in front of the projection plane or monitor, the situation is reversed. They have a *negative parallax*.

A computer can also create a *divergent parallax* by showing an object left of the left eye and right of the right eye which is impossible in reality.

A general problem of computer monitors for stereoscopic viewing is the frame or boundary of the monitor. For objects with positive parallax, the monitor is like a window through which the objects are seen. Objects with negative parallax are simply cut off at the edge of the monitor.

9.11 Exercises

Exercise 9.1

Create a scene with fog and let an object move away from the viewer until it vanishes in the fog.

Exercise 9.2

Create a simple light switch in a scene. Clicking the light switch with the mouse should switch on and off a light source. The light source should be assigned to the `BranchGroup the Scene` and not the `BranchGroup bgLight`.

Exercise 9.3

Specify bounding volumes in the form of a box and a sphere for the object in figure 9.3. The cylinder has a radius of one unit and a height of three units. The cone is two units high.

Exercise 9.4

Modify the program `CollisionExample.java` in such a way that the sphere becomes transparent when it collides with the cube.

Exercise 9.5

Create a simple model of a megaphone in the form of a cone and assign a `ConeSound` to it. Change the viewer's position interactively.

Appendix: Useful links

Online service of the book: The online service with the source code of all example programs, additional programs, supplementary files, exercises with solution and slides for teaching is available under

http://public.rz.fh-wolfenbuettel.de/~klawonn/computergraphics

Java 2D: Further information concerning Java 2D can be found in the Java tutorial at

http://java.sun.com/docs/books/tutorial/2d/

Java 3D: The homepage of Java 3D has the URL

http://www.java3d.org

Numerous links in connection with Java 3D can be found there like links to the Java 3D tutorial, the Java 3D API, to books, example programs, additional information for loading different file formats as well as a scenegraph editor. Of course, the link for downloading Java 3D

http://java.sun.com/products/java-media/3D/

can be found there, too.

3D modelling: Apart from CAD tools, the commercial program Maya is very popular for developing models for games, animations and movies. Maya resides under the URL http://www.alias.com

Blender3D is a free Open Source Product for 3D-modelling that can also export Wavefront Object files. Blender3D can be downloaded at

http://www.blender3d.com

Wavefront Object files: At

http://www.3droad.com/3d_models_OBJ.htm

various examples of files in Wavefront Object Format can be found for free download for noncommercial use.

OpenGL: The OpenGL homepage has the address

http://www.opengl.org

Appendix: Example programs

All programs mentioned in the book and additional ones can be downloaded at the online service to this book. The following tables refer to the pages where the programs are mentioned in the book. There is one table for Java 2D and one for Java 3D programs. The programs are listed in alphabetical order.

Java 2D		
Java class	**Topic**	**Page**
ArcExample	Ellipse arc and segment	22
AreaExample	Union, intersection, difference and symmetric difference for areas	23
BufferedImageDrawer	Generic class for the use of double buffering for drawing a `BufferedImage`	93
ConvexCombTransforms	Animation based on convex combinations of transformations with an example of transforming two ellipses	44
CurveDemo	Drawing of lines, quadratic and cubic curves	18
DoubleBufferingClockExample	Animation with moving objects using double buffering with a moving clock as an example	93

Java 2D		
Java class	**Topic**	**Page**
DToCMorphing	Transformation of one object into another. The objects are modelled by curves defined over control points. The letter D is transformed into the letter C.	45
GeneralPathCar	Example of a `GeneralPath` for the silhouette of a car	20
GradientPaintExample	Use of colour gradients	110
ImageLoadingExample	Loading a JPEG image	94
ImageSavingExample	Saving a JPEG image	95
LineEndings	Line endings and joints for thick lines	85
MorphingCandS	Uses the class `TriangulatedImage` for transforming two triangulated images into each other	111
MyFinishWindow	Class for closing a window	12
NonSynchronizedClock	Movements of a simple clock	39
RectangleEllipseExample	Rectangle and ellipse	21
RotationExample	Rotation	36
ScalingExample	Scaling	36
ShearingExample	Shear transformation	36
SimpleJava2DExample	First Java 2D example program	11
SimpleLetterC	Representation of the letter C with quadratic curves	45
SimpleLetterD	Representation of the letter D with quadratic curves	45
StrokingExample	Various dash patterns	67
TextExample	Drawing and modifying text	99
Texture2DExample	Drawing of textures	95
TransformationOrderExample	Importance of the order for transformations	36

Java 2D		
Java class	**Topic**	**Page**
TransformationOrderExampleR	Importance of the order for transformations	36
TransformationOrderExampleRT	Importance of the order for transformations	36
TransformationOrderExampleT	Importance of the order for transformations	36
TransformationOrderExampleTR	Importance of the order for transformations	36
TranslationExample	Translation	36
TriangulatedImage	Class for triangulated images which can be transformed into each other by pixel and colour interpolation	111

Java 3D		
Java class	**Topic**	**Page**
BackgroundExample	An image from file as background. This program requires the file `sunset.jpg`. A background with a homogeneous colour can be found in the program `StaticSceneExample`.	231
ClippingPlanes	Modification of the clipping volume by the angle for the field of view and the front and the back clipping plane	182
CollisionBehaviour1	A class that is used in `CollisionExample` in order to change the colour of an object when a collision occurs. A `Switch` is used here.	253
CollisionBehaviour2	A class that is used in `CollisionExample` in order to move an object when a collision occurs	251
CollisionExample	Example for the application of collision detection. Uses also a `Switch` and navigation via keyboard commands. The classes `CollisionBehaviour1` and `CollisionBehaviour2` are needed.	250

Java 3D		
Java class	**Topic**	**Page**
ExpFogExample	Exponential fog and the multiple use of transformation group in a scene as a `Link`	242
Extract3DExample	Loading an object from a file in Wavefront Object Format. Only a selected part of the whole object is included in the scene. The file `schiff.obj` is required.	163
GeomArrayExample	Definition of an object (tetrahedron) with triangles	161
InteractionExample	Picking objects with the mouse and initiating movements. The class `PickingExample` is needed.	248
InteractionTest	Picking objects with the mouse. Using the class `PickingTest` the name of the picked object is printed.	248
LightingExample	Use of different light sources and different reflection properties of surfaces	217
LightingExample2	A rotating light source causing unrealistic colour effects for objects with badly modelled reflection properties	217
LinFogExample	Linear fog and the multiple use of transformation group in a scene as a `Link`	242
Load3DExample	Loading and displaying an object from a file in Wavefront Object Format. Printing out the names of all subobjects. Assigning a new colour to one of the subobjects. The file `schiff.obj` is needed.	163
MovingLight	A moving light source	207
MovingSpotLight	A spotlight rotation around the scene. The intensity in the cone of light is constant and drops abruptly to zero at the edge.	217
NormalsForGeomArrays	Definition of an object (tetrahedron) with triangles. Normal vectors are interpolated.	177

Java 3D		
Java class	**Topic**	**Page**
PickingExample	A class needed for `InteractionExample` for initiating movements and scalings for picked objects	249
PickingTest	A class needed for `InteractionTest` in order to print out the names of picked objects	248
ShadingExample	Use of constant instead of Gouraud shading	222
SimpleAnimation3d	A simple animation with a starting and landing helicopter	139
SoundExample	Incorporating sound effects into a scene in the form of a `BackgroundSound` and a `PointSound`. The files `bgsound.wav`, `psound.wav` and `darkclouds.jpg` are needed.	258
StaticSceneExample	A static scene with a helicopter and a tree	127
TesselationBWExample	Wire frame model of a static scene with a helicopter and a tree	159
TesselationExample	Part of a static scene with a helicopter and a tree shown as a wire frame model	159
TesselationResolution	Approximation of the surface of a sphere with different numbers of triangles	160
TextureExample	Loading a texture from a file and mapping it to an object's surface. The file `myTexture.jpg` is needed.	230
TransparencyExample	Example for interpolated and screen-door transparency	227
ViewParallelProjection	Parallel projection for displaying a static scene with a helicopter and a tree	146

Appendix: References to Java 2D classes and methods

Appendix: References to Java 3D classes and methods

Bibliography

[1] J. Barrilleaux: 3D User Interfaces with Java 3D. Manning Publications, Greenwich, CT (2002)

[2] A. Beuthner: Displays erobern die dritte Dimension (in German). Computer Zeitung 30/2004, 14-14

[3] J.F. Blinn: Simulation of Wrinkled Surfaces. In: Proc. SIGGRAPH'78, Computer Graphics 12 (1978), 286-292

[4] A. Bogomjakov, C. Gotsman, M. Magnor: Free-Viewpoint Video from Depth Cameras. Proc. Vision, Modeling, and Visualization (VMV'06), Aachen (2006), 89-96

[5] J.E. Bresenham: Algorithm for Computer Control of a Digital Plotter. IBM Systems Journal 4 (1965), 25-30

[6] J.E. Bresenham: A Linear Algorithm for Incremental Digital Display of Circular Arcs. Communications of the ACM 20 (1977), 100-106

[7] R. Brons: Linguistic Methods for the Description of a Straight Line on a Grid. Computer Graphics and Image Processing 3 (1974), 48-62

[8] R. Brons: Theoretical and Linguistic Methods for Describing Straight Lines. In: [16], 19-57

[9] K. Brown, D. Petersen: Ready-to-Run Java 3D. Wiley, Chichester (1999)

[10] H.-J. Bungartz, M. Griebel, C. Zenger: Einführung in die Computergraphik (2. Aufl.) (in German). Vieweg, Wiesbaden (2002)

[11] H. Chen, S.S. Fuller, C. Friedman, W. Hersh (eds.): Medical Informatics. Springer, Berlin (2005)

[12] M.F. Cohen, S.E. Chen, J.R. Wallace, D.P. Greenberg: A Progressive Refinement Approach to Fast Radiosity Image Generation. In: Proc. SIGGRAPH'88, Computer Graphics 22 (1988), 75-84

[13] M.F. Cohen, D.P. Greenberg: The Hemi-Cube: A Radiosity Solution for Complex Environments. In: Proc. SIGGRAPH'85, Computer Graphics 19 (1985), 31-40

[14] M. Cyrus, J. Beck: Generalized Two- and Three-Dimensional Clipping. Computers and Graphics 3 (1978), 23-28

[15] Y. Dobashi, K. Kaneda, H. Yamashita, T. Okita, T. Nishita: A Simple, Efficient Method for Realistic Animation of Clouds. In Proc. SIGGRAPH'2000, Computer Graphics 34 (2000), 19-28

[16] R.A. Earnshaw (ed.): Fundamental Algorithms for Computer Graphics. Springer, Berlin (1985)

[17] O. Etzmuß, M. Keckeisen, W. Straßer: A Fast Finite Element Solution for Cloth Modelling. In: 11th Pacific Conf. on Computer Graphics and Applications, IEEE, Piscataway (2003), 244-251

[18] J.D. Foley, A. van Dam, S.K. Feiner, J.F. Hughes: Computer Graphics: Principles and Practice. Second Edition in C. Addison-Wesley, Boston (1996)

[19] C. Geiger: Helft mir, Obi-Wan Kenobi (in German). iX 5/2004, 97-102

[20] C.M. Goral, K.E. Torrance, D.P. Greenberg, B. Battaile: Modeling the Interaction of Light Between Surfaces. In: Proc. SIGGRAPH'84, Computer Graphics 18 (1984), 213-222

[21] H. Gouraud: Continuous Shading of Curved Surfaces. IEEE Transactions on Computers C-20 (1971), 623-629

[22] S. Gupta, R.E. Sproull: Filtering Edges for Gray-Scale Displays. Computer Graphics 15 (1981), 1-5

[23] R.R. Hainich: The End of Hardware: A Novel Approach to Augmented Reality (2nd Edition). BookSurge Publishing, Charleston, SC (2006)

[24] V.J. Hardy: Java 2D API Graphics. Prentice Hall, Upper Saddle River, NJ (2000)

[25] D. Hearn, M.P. Baker: Computer Graphics with OpenGL (3rd Edition). Pearson Prentice Hall, Upper Saddle River, NJ (2004)

[26] M.R. Kappel: An Ellipse-Drawing Algorithm for Raster Displays. In: [16], 257-280

[27] G. Kim: Designing Virtual Reality Systems: The Structured Approach. Springer, Berlin (2005)

[28] F. Klawonn, V. Chekhtman, E. Janz: Visual Inspection of Fuzzy Clustering Results. In: J. Benitez, O. Cordon, F. Hoffmann, R. Roy (eds.): Advances in Soft Computing: Engineering Design and Manufacturing. Springer, London (2003), 65-76

[29] J. Knudsen: Java 2D Graphics. O'Reilly, Beijing (1999)

[30] H. Kopka, P.W. Daly: A Guide to LaTeX: Document Preparation for Beginners and Advanced Users (3rd ed.) Addison-Wesley, Reading, MA (1999)

[31] K. Larson: The Technology of Text. IEEE Spectrum (INT) 5/2007, 20-25

[32] T. Nishita, E. Nakamae: Continuous Tone Representation of Three-Dimensional Objects Taking Account of Shadows and Interreflection. In: Proc. SIGGRAPH'85, Computer Graphics 19 (1985), 124-246

[33] I. Palmer: Essential Java 3D Fast. Springer, London (2001)

[34] B.-T. Phong: Illumination for Computer Generated Pictures. Communications of the ACM 18 (1975), 311-317

[35] M.L.V. Pitteway: Algorithms for Drawing Ellipses or Hyperbolae with a Digital Plotter. Computer Journal 10 (1967), 282-289

[36] M.L.V. Pitteway, D.J. Watkinson: Bresenham's Algorithm with Gray Scale. Communications of the ACM 23 (1980), 625-626

[37] W.T. Reeves: Particle Systems – A Technique for Modelling a Class of Fuzzy Objects. In: Proc. SIGGRAPH'83, Computer Graphics 17 (1983), 359-376

[38] W.T. Reeves, R. Blau: Approximate and Probabilistic Algorithms for Shading and Rendering Structured Particle Systems. In: Proc. SIGGRAPH'85, Computer Graphics 19 (1985), 313-322

[39] F. Rehm, F. Klawonn, R. Kruse: POLARMAP – Efficient Visualisation of High Dimensional Data. In: E. Banissi, R.A. Burkhard, A. Ursyn, J.J. Zhang, M. Bannatyne, C. Maple, A.J. Cowell, G.Y. Tian, M. Hou: Information Visualization. IEEE, London (2006), 731-740

[40] C.W. Reynolds: Flocks, Herds, and Schools: A Distributed Behavior Model. In: Proc. SIGGRAPH'87, Computer Graphics 21 (1987), 25-34

[41] D. Selman: Java 3D Programming. Manning Publications, Greenwich, CT (2002)

[42] H. Sowizral, K. Rushforth, M. Deering: The Java 3D API Specification. Addison-Wesley, Boston (2000)

[43] T. Soukup, I. Davidson: Visual Data Mining. Wiley, New York (2002)

[44] A. Sullivan: 3-Deep. IEEE Spectrum (INT) 4/2005, 22-27

[45] N. Thibieroz: Deferred Shading with Multiple Render Targets. In: W.F. Engel (ed.): Shader X2, Shader Programming, Tips & Tricks with DirectX 9. Plano, USA (2004), 251-251

[46] S.E. Umbaugh: Computer Imaging: Digital Image Analysis and Processing. CRC Press, Boca Raton (2005)

[47] J.R. Van Aken: An Efficient Ellipse-Drawing Algorithm. IEEE Computer Graphics and Applications 4 (1984), 24-35

[48] A.E. Walsh, D. Gehringer: Java 3D API Jump-Start. Prentice Hall, Upper Saddle River, NJ (2002)

[49] D.R. Warn: Lighting Controls for Synthetic Images. In: Proc. SIG-GRAPH'83, Computer Graphics 17 (1983), 13-21

[50] G. Wyszecki, W. Stiles: Color Science: Concepts and Methods, Quantitative Data and Formulae (2nd ed.). Wiley, New York (1982)

Index